THE
GNOSTIC GOSPEL
OF ST. THOMAS

ABOUT THE AUTHOR

Malachi Eben Ha-Elijah is a modern mystic. His journey on the spiritual path began when he was a young boy, when he encountered a Tau of the Sophian Tradition of Gnostic Christianity, Tau Elijah Ben Miriam. He received the oral tradition of Sophian Gnosticism from Tau Elijah, and has been a student and practitioner of Gnostic Christianity for over thirty-four years. In 1983 he founded Sophia Fellowship as an expression of the tradition, and has been teaching and initiating others into Christian Gnosticism, Rosicrucian Philosophy, and the holy Kabbalah since that time. He is an initiate of Ordo Sanctus Gnosis and holds the recognition of an Elder and Tau of the Sophian Tradition.

Along with his studies in the Western Mystery Tradition, Tau Malachi has studied extensively in several Eastern Traditions, such as Vajrayana Buddhism and Vedanta, as well as studying and practicing a Middle Eastern Tradition of Sufism. While Gnostic Christianity has always been his heart-path and spiritual home, Malachi speaks of himself as a traveler and explorer of the Spirit and Truth, and his journey has taken him to many sacred places and into diverse Wisdom Traditions.

For many years Tau Malachi served as a hospice volunteer, a volunteer trainer, and for a period of time as a hospice chaplain. Although he worked with patients suffering from various forms of terminal illness, much of his work focused on individuals living with HIV and AIDS.

Today he lives in the Sierra foothills, in Nevada City, California.

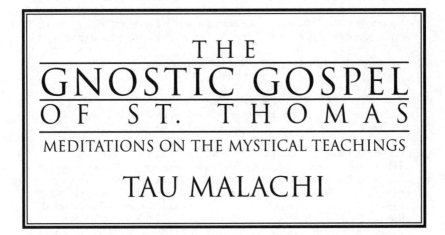

THE
GNOSTIC GOSPEL
OF ST. THOMAS
MEDITATIONS ON THE MYSTICAL TEACHINGS

TAU MALACHI

2004
Llewellyn Publications
Saint Paul, Minnesota, U.S.A. 55164-0383

FIRST EDITION
First Printing, 2004

Cover design by Gavin Dayton Duffy
Cover painting "Woman of Samaria" by Carl Henrich © SuperStock
Editing and interior design by Connie Hill

Permission for use of copyrighted text has been granted as follows:
THE GOSPEL OF ST. THOMAS [114 verses] from *The Nag Hammadi Library In English, 3rd, Completely Revised Ed.* by James M. Robinson, General Editor. Copyright © 1978, 1988 by E. J. Brill. Leiden, The Netherlands. Reprinted by permission of HarperCollins Publishers, Inc. Permission also granted for James M. Robinson (ed.), *The Nag Hammadi Library in English*, 3rd edition, Brill Academic Publishers, 1996, pp. 126–38 (all 114 verses from the Gospel of St. Thomas), by Brill Academic Publishers.

Library of Congress Cataloging-in-Publication Data
Malachi, Tau.
    The gnostic Gospel of st. thomas : meditations on the mystical teachings / Tau Malachi — 1st ed.
        p.   cm.
    Includes bibliographical references.
    ISBN 0-7387-0499-7
    1. Gospel of Thomas (Coptic Gospel)—Meditations. 2. Gospel of Thomas (Coptic Gospel)—Commentaries. I. Title.

BS2860.T52M35   2004
229'.8—dc22   2004040880

Llewellyn Worldwide does not participate in, endorse, or have any authority or responsibility concerning private business transactions between our authors and
    All mail addressed to the author is forwarded, but the publisher cannot, unless specifically instructed by the author, give out an address or phone number.
    Any Internet references contained in this work are current at publication time, but the publisher cannot guarantee that a specific location will continue to be maintained. Please refer to the publisher's website for links to authors' websites and other sources.

Llewellyn Publications
A Division of Llewellyn Worldwide, Ltd.
P.O. Box 64383, Dept. 0-7387-0499-7
St. Paul, MN 55164-0383, U.S.A.
www.llewellyn.com

Printed in the United States of America

CONTENTS

ACKNOWLEDGMENTS

First and foremost I'd like to give my thanks and praise to my beloved teacher, of blessed memory, Tau Elijah Ben Miriam, and to the companions of his circle, who taught and initiated me into the path of Gnosticism and the Christian Kabbalah. My own work is merely the continuation of his divine labor, and whatever knowledge, understanding, or wisdom in spirit I may be able to share, in truth, all flows from my sacred friendship with him. He was my spiritual grandfather and best friend in my youth, and the guidance and inspiration I received from him remains with me to this day.

I'd also like to give special thanks to Phillip Taylor, Penelope Amadali, Christopher Derks, and Michael Zysk, who worked with me to prepare the manuscript of this book for submission, without whose help it would not have been possible. Along with these friends I'd like to thank all of the companions of Sophia Fellowship, whose love, encouragement, and support made this possible. I truly am blessed with wonderful friends and a delightful spiritual community.

Llewellyn Publications and all of the staff at Llewellyn also deserve my gratitude and thanks for their refinement and publication of this project. Llewellyn facilitates a voice for peoples of alternative spirituality, which is sorely needed, and they are exceptional at what they do. Thank you all!

Considering all of the people involved in the publication of a book it is impossible for me to think of it as "my book." In truth, it is our book!

My heartfelt thanks!

Sincerely,
Tau Malachi Eben Ha-Elijah

INTRODUCTION

The wind blows where it chooses, and you hear the sound of it, but you do not know where it comes from or where it goes. So is everyone who is born of the Spirit.

Gospel of St. John 3:8

There is a need for a new gospel, a Gospel of the Cosmic Christ—one that restores the mystical and magical elements to Christianity, and yet more, one that teaches a path of conscious evolution toward the enlightenment experience that Yeshua Messiah (Jesus Christ) himself embodied—the state of Christ-consciousness. I would go so far as to say that it is not only our need but God's Will that a new gospel emerge and that there are voices of a new gospel who boldly proclaim even better "good news."

In speaking about a new gospel, I'm speaking about a shift in paradigm that requires us to look at the Scriptures we have with new eyes and to listen to their words with new ears. I am also speaking about seeking to understand the Scriptures through the inspiration of the Spirit so that we might glean something of their deeper and mystical meaning. The truth is that the Holy Scriptures have many levels of meaning, from the surface and literal meaning, to the metaphorical level, and deeper still, to the secret and mystical level. At each level, there are many different spiritual teachings that can be drawn out of any verse of the Holy Scriptures, all according to the inspiration of the Spirit in the moment and one's own capacity to receive. In effect, each verse is like an endless well of Wisdom into which one can dip one's cup again and again, continually bringing forth new Wisdom—the very living waters of which Jesus spoke.

While we can speak of the verses comprising the Scriptures as the well from which the living water of Wisdom is being drawn, we can also speak of one's own soul as the well, and the verse being like a cup that is drawing out the Holy Wisdom from within oneself. While we may look to see the depth of Wisdom contained in a verse, and gain an understanding of various levels of meaning intended, we can also seek what the verse draws out from the depths of our own being—an expression of our holy soul or Divine self. Jesus said, "He who drinks from my mouth will become like me. I myself will become he, and the things that are hidden will be revealed" (Gospel of St. Thomas, Verse 108). To "drink" from the mouth of the Master and to become like him is to draw out the various teachings to be found in the different layers of meaning in the Scriptures, the Master becoming the person who is drawing forth the Wisdom of one's own holy soul and Christ-self. Only in this way are "the things that are hidden" revealed.

This process of seeking knowledge, understanding, and wisdom must be more than merely the formation of mental concepts. While the mind and mental being needs to be involved in the process, the heart and soul-being needs to be primary. As we seek to draw out the Wisdom contained within the Scriptures and seek to draw out the Wisdom from within our holy soul, we need to make ourselves open and sensitive, and seek to enter into the spiritual experience from which the Scripture itself was written. The heart, with its capacity to feel and intuit, and the soul-being, with its capacity to perceive within metaphysical dimensions through interior senses, are crucial to making the process experiential. When it is experiential, we restore our own Spirit-connectedness and are transformed in the process. We progress in the gospel.

What I am describing here is the way initiates of mystical and gnostic Christianity approach the Holy Scriptures and use contemplative meditation on the Scriptures, along with other forms of spiritual practice, as a vehicle of direct self-realization. This is something much more than a religion based on faith in dogmatic doctrine or creed; rather it is an authentic spirituality that seeks gnosis, which is the knowledge acquired through direct spiritual or mystical experience. It is knowledge of higher states of consciousness and the soul of Light within oneself; and it is knowledge of the metaphysical dimensions of the universe and the play of hidden spiritual forces upon which the universe is founded. Ultimately, gnosis is a state of Truth-consciousness in which the Spirit and Truth is inwardly known, hence a state of enlightenment or self-realization.

Here, we come to a central point where gnostic Christianity diverges from exoteric and orthodox forms of Christianity. Where there is a belief in Christ as something coming only from outside of oneself, a religion of faith in the Christos through fixed or static interpretations of the Scriptures, dogmatic doctrine and creed comes into being. However, where there is a belief in Christ as something within oneself—within, yet beyond, creature and creation, a spirituality of gnosis comes into being—the Gospel of the Cosmic Christ. To one who believes the Christos, as something within, as the truth of the soul and Divine self, the Christos is something to be experienced, known, and realized inwardly as much as something to be experienced, known, and realized outwardly. In this gnostic view, not only is one to believe in the Divine incarnation of the Christos in the person of Jesus Christ, but one is to seek the gnosis of Jesus Christ, which means to incarnate the Christos within oneself and consciously evolve toward Christhood.

Faith has a very different meaning to the gnostic initiate. It means a "sense of the mystery" or "an intuition of an experience not yet had." Thus, it is a guiding light into the mystery or experience (gnosis). Once initiated into something of this mystery, faith unfolds a higher consciousness from day to day, drawn from the Truth and Light revealed in one's experience. This facilitates a progress from one degree or grade of the enlightenment experience to another until a complete realization of Christ-consciousness is attained.

Based on this discussion, one may understand that tradition has a different meaning to a mystic or gnostic Christian than the orthodox counterpart. Gnostic Tradition provides a cosmology, a mysticism and magic, through which an aspirant can gain knowledge through direct spiritual or mystical experience—gnosis. On the one hand, tradition is a language that communicates something of the gnosis that has been acquired by previous generations of initiates, like a "finger point-ing at the moon," as a Buddhist saying goes. On the other hand, tra-dition provides methods of spiritual practice and spiritual living through which one can acquire gnosis for oneself and gives a context into which one can place such experience. However, tradition is not a fixed or static doctrine. Rather, it is a vehicle for the transmission of a living presence and power, and is itself alive, ever growing and chang-ing as each generation of gnostic initiates adds its own gnosis to the stream of Light-transmission. Gnostic Tradition is, ultimately, some-thing fluid and flowing and does not stand still, any more than any-thing else in life. In essence, it is an ongoing Divine revelation, a continual emergence of a new gospel, which unfolds in the experi-ence of those who practice the tradition.

Although initiates of the same tradition may have much in com-mon in terms of their views and beliefs, and share the same mystical or symbolic language, it is not uncommon to find, from one initiate to another, very different views and beliefs. In fact, many Gnostic Tradi-tions teach radically different ideas about the same subjects and see no contradiction in so doing! Why? Because the emphasis is on indi-vidual spiritual or mystical experience and, specifically, a process of enlightenment and liberation. No two individuals' experience is going to be exactly the same, as each individual is unique, and each individ-ual will enter into the experience of gnosis from a different angle. Likewise, there are souls at various grades of evolution, and thus vari-ous grades of knowledge, understanding, and wisdom. Tradition, cos-mology, myths, spiritual teachings, methods of practice, rituals of initiation, and the Holy Scriptures are merely vehicles of spiritual or mystical experience and are not the enlightenment experience or gnosis itself. Such things may reflect and embody something of the experience to a degree, but they are not the actual experience.

"Come and see . . ." "follow me . . . ," these are terms Jesus himself is said to have used in calling his disciples, both of which suggest a "knowing" through a direct spiritual or mystical experience. This is exactly what a gnostic teacher will say to an aspirant, understanding that it is the experience of a living presence that imparts true Gnosis. For this reason, gnostic teachers of many traditions tend to rely more upon an oral tradition than written tradition, and on the shared experience that only a more personal relationship can facilitate. Even where there is a written tradition, typically it is coupled with a larger oral tradition, so that, to fully receive the teachings and initiations of the tradition, one must have an adept or master of the tradition (a tau or elder) as a close spiritual friend.

By now, you may surmise why the verse from the Gospel of St. John was chosen to begin this introduction. It speaks directly to how Christian Gnostics live and how Christian Gnostic Traditions work. Many of the traditions of Christian Gnosticism are like the wind, so that one does not know where they have come from or where they are going. It is as though they appear out of nowhere and, just as swiftly, vanish from sight if one tries too hard to pin down their origin. They are elusive creatures!

The tradition I encountered in my youth is a fine example. I became friends with an elderly gentleman who was a tau (master) of a living Gnostic Tradition, which he and the circle of initiates around him called the Sophia Tradition, because of the central role that St. Mary Magdalene holds. Through him and the spiritual companions gathered around him, I came into contact with an esoteric order—a lineage of mystical or Gnostic Christians. This delightful elderly man, who everyone called either the "Old Man" or Tau Elijah, took me on as a disciple or spiritual companion. Through personal or individual conversations, group discourse, instruction on methods of mystical prayer, prophetic meditation, rituals of initiation, and such, he imparted the teachings of the tradition. Although classical source-works were referenced and studied, from which much of the tradition was drawn, nothing at all of the tradition was committed to writing—it was completely an oral tradition. I studied with Tau Elijah for eight years, until his death in 1978. Before he died, he imparted to me the blessing of being his successor. After his death, coinciding with my relocating, all of his companions went separate ways like the fruit of the Tree of Life going to seed; the seeds fell into the earth so as to sprout and generate new trees. In this way, the lineage of the holy order passed on to a new generation of initiates, the circle from which they were born vanishing from sight.

As for knowledge of the tradition's origin? Well, I experienced for myself the living presence and power in my teacher, Tau Elijah, and he spoke often of his teacher, Tau Miriam. Occasionally he made passing references to the Frenchman who was her holy apostle, and once he mentioned a German fellow who taught and initiated this Frenchman. My teacher spoke of the origin of the tradition as taking place during the seventeenth century, inspired by the Rosicrucian Enlightenment of that era, and alluded to an origin in the more distant past. In terms of the history of the order and tradition, that is about all I know. It is rather like a ghostly figure that vanishes from sight when stared at directly! Yet I was left with the teachings and initiations of the Sophian Tradition as I received them from Tau Elijah and the gnosis I have acquired through my practice of the Tradition. If it were not for the complete transformation of me and my life, the knowledge and understanding of the tradition that I have been left with, and the living presence in my experience today, I would no doubt be wondering if the whole encounter of some eight years was only an intense lucid dream, and, in the end, who is to say that it wasn't? As I understand it, there are many mystical and gnostic Christian Traditions that function in this way.

The Gospel of St. Thomas opens with a verse proclaiming, "These are the secret sayings which the living Jesus spoke and which Didymos Judas Thomas wrote down. And he [Jesus] said, 'Whoever finds the interpretation of these sayings will not experience death.'" This verse characterizes Gnostic Christianity, which represents an inner tradition of secret knowledge orally imparted from apostle to disciple through discourse and initiation. At the heart of this inner tradition is a spiritual art of conscious living and conscious dying, and the development of consciousness beyond the body, through which the initiate is able to consciously enter into higher planes of existence, both in this life and the afterlife. The result is a conscious continuity of self-awareness throughout all states of existence, including what we call "death," so that, in effect, there is no more death and no more need for physical incarnation. When we speak of enlightenment and liberation, self-realization or Christ-consciousness, this is ultimately what is meant. Like many Eastern schools, the Western Tradition of Chris-

tian Gnosticism agrees that our primary purpose in life is to free ourselves from the cycles of transmigration (reincarnation) and to tran-
scend the material plane of existence as exactly demonstrated by Jesus
through his resurrection.

An orientation of oneself and one's life to the development of a
consciousness beyond the body and the ascent of consciousness to a
higher plane of existence is something quite opposite to the way of
the establishment in the world or of unenlightened society. Having
received our education from the establishment, and founded our self-
identification and the values of our lives upon it, when we first encounter a Christian Gnostic Tradition, while illuminating, it will also
be disorienting and bewildering. The disorientation or bewilderment,
and the discomfort that comes with it, cannot be avoided by the new-
comer. Authentic mysticism, and the Gnostic style of teaching, is
founded upon a play of illumination and bewilderment, and bewilderment is considered crucial to any actual development or progress in
self-realization. Bewilderment invokes new questions—questions one
would not have thought to ask before. One's questions turn into a sacred quest for greater knowledge, understanding, and wisdom—a
deeper penetration of the mystery. This leads to a breakthrough into
a higher degree of the enlightenment experience, or gnosis.

The traditional style of gnostic teaching in the Sophian Tradition is,
therefore, distinctly different from the way of modern academic education or scholarly presentation. Whereas the way of modern academics focuses primarily on the rational mind and a linear presentation, the
gnostic style of teaching focuses more on the feelings and intuitions of
the heart and the perceptions of the soul—a multilayered and nonlin-
ear presentation. While in a modern academic method everything
mentioned is thoroughly explained, in the gnostic method that is not
the case. A gnostic teacher will clearly and openly explain many
things, while other things he or she will allude to only in a veiled way.
The intention is to create bewilderment as much as to illuminate and
to facilitate a reliance of his or her students upon their own feelings
and intuitions, and their own process of spiritual study and practice
through which the interior senses of the soul might be opened. While
the spiritual friendship and connection with the physical teacher (holy

tzaddik or apostle) is considered very important in the Sophian Tradition, it is one's relationship and connection with the inner teacher or Christ-self that is crucial, which a physical teacher is constantly seeking to reflect within the aspirant.

In this book, the reader is encountering a living Gnostic Tradition and a gnostic style of teaching. It is as though one has come in contact with a gnostic tau or elder and is receiving correspondence from him or her on mystical insights drawn from the verses of the Gospel of St. Thomas, or as though one is attending meetings of a gnostic circle in which a discourse of the verses is occurring. In effect, through this book, that is exactly what is happening. The letters composing this volume were written to initiates of a gnostic circle. In so doing, a body of commentary was generated that would form a book that could be published for a larger audience, and thus extend the knowledge and wisdom of the tradition beyond the boundaries of the esoteric order that has developed and preserved it. It is part of a larger work to transcribe the oral teachings of the Sophian Tradition and make them more accessible.

In this process, I attempt to maintain something of the way the teachings have always been imparted. Being an oral tradition, it has been transmitted by word of mouth from the tau or elders of the tradition to their spiritual companions in the form of individual and group discourse. These transmissions have never come from any fixed outline of the points to be covered or what is to be shared, but rather have always flowed forth from a contemplative meditation in the moment of the discourse. This allows opportunity for inspiration of the Holy Spirit, space for new insights, spontaneous creativity, and involvement of the student in the process of sharing. These letters on a mystical gospel have been written in the same way.

Being composed of a series of letters, this book is not really meant to be read cover to cover, in one fell swoop. The intention, more practically, is an exercise using these letters as a series of contemplative mediations. To read letter by letter, perhaps taking one verse and its commentary per day as a source of contemplation, is a practice in listening to the Holy Spirit. In doing this, one will learn how to listen to her speak in one's own thoughts, feelings, and intuition throughout the circumstances of the day, which will vary in accordance with every verse and contemplation! These letters were written to facilitate the reader's own spiritual exploration. They are meant to illuminate and inspire, as well as to invoke questions of one's own sacred quest—even to provoke debate or an inner wrestling. The commentary is by no means meant as a final word, but rather as only a beginning—the initiation of a process. This is exactly how initiates of Christian Gnosticism receive teachings, the process of reception being a spiritual practice itself.

A daily application of such a practice would be to take one verse and its letter per day as a contemplative meditation. It is best to read the verse first by itself several times, contemplating and meditating upon it with prayer for insight and understanding. Having considered the verse by itself, extend your contemplation to the letter. Concluding this practice, you can return to the verse and read it one more time, carrying its message into your day. In doing this, you transform reading this book into a spiritual practice through which something of a more direct spiritual or mystical experience might unfold.

As one reads and contemplates these letters, one will become aware of a very rich and vast body of mystical and magical teachings. The Sophian Tradition, as stated above, has its origin in the Rosicrucian Enlightenment of the seventeenth century; this is well articulated in *The True and Invisible Rosicrucian Order* by Paul Foster Case. At the heart of Sophian Tradition is the holy Kabbalah, the tradition of Jewish mysticism, which can be traced back to the prophets in ancient Israel and the early Merkavah mystics of first-century Palestine. Because the historical Jesus and his circle of apostles were not "Christian," but Jewish, initiates of the Sophian Tradition, seeking the way of that original first circle, find their logical beginning in the holy Kabbalah. Therefore, while one will find specifically Gnostic ideas in these letters, along with principles of a Rosicrucian Philosophy, one will find a great deal of Kabbalistic teachings presented. This is what the Christian Gnosticism of the Sophian Tradition is—a weave of Gnosticism, Kabbalah, and Rosicrucian philosophy.

Anyone who reads and contemplates these letters and who has a background in a mystical or Gnostic Christianity and the Kabbalah will certainly see layers of the teachings presented that the novice will not. However, such a background is not necessary in order to read this book. The same teaching is presented to both the novice and the adept in the traditional style of Gnostic teaching, and each person naturally receives according to his or her capacity and need. To help the novice, I have included a glossary of terms with simple definitions of those words that are likely to be unfamiliar. Likewise, I have also included a suggested reading and reference list for those who might like to extend their exploration of the ideas and teachings presented in this book.

It is my hope and prayer that this book is a blessing upon those who read it, and that it serves to help bring forth a new gospel of Light in the experience of those who read it. May the Lord of Spirits bless you!

Tau Malachi Eben Ha-Elijah
Sophia Fellowship, O.S.G.

VERSE 1

These are the secret sayings which the living Jesus spoke and which Didymos Judas Thomas wrote down.

And he said, "Whoever finds the interpretation of these sayings will not experience death."

The Living Yeshua is speaking in secret, within, behind your heart. Christ dwells there within you, and when you go within, Christ will speak the secret teachings to you and lead you in the path of awakening. To listen and hear, you must be silent. You must empty yourself of yourself and let the Christ-Spirit fill you. Dying to yourself, you must be conceived and reborn of the Holy Spirit as the Living Yeshua. Indeed, you must experience the same conception, gestation, and birth as the Living Yeshua so that you also might be his twin, born of the same birth from the Holy Virgin, Mother Wisdom. Only in this way can you receive the Light-transmission from the Master and become a Gnostic yourself.

Everyone is the Living Yeshua. The ordinary person is ignorant of this, but the apostle of God knows it and lives according to the Truth and Light revealed through experience. Likewise, the kingdom of heaven is here and now, within you and all around you. It is present within everyone. The ordinary person does not have eyes to see it, but the Gnostic perceives it and so dwells in the kingdom of God here and now. Logos (Word) and Sophia (Wisdom) are to be found within

everyone and everything, and so also within you. There, within your
secret center, at the core of your being, is the Holy One of Being.
The Christ-self is your true self, the self of every self and soul of every
soul. All are united with him in the Sacred Unity that is God, the Father-Mother. Through him, the Holy Spirit indwells the whole of
Creation. Knowing this, you will not experience death.

This is the truth that is contained in these sayings or verses, the essential reality of which they speak. The secret is openly spoken, but
who can listen and hear and so receive it? Written or spoken, the secret remains a secret until it is part of your own experience. The
teachings are received only when they are your own experience.
Then they become a living initiation—a Light-transmission. This is
the aim of the mystic, that he or she should directly experience the
Living Yeshua and become as the risen Christ.

What will death mean to that one who experiences Messianic consciousness and dwells in the kingdom of God while in this life? Indeed,
death will not mean what it means to the ordinary person, for that one
is not so self-identified with mortal name and form, but knows oneself
as an immortal Spirit, a bornless and therefore deathless Spirit. Likewise, this person knows that the kingdom of heaven is present within
and all around, always—that upon death one's experience of Christ
will continue in a more subtle and sublime form, having shed the physical body. With this knowledge, death is no longer death and the adversary has no power over the soul, whether in this world or in the
world to come. Such a person is awakened and therefore free, having a
continuity of awareness throughout all states of existence. Death will
come, as it has for all prophets and saints, but it will just be an appearance of departure—a transition to another mode of existence, no more
or less real than falling asleep, only to dream and awaken again. Death,
for the Gnostic, is not an end as much as a new beginning. Ultimately,
death has no substantial reality, but is merely a natural moment of transition. Knowing this changes everything. Meditate upon it and you
will see!

Grace accomplishes this awakening and the transformation that
follows it. Nothing one does accomplishes this self-realization. Yet
spiritual practice and spiritual living are the conditions that allow

Grace to act, without which it is unlikely that the Holy Spirit can work within and through oneself to accomplish the great work. More profoundly, spiritual practice and spiritual living are, themselves, the goal or attainment sought; so that in practicing and living according to the Truth and Light, one naturally awakens and receives the Light-transmission. It is not so much a matter of receiving something that one does not already have as much as it is creating the conditions necessary for the Word (Logos) and Wisdom (Sophia) to pour forth from within oneself. Hence, it is letting the Christ-self that is already present deep within come forward and live this life. Spiritual practice and spiritual living do just that. Practice living as Christ and you will see!

VERSE 2

Jesus said, "Let him who seeks continue seeking until he finds. When he finds he will become troubled. When he becomes troubled, he will be astonished, and he will rule over the all."

You must seek in order to discover the Spirit and Truth and must continue seeking until you realize the Spirit in-dwelling you and know the Truth in your own experience. It is not enough that another person has discovered the Truth. Each individual must seek and strive to discover it and so en-gage in the Divine labor of salvation of one's soul, that is to say, the awakening and liberation of one's soul in conscious union with God.

This seeking is the sacred quest for the Holy Grail, which is not a physical relic or holy cup outside of oneself. Rather, the Holy Grail is a purified and consecrated heart, soul, mind, and life; it is oneself open and sensitive to the Christ-Spirit so that one lives the life of Christ. The Grail is the heart in which the Lord dwells, the person who has dis-covered an innate Spirit-connection and who lives within. It is the Christ-self, the Logos and Sophia of God, the inner or higher self that is one's secret center and holy root.

Now these are just words, concepts in the mind. The na-ture of this sacred quest is such that you may have a word, name, or concept of what it is you are looking for, some idea of what it is, how and where it may be found. Yet, in fact, you do not know what it is you are looking for, how, where, or when it may be found. Whatever idea you may have of it is more likely a hindrance or obstruction to finding what you seek, misleading rather than helpful.

When seeking is based upon preconception, precondition, and expectations, upon who and what you think you are and who and what you believe reality or God to be, then seeking itself becomes an obstruction and what is sought cannot be discovered. If you go looking for something that does not exist or go seeking in a way or in a place it cannot be found, then, indeed, you will not find it.

At the outset, you must understand that the very nature of God is different than anything you might conceive and that you yourself are not who or what you might think you are. Whatever your preconceptions, preconditions, or expectations, the reality-truth-continuum is yet more and cannot be contained or comprehended by the linear reasoning mind or dualistic consciousness. God will forever be a mystery, the nameless and unknown. God is completely other than what we might think. Discovering this is a troubling thing, shaking one to the core!

To draw near to the Lord is a deeply troubling thing, for I must become no-thing, empty of myself, that the Lord might enter and the Holy Spirit fill me. God is No-thing (Ain) and I must become no-thing to enter into union with the Holy One of Being

If you think you are something, if you think you are a substantial and independent self-existence, a solid or fixed entity, it is greatly troubling to discover that your secret center is no-thing, that you are empty of any substantial or independent self-existence. Discovering this, however, you then realize that this is the very nature of everything in existence. You discover that everything is impermanent, that everything changes. Reality is empty of any substantial and independent self-existence. There is only the Holy One of Being, the One-Without-End (Ain Sof). Yet in this gnosis, the prophet or apostle of God attains dominion over the all, for everything is the magic-display of the Divine mind, the mind of Christ.

There is another sort of troubling that may come with the dawn of higher awareness and drawing near to the Lord. In the Sacred Unity that God is, you encounter absolute and ultimate perfection, the primordial emptiness that is at one and the same time Divine fullness. Before the perfection of the Lord, your own imperfection is glaring and stark in contrast, a profoundly troubling thing to discover and, indeed, painful. Drawing nearer to the Lord, you discover how very far away from God you are. This is the cause of the dark night of the soul of which the mystics speak in their journey.

Anyone who seeks must be willing to endure the trouble that comes with finding, willing to endure the dark nights of the soul and the ordeals of initiation. A mystical death precedes a resurrection; a descent into the depths precedes every ascension. The Living Yeshua has opened the way before us and revealed the path to us. We also must die and be reborn, descend into the depths and ascend; we must be willing to take up our cross daily and follow the Christ-self within us. Only in this way is salvation attained.

This is not something new. Life teaches this very lesson. Birth itself is a troubling and painful thing, yet the great joy of life comes from it. So it is with everything in this life. The pain is part of the pleasure, the sorrow part of the joy. Dying is part of living. You cannot have one without the other. Everything is interconnected and interdependent; it is the nature of things ever-becoming. You must learn to accept and embrace the whole of life and the whole of yourself if you would discover the Spirit and Truth. The Light and the Darkness must be joined and you must realize the Sacred Unity.

Now I tell you this, when you seek, what you find will be disturbing, for you will discover that all the ways of mortals and their pomp is vain and futile, mere vanity under the sun. Virtually everything unenlightened human society values so dearly is ultimately meaningless, and what we ourselves value and believe so important is not important at all. It is all arbitrary. Everything is dust in the wind with the passage of time. In the hour of reckoning, the moment of death, what will it all mean? The world will be nothing and you will be nothing. If you do not know the Christ-self as your very own self in that hour, where will you be? What will become of you?

I will tell you plainly, the outer person I am is nothing. This name and form is a transitional state that in and of itself means nothing.

Save that I know the inner person, the soul-being and Christ-self within, this outer person and life are but vanity under the sun. To love, to gain knowledge, to uplift humanity Godward, is the purpose and meaning of this life. This name and form have meaning to the extent that Messianic consciousness is embodied. That is why the soul enters into this life, so that the being of the becoming that is within you might incarnate and the world to come might manifest. If you accomplish something of this great work, then all that you do in this life will be filled with meaning. Yet if you accomplish many things and, by the judgment of mortals, are considered great in this world, but you do not accomplish anything of this great work, all that you might do will be meaningless, pure vanity. It is a simple truth.

"Ask, and it will be given to you; search, and you will find; knock, and the door will be opened for you. Everyone who asks receives, and everyone who searches finds, and for everyone who knocks, the door will be opened" (Matthew 7:7–8).

Asking is receiving, seeking is finding, knocking is the opening of the door that you might enter. It is not *you* who is asking or seeking or knocking but the Christ-Spirit in you, and it is Grace that answers, Grace that finds, the Holy Spirit that knocks and enters and accomplishes everything. Therefore, this promise is certain—the one anointed in the Supernal Light attains dominion over the all. Of myself, I can accomplish nothing; Christ in me accomplishes everything. This is an astonishing discovery and it comes with holy awe and wonder!

"Listen! I am standing at the door, knocking; if you hear my voice and open the door, I will come in to you and eat with you, and you with me. To anyone who conquers I will give a place with me on my throne, just as I have conquered and sat down with my Father on his throne" (Revelations 3:20–21).

VERSE 3

Jesus said, "If those who lead you say to you, 'See, the king-
dom is in the sky,' then the birds of the air will precede you. If
they say to you, 'It is in the sea,' then the fish will precede
you. Rather, the kingdom is inside of you, and it is outside of
you. When you come to know yourselves, then you will be-
come known, and you will realize that it is you who are the
sons of the living father. But if you will not know yourselves,
you dwell in poverty and it is you who are that poverty."

Malkut, the kingdom of heaven, is within you and all
around you—yet, if you do not know that the kingdom is within you, then you will not see the kingdom outside
of you. Such is the nature of reality, this magical display of
consciousness. The inside and the outside are not separate
but are intimately connected. The reality of your experience
is the magical display of your own consciousness. A change
in consciousness brings about a corresponding change in the
reality you encounter. A change in the reality you encounter
is an expression of a change in consciousness.

In the world and waking consciousness there are many co-
creators of the magical display. There is the individual and the
collective creation of this magical display—and the individual,
the collective, and the universal consciousness are completely
interconnected and interdependent. You alone are not the creator of the reality you experience. Every living being is a
unique individual expression of the Life-power, the Holy One.

of Being, and a co-creator with God of the reality you experience. Nevertheless, when there is a transformation in your own consciousness, there is a proportional and corresponding transformation in the world, in the reality of your experience. In transforming yourself, you transform the world in which you exist. Do you want to change the world? You are the world and the world is you. If you want to change the world, make a change in your own consciousness.

Whether heaven or hell or a world of admixture, it is all a state of mind, a condition of consciousness-being. The kingdom of heaven is not a place, but a spaciousness in consciousness, just as hell is a severe confinement and limitation upon consciousness. There are worlds within worlds and worlds beyond, heavens and hells and spaces in between. All are an expression of consciousness-being, which is the radiant nature of consciousness, and all exist within consciousness.

There are higher, holier worlds than this one. No one can know how many there are. Nor can anyone be certain that any given world or level of consciousness is the same for different persons. Heaven could well be a dread and terrible thing for the wicked person, and for a saint, "hell" could be the most intense joy. What is known is that, most of the time, people are too busy here in this world to notice what is transpiring within it and beyond it, too lost in distraction to know themselves and so realize the wealth of higher and holier worlds that occupy the same space. Most ordinary individuals do not know the creative power that is in them and do not know that they are the world and the world is them. In ignorance, they remain bound to lesser gods and shadow lands, and do not know the world of Supernal Light within and all around them.

So many souls are asleep and dreaming strange and fitful dreams. They are asleep and do not know that they are dreaming and so cannot awaken in the dream to transform it. To the awakened ones, the holy ones, it is a sad and sorry sight. It is a vision of sorrow to behold the nightmares created by self-grasping, desire, and fear, and all of the suffering that naturally follows. The awakened ones know the world of Supernal Light here and now, yet they also know how very real the suffering is of those who remain ignorant and asleep. It is not an issue of personal salvation. No one is perfectly free until everyone is free.

"The first shall be last and the last shall be first" (Mark 10:31). Until the last "wicked" person repents and seeks righteousness, the great transformation of the Second Coming shall not be complete.

The force that binds is the force that will set everyone free. It is the same consciousness-force that manifests as the adversary or the Messiah, as heaven or hell. Enlightenment or unenlightenment are expressions of the very same consciousness-force, the one Life-power. There is one Divine mind, but two paths. This world stands on the threshold in between. It could go either way at any moment—toward heaven or toward hell—yet salvation is always at hand, the Second Coming ever near, as near as your breath and the beat of your heart, as close as the very nature of your consciousness-being!

Now listen and hear the Word of the Lord. You are free to choose! It could be heaven or it could be hell, but everyone must choose. Within you are the powers of salvation and damnation, the Light and the Darkness. When you are at last transparent, there will only be the Light and Life. That is the certainty of salvation in our Lord. Yet the suffering of damnation is all too real until salvation is attained. You must choose each moment. You must know the creative power that is in you and live in remembrance of the Spirit and Truth.

What is to be attained? Knowing and experiencing yourself as part of the Sacred Unity that is God, here and now. You have always been part of that Sacred Unity, are and always will be part of that Sacred Unity, the Holy One of Being. Never have you been separate from the Holy One. Union with God is not really an attainment; it is a present reality and truth. You need only remember the Spirit and Truth. You need only awaken and live with this awareness. It is not something you lack, but who and what you most truly are, the son or daughter of the Living God—the child of the Light, the Light of awareness itself.

Who are lost that they should be found? I tell you, none are lost that they should be found. The one who is lost has never existed, and the one to be found was never born. You are what you are seeking, the bornless Spirit.

This is the good news! Malkut, the kingdom, is within you and all around you. Eternal life is the Truth of your inmost being. Death has never existed. You are free!

VERSE 4

Jesus said, "The man old in days will not hesitate to ask a small child of seven days old about the place of life, and he will live. For many who are first will become last, and they will become one and the same."

An infant is not involved in, nor attached to the world. A babe of seven days old is not in bondage to name, form, and limited self-identity. Such a soul is undistracted and moves freely between worlds, neither bound to one nor forgetting the other, but naturally near to the source of life and light. If the small child of seven days old, as yet uncorrupted by the mind of the world, could speak, surely wisdom would pour forth, a wisdom people of the world would undoubtedly call folly or crazy. Yet such wisdom would come directly from the inmost part of the soul and God itself.

Now, indeed, the suggestion that an old man should inquire of an infant about the place of life is an impossible and crazy thing. Everyone knows an infant cannot speak and most would say an infant knows nothing. Yet the knowledge that the baby cannot speak and cannot hold in conscious awareness is a knowledge that is deep inside you. It is a gnosis in the inmost part of the soul that you can touch upon when, at last, you abide open and sensitive, completely undistracted.

Listen and hear. The holy child, the baby Messiah, is within you. There, in your inmost part, is the Spiritual Sun, the holy child. If you follow the star of Grace, the sense of the mystery in you, and you listen and hear, the holy child will speak to you and teach you about Mother Wisdom.

What the old man would seek to hear from the small child of seven days old is within himself. He has forgotten the wisdom of his soul, having become involved and attached to the world, his name and form, his self-identity, and his ambitions. He has forgotten why he has come into the world, the purpose and mission of his soul, and becoming distracted, he is lost to himself.

So it is with every ordinary person in the world intoxicated and distracted by self-grasping, desire, and fear, completely in bondage to a limited and mortal self-identity, and so remaining under the power of death. Yet, if one can let go and let be and go within, one will remember what has been forgotten and so set oneself free. This is true for anyone. It is true for you as well.

Now, there is also a secret meaning hidden in this saying. When it is said that the old man will ask a small child of "seven days old," the seven days are the days of Creation, the seventh day being the holy Sabbath, the day of repose. Yes, indeed, the holy child, the Spirit of the Messiah that is within you, is Lord of the Sabbath. The seventh day of Creation is the eternal Sabbath, of which every Sabbath occurring in space-time-consciousness is a gate.

So, here, the Master is speaking of entering into repose and seeking the Wisdom of the Divine presence and power that enters the holy abode on the Sabbath. Yet one must understand that the meaning of the holy Sabbath is more than it appears to be. It is not merely one day in the week. Rather, it is living from within in such a way that you are no longer the doer in life. The Spirit of the Messiah is the doer and the holy Shekinah is your faithful companion and guide. The eternal Sabbath has neither beginning nor end, nor does the Divine presence and power distinguish between days of the week. At any moment, whenever you remember the Lord, in that instant the Holy Spirit moves within you and through you and uplifts you into Malkut, the seventh holy Sephirah. Any time you enter into repose, the holy Sabbath dawns for you and the holy Shekinah comes to rest upon you.

The commandment of the Sabbath exists to remind you. It is given as a gift, so that perhaps at least one day in the week you might let go of involvement in the world and the natural distractions of such involvement and go within, seeking repose and communion in God. Then, perhaps, if you remember yourself as part of the Sacred Unity that God is, you might live according to that awareness. For the inmost part of the soul, the Holy Sabbath is every day; for the outer person, it is once a week. Such is the difference between timeless eternity and time eternity. In time, there are beginnings and endings, the first and the last, but in eternity, there is no such distinction. All is the same. When you realize yourself in Sacred Unity, when you awaken the Christ-Spirit in you, you will know yourself one with all and the same in essence. In that instant, you will experience eternal life.

Now I will share a further secret with you. Everything that has happened, is happening, or ever will happen, transpires on the seventh day of Creation, the eternal Sabbath. The knowledge is within you, the knowledge of your divine destiny and the destiny of all Creation. It is the vision of Creation from one end to the other, the awareness of a beginningless and endless reality-truth-continuum. It is the gnosis of Adam Kadmon, the primordial human being. This forms the basis of a worthy meditation.

VERSE 5

Jesus said, "Recognize what is in your sight, and that which is hidden from you will become plain to you. For there is nothing hidden which will not become manifest."

Imagine that the Lord himself is standing in front of you, along with Lady Mary Magdalene, speaking these words. There, in your sight, is a man and a woman, a spiritual teacher (a rabbi) and his consort. In plain sight are a husband and wife. Yet hidden within the ordinary appearance of a man and woman, Logos and Sophia are present, standing before you and speaking with you. If you recognize what is in your sight, the Divine presence and power manifesting as a man and woman, then in the instant of recognition, what is hidden is revealed to you and becomes clear. You realize the presence of the Messiah and receive something of the Spirit of the Messiah. In that very moment, the Light-transmission occurs.

You must understand, the Lord appears as any man and Lady Mary appears as any woman. They are completely ordinary in appearance, although, indeed, Lord Yeshua appears as a strong man and Lady Mary as a most beautiful woman. Yet, in appearance, there is nothing extraordinary about them. They look like you or me, or anybody. You could pass them on the street and never know how near to the Messiah and kingdom of God you had come. In order to know what is hidden within them, you would have to recognize what is in your sight. You would have to encounter them with a presence of awareness and then pay attention to perceive the Divine presence and power moving with them. Only then would you know to seek teachings and initiation and so invoke the Divine revelation.

Now, truly, such recognition is a gift of the Holy Spirit and is dependent upon the evolution of the soul-being. Few are they in any generation who recognize the prophets and apostles of God. Fewer still are those who actually seek teachings and initiation. Recognition is the beginning of initiation and self-realization. Having recognized a holy one who embodies something of the Divine presence and power, one must then abide and develop a strong connection with the holy one, and bring recognition to fruition, realizing the Divine within oneself. One must become a true and faithful disciple.

What does it mean to be a disciple? It means that you consciously participate in a mystery drama, a living myth that brings forth the Divine in life. Not only does it mean that you recognize one who embodies a higher form of consciousness and seek to receive teachings and initiations, but that you, yourself, seek to embody something of that Divine presence and power and act as an apostle of God yourself. The disciple is the servant of the spiritual master and labors in the work of the master. Yet, what the master is, in truth, is the truth of the disciple, the disciple's own inner teacher manifest. Hence, in recognition of one's master, one perceives one's own purpose and destiny in life. Discipleship means a journey of self-knowledge and self-realization, the realization of the Christ-self within oneself.

Here, I will tell you a secret. You can only recognize what is within you. If you are able to recognize something of the Divine presence and power within a holy person, it is that same presence and power within yourself that is recognizing. The holy person in you recognizes the holy person of the Master. The Supernal Light in you recognizes the Supernal Light in others and in the world around you. In the moment of recognition, you enter, to some degree, into the higher form of consciousness you are noticing. To some degree, that higher state of awareness dawns in you. If there is a difference between you and the apostle in whom you have recognized something of the Divine, it is only that the apostle has learned to abide in that Divine presence and power and to consciously unite with it, and, as yet, you have not learned to do so. At the outset, for you, it is a potential, while, for the apostle, it is actual. That is the only difference. Nevertheless, what you perceive is the Truth about yourself.

This is what is happening for everyone. Everyone is perceiving something about themselves all of the time. How we perceive others and the world is how we perceive ourselves. What is perceived depends upon our own state of consciousness, whether a lower or higher state. If we want to recognize what is in our sight so that what is hidden is revealed, we need only change our own consciousness.

Now there is a greater mystery revealed in this saying, for the kingdom of heaven is not merely something experienced in the afterlife states, nor is the world of Supernal Light something distant and removed from you. Matter and Spirit are not separate. Mundane reality and sacred reality are one and the same reality-truth-continuum. This very life you are living is a Divine drama, the play of a Living God. The whole of life is sacred. The whole of life is a Divine revelation, God revealing itself. The mystery is revealed in plain sight—in life itself, for those who have the awareness to perceive it.

Jacob discovered the Truth of the Master's saying at Bethel. God is in this place, whenever you are. God is present within all that transpires. There is no place devoid of God. If there were such a place that God did not exist, that place would not exist. Nothing happens save through the presence and power of God, for if there were an event in which God was not present, then the event could not take place. No place exists without God, nor does anything happen without God. God is the presence and power of everything, the source and foundation of all. God is within, yet ever beyond all that is. All that is, all that transpires, exists only in God. Something of God exists in everything, everywhere.

Jacob laid himself down to sleep somewhere in the midst of his journey. In the middle of nowhere, he laid down, taking an ordinary stone for a pillow. There, he dreamt of a Ladder of Lights and angels of the Lord ascending and descending upon it, and there God revealed itself to him. One end of this ladder was upon the earth and the other end was in the heights of the heavens. Messengers of the

Lord God ascended from the earth to heaven and returned with the Word of the Lord, with Divine revelation. There, in that nameless place, God revealed itself to Jacob and revealed the spiritual forces within and behind events in the world. So Jacob named that place Bethel, the "House of God."

Everywhere is a gate to heaven. The whole of Creation is the house or body of God, and God dwells in it and reveals itself through it. God is speaking through you and me, through everyone and everything. All is the self-expression of God. Thus, rightly, God has been called the Almighty Living God, for God lives in Creation, within, yet ever beyond it.

"For there is nothing hidden that will not become manifest"—the Divine potential will always tend to manifest itself. The purpose of God will always play itself out and ultimately be fulfilled. God will reveal itself in full. God is revealing itself all of the time!

Much more could be said, but this is enough. You will discover more of the Divine in life, your ordinary daily life, and the world, than in a book. Look and see what is in your sight, and what is hidden will be revealed!

VERSE 6

His disciples questioned him and said to him, "Do you want us to fast? How shall we pray? Shall we give alms? What diet shall we observe?"

Jesus said, "Do not tell lies, and do not do what you hate, for all things are plain in the sight of heaven. For nothing hidden will not become manifest, and nothing covered will remain without being uncovered."

Religious doctrine and observance is a human invention. It does not necessarily have anything to do with spirituality and the Divine life. Spiritual practice, devoid of spiritual living, will not bring about the necessary change in consciousness for enlightenment. The foundation of a true spirituality is the cultivation of your humanity and of the Divine potential within your humanity. Only when you cultivate your humanity and practice truth in your daily living is there fertile ground for spiritual practice to take root and bear fruit.

Receiving oral transmission of teachings and initiation is important. If you receive teachings and initiation but do not practice spiritual living and the cultivation of your humanity, there will be no change in you and higher awareness will not dawn. What do receiving teachings and initiation or engaging in prayer, meditation, and ritual mean if one does not live the Spirit and Truth of these practices daily? To learn about love and compassion, but not actively practice love and compassion in one's life, has no relevance. To study spiritual and esoteric teachings, yet not cultivate such qualities as patience, tolerance, understanding, generosity, kindness, compassion, forgiveness, and so on, has no relevance. The real meaning of whatever we might do spiritually, the teachings and initiations we might receive, the spiritual practice we might perform, lies in our ability to integrate the Truth and Light revealed in our experience and live according to it.

Here, the Master speaks of a spiritual life that anyone can practice. Fundamentally, he says, "Practice speaking the truth and treat others as you yourself would want to be treated." He tells you to live in an open and honest way and to practice the Golden Rule. Who can say that they do not understand what this means or that they are incapable of practicing it? Indeed, it is a way that everyone who is willing can follow.

Now here is a secret. Your ultimate health and happiness is completely interconnected and interdependent with the health and happiness of everyone else. Your own well-being and the well-being of others is connected. You are not separated and isolated from anyone or anything else in existence. All of Creation is intimately interconnected and interdependent. What you do to anyone or anything you see, you do to yourself. What you do to your environment and the world, you do to yourself. When dealing with others and your environment, you are dealing with yourself, so, in reality, acting toward others as you would want to be treated is giving to yourself what you most desire. Indeed, it is a practice of a true or enlightened selfishness, as opposed to the ignorant selfishness we practice that brings harm to ourselves, others, and our environment. The Master is speaking from an awareness of Sacred Unity and encouraging the truth seeker to live in such a way as to cultivate that same awareness.

Suppose what you are doing is writing a book as you live your life—a book of your life? It is a book that is finished and made complete only at the moment of your death. Now reflect upon this book and consider the possibility of studying and rereading this book in the afterlife. Is it an interesting book? Do you like the central character and what he or she is accomplishing? Is the book uplifting? What sort of book is it? Is it a book akin to the Holy Scriptures that you could reread and study forever, or is it a book you would never be inclined to read again?

What sort of book is being authored with your life and the way you live it? It is good to inquire what you would change of this book and to set about making that change, for when you die nothing can be changed. All is said and done and that is it—and it goes with you.

Truly, it is a dangerous thing to live as though there is no conse-quence for one's actions or as though there is no accounting for how one has lived. The masters of all Wisdom Traditions tell us that our future is born of our present actions, that the nature of our existence beyond the threshold of death is determined by how we are living now. Living without this awareness, one may, indeed, bring great harm and suffering upon oneself.

Gnostic Christianity does not believe in eternal damnation but rather in reincarnation, which is to say a journey of consciousness through diverse states of existence that tend toward a progressive de-velopment and evolution of the soul or of consciousness itself. In the midst of this journey, there are heavens and hells and realms of admix-ture, as in the life of our present experience. Whether heaven or hell or something of admixture, each individual generates the causes and conditions of their own experience. One's own state of consciousness, one's own self-grasping, desire, and fear, brings one's experience. The creative power in oneself generates one's experience and manifests it. It is all a question of how one uses the Life-power. The soul enters into the experience and becomes the sentient being, corresponding with what one most desires. The soul travels the path one's desire follows.

Here, the Master speaks the plain and simple truth. It is a truth in your present experience, if you have eyes to look and see it. Anyone with any degree of understanding will surely seek to live with this awareness. This awareness might be spoken of as living as though you were going to die tomorrow. How would you live today if you knew you were going to die tomorrow?

VERSE 7

Jesus said, "Blessed is the lion which becomes man when consumed by man; and cursed is the man whom the lion consumes, and the lion becomes man."

One might rightly call this verse a prophecy for everyone, a simple Truth of blessing and curse based upon the principle of free will in human consciousness. Indeed, this very thing of which the Master is speaking is the cause of Armageddon, the final conflict.

You must understand what Armageddon is. It is a conflict being waged within you and within every human being. It is a conflict between the forces of ignorance and the forces of gnosis, between our evolutionary past and our Divine destiny, between dark and hostile forces and the Divine presence and power. Although it will very likely be externalized in dark and horrific times ahead, it is already transpiring within the human spirit and vital soul. Whatever is externalized in these outward events will be the product of the internal conflicts that human beings have not resolved within themselves. Hence, the darkness and horror that may transpire in the world will come from within human beings. Thus, truly, humanity brings forth blessings or curses upon itself, becoming its own blessing or curse, depending upon how it uses the creative Life-power.

The root of this duality and conflict is found within Nefesh, the vital soul or desire nature. From time to time, everyone notices this duality or conflict within themselves. Whenever you notice yourself consumed with negative thoughts and emotions or behaving in a way you do not truly believe is right, when you notice a tendency to violence or hostility arising, or when you find yourself carried away by self-concern, disregarding others, in that instant you are seeing and becoming aware of an internal conflict between two aspects of Nefesh. That aspect consuming you with negative and violent thoughts and emotions is Nefesh Behamit, the bestial soul. That deeper part of you, which is noticing and becoming aware, is Nefesh Elokit, the godly soul.

This duality becomes most apparent in moments of crisis, or when you are tired or ill, or when life just does not seem to be going your way. When you become aware of this conflict, in that moment, what you will notice is that the negative thoughts and emotions consume you and that, in effect, you become them. It is the same with any extreme manifestation of desire or fear. The desire or fear tends to completely consume the consciousness, and one becomes almost entirely that fear or desire, often in total disregard for everyone and everything else and even forgetting oneself. This is Nefesh Behamit, the lion that consumes the human being and becomes the human being. In any instant you are aware of this and notice what has happened or is happening, that noticing and inclination to redirect desire energy is your Nefesh Elokit awakening and coming forward. The natural result of Nefesh Elokit becoming active is the transformation of Nefesh Behamit. This transformation is a restraint put upon the bestial aspect of Nefesh so that it acts in harmony with your inner being. Thus the human being consumes the lion and the lion becomes a human being.

It must be said that Nefesh Behamit is not inherently evil, though, indeed, the evil inclination and dark and hostile forces tend to possess and act through it. Nefesh Behamit is your survival and self-preservation instinct, as well as your tendency toward selfishness or the desire to receive for yourself alone. In truth, your inclination for survival and self-preservation is absolutely necessary for life in this world, and the desire to receive is also necessary. When this desire nature is manifest unconsciously and in an unbalanced way, so that we are unwilling to share and give to others or concerned only with ourselves in disregard of others and our environment, and perhaps even in disregard of our own true well-being, then Nefesh Behamit tends to generate evil and connects itself with forces of ignorance—dark and hostile powers. Yet when the desire to receive is transformed and manifest in a conscious and balanced fashion, so that one desires to receive, not for oneself alone, but for the sake of sharing and giving to others, then Nefesh Behamit is integrated into Nefesh Elokit and acts in harmony with the Divine intention in the soul or God's Will for the soul.

Now what is the nature of the blessing in store for an individual who masters the bestial inclination and desire energy? It is the blessing of becoming truly human and receiving the Neshamah, the heavenly soul, and through the Neshamah, consciously uniting yourself with God.

All who live according to the righteousness of Nefesh Elokit receive their Ruach, their spirit or human intelligence, and a greater intelligence of intuition is added to them. Through the lower and upper Ruach, they are linked to and receive the influence of their Neshamah. The Neshamah is the dwelling place of the Holy Spirit, the Spirit of the prophets and Spirit of the Messiah. There, in the inmost sanctuary of the soul, Godhead and God dwells.

Thus, the nature of the blessing is God dwelling in you and a constant communion in God. To enter this enlightened awareness is to enter into the kingdom.

When desire energy is scattered and directed to things of the world outside of oneself, the dawn of this enlightenment is impossible. Rather there must be a metanoia, a radical change in consciousness or conversion of consciousness, in which the desire energy is gathered up and turned inward and Godward. As long as you desire anything in the world more than God, you cannot attain Messianic consciousness. It is this transformation of desire in a spiritual conversion of which the Master is speaking.

The nature of the blessing and the nature of the curse are the experience of heaven or the experience of hell, not so much in the afterlife states, but here on earth. At any moment you are aware of the Sacred

Unity that God is, then surely you experience something of heaven. Likewise, any moment you forget and are unconscious of the Sacred Unity that God is, surely is a glimpse of hell. It is all a state of consciousness—a state of the heart and soul, mind and life.

Let us be clear. The battle of Armageddon is ongoing as this internal conflict within you. It is a battle being waged each day in the choices you, I, and everyone else make. If there is to be a victory for Christ, you must act as a spiritual warrior and master the great beast within yourself. Only then will Messianic consciousness dawn for you and only when a sufficient number of individuals so awaken will the Second Coming of Christ transpire—that is to say, the dawn of Messianic consciousness on earth. The prophecy of the Master is that it is all up to you and me and everyone, for we are masters of our destiny, whether conscious of it or unconscious, whether a blessing or a curse!

VERSE 8

And he said, "The man is like a wise fisherman who cast his net into the sea and drew it up from the sea full of small fish. Among them the wise fisherman found a fine large fish. He threw all of the small fish back into the sea and chose the large fish without difficulty. Whoever has ears to hear, let him hear."

This person is the one who has consumed the lion, transforming the beast into a human being. Such a person has let go of attachment to all lesser and petty desires in order to fulfill the inmost heart's desire, all desire energy drawn inward and upward into one holy desire, passion for the Beloved. For one who has transformed and integrated Nefesh Behamit into Nefesh Elokit, this is not a difficult thing; yet when Nefesh Behamit remains strong and dominant in oneself, it is a most difficult thing indeed.

The difficulty and the internal conflict you experience in the form of desire and fear reflects the opposition between the bestial part of Nefesh (the vital soul) and the inward godly part. All sorrow and suffering comes from this duality, which is the product of fundamental ignorance. In ignorance, one cannot discern between lesser desires and the greater desire, and so desire energy remains scattered and consciousness remains fragmented. As desire energy is gathered up and the fragments of consciousness are integrated into an authentic individual center, the power of ignorance and forgetfulness dissolves, along with the internal conflict.

What is the "big fish"? It is your Neshamah, the heavenly soul, and the Christ-self that dwells in it. Indeed, the fundamentalist would say it is Yeshua Messiah, the Son of God and Savior, yet what the fundamentalist would not understand is that the only-begotten Son, the child of the Living God, is that Divine self within each and every person. This, the Master has revealed through himself, though what is revealed is not exclusive to himself; it is the Truth of one and all in attainment.

You must understand that faith in Yeshua Messiah is faith in the Divine potential within yourself and that to follow him is to follow the way of the Spirit of the Messiah within yourself. The path he has revealed is a path to enlightenment, a conscious development and evolution of the soul into Messianic consciousness or Christhood. You are called to shape yourself in imitation of Christ and to embody the Christ-Spirit, thus, ultimately, becoming one anointed with the Supernal Light. Faith in the Spirit of the Messiah is the beginning of salvation, but it is conscious evolution into Messianic consciousness that is salvation itself.

Listen and hear what the perfect Master is saying, for you are called to a Divine labor in Spirit and Truth, and your faith must come to fruition in gnosis. It is not enough to believe, but you must become what you believe in. The Lord himself has shown us the way.

You do not live one life, but many lives. Your soul passes from one life to the next until it fulfills its Divine destiny. You have not come into the world for the sake of the world, but for the development and evolution of your soul. The challenge in entering into the world is to remember why you have come and to remain undistracted so that you might accomplish the purpose for which you have come. The world is a darkness wrapped in glittering lights and the power of ignorance and forgetfulness is strong in it, but the true Light is within you and it is the extension of this Light you must seek in the world and so resurrect yourself and the world.

To suggest that there is an enlightenment or resurrection to eternal life without a labor in Spirit is ignorant. Faith devoid of spiritual practice and spiritual living cannot come to fruition in true Gnosis. In the absence of spiritual practice and spiritual living, it is clear that one's desire is not for the Beloved, but rather that one's desire is for the world and the things of the world. Surely this is ignorance, for everyone knows that this world and everything in it will pass away. Knowing this, one must inquire what is most valuable. So it must be said that, while it is the pleasure of the Lord that we live life abundantly and enjoy creation and the life the Lord has bestowed upon us, nevertheless, you must know what the most valuable thing is and not be distracted so that you might attain it. This, in essence, is what the Master is saying.

In closing, I will share the secret teaching associated with this verse so that you might pass beyond the obvious. Here, the Master is speaking of the Hebrew letter Nun, the mystical death and rebirth in the Holy Spirit. He is also speaking of the difference between Nefesh and Neshamah, and of their ultimate union. In so doing, perhaps more, he indicates shifts in consciousness that allow one to enter into other worlds. Thus, while speaking of mystical attainment, the Master is also indicating the development of a knowledge of occult or hidden forces (magical development) and the mastery of those forces necessary in the great work. With regard to Nun, the fish, there is an inner and secret discourse associated with this verse. For one who seeks some knowledge of it, contemplation and meditation upon Nun will reveal many insights.

VERSE 9

Jesus said, "Now the sower went out, took a handful (of seeds), and scattered them. Some fell on the road; the birds came and gathered them up. Others fell upon rock, did not take root in the soil, and did not produce ears. And others fell on thorns; they choked the seed(s) and worms ate them. And others fell on the good soil and it produced good fruit: it bore sixty per measure and a hundred and twenty per measure."

The seed of Light, the Living Word and Wisdom, may be sown in one's consciousness, yet not take root and come to fruition. Teachings and initiations may be imparted but not be integrated and received. Receptivity is dependent upon the state of one's consciousness, the development of the desire to receive and impart. To receive the teachings of secret wisdom and initiation, one must prepare one's consciousness, purify and consecrate oneself to Spirit and Truth.

"Some fell on the road; the birds came and gathered them up." This is the situation of a person who has links to dark and hostile forces, and who is open to extremely negative influences. The demonic beings-forces will immediately devour and dispel the influence of whatever teachings and initiations might be imparted. Indeed, there are some who will approach a holy teacher, a tzaddik, not led by a sincere desire to receive, but for extremely distorted and negative ulterior motives. The dark and hostile forces are attracted like moths to a bright flame and compel the person to approach under the false appearance of a true seeker. Not only will the dark and hostile forces prevent reception of any teachings or initiations, but may also act to attempt to harm the tzaddik, disrupt the continuum, or cause discord in the spiritual community that forms around the tzaddik.

Entering into the mystical path, you must understand that you exist in a play of cosmic forces, Divine forces, demonic forces, and forces of admixture. Behind everything that appears and transpires in this world is the play of these cosmic forces, forces of which the ordinary individual is completely ignorant and unaware. So long as one lives in disbelief or unconscious of these forces, that soul tends to be driven and unconsciously compelled by these forces, held in bondage, as it were, by the play of these forces. It is for this reason that initiates of our tradition seek not only a mystical attainment, that is to say a conscious awareness of unity with God, but also seek knowledge and mastery of the occult or hidden forces, so that they might liberate themselves and others from bondage to these cosmic forces of ignorance and direct the cosmic forces according to the Divine Will. Here we come to understand why there is both a mystical and magical side to initiates in a Gnostic Christian Tradition, and why Divine theurgy plays such a strong part in the spiritual practices taught.

"Some fell on rock, did not take root in the soil, and did not produce ears." This is the state of the person who is completely disinterested and unreceptive to spiritual teachings. Such a state of complete nonreceptivity can occur for many reasons. It could be on account of severe grief that the individual refuses to let go and heal, finding a perverse sort of security in their suffering and being unwilling to seek healing and redemption. Likewise, it could be due to being too caught up in the world and self-cherishing or complete disbelief in anything spiritual or divine. It could also occur to a religious person bound to dogmas generated by mortal human beings and confused about the Truth of enlightenment or God. Preconceptions, preconditions, and expectations of all sorts could cause this unreceptive condition, even a concept appearing so innocent as unworthiness or believing oneself incapable could make the heart and mind dense like stone before the Light-transmission.

What is being spoken of is a dense or dull state of consciousness that does not allow the penetration of the Word and Wisdom of God and thus completely prevents the possibility of the Light-transmission. This is the most common state of the ordinary person in the world. While the first state the Master speaks of is due to extreme negativity, extremely negative actions, and karma, this state is due to a lack of development and evolution of the soul-being. Not everyone necessarily has a level of soul development adequate to receive the inner teachings and initiation. Likewise, it is possible that even a soul that is at that level could stop itself from receiving these things due to ignorance and forgetfulness.

"And others fell on thorns; they choked the seeds and worms ate them." In this situation, the person does have the capacity to receive and, indeed, is destined to meet a spiritual teacher and guide in this life. But although one may have the capacity to receive and the necessary level of soul development, one is distracted by the world and petty lesser desires, to such an extent that one forgets and betrays the seed of Light received. A choice for one's desire and the world seems harmless enough, yet it naturally causes stagnation and regression in the soul's development and evolution and, in a certain sense, can be more harmful than in the first instance of which the Master speaks. Greater damage is done to oneself when there is knowledge of what one is doing, and it is a completely conscious choice, than when an action is performed in ignorance and unconsciously. For this reason, the Master speaks in such a way as to make this sound more horrible than in the case of one under the compulsion of the dark and hostile forces.

Here you will understand that, in receiving teachings and initiations, you must guard, cultivate, and integrate what you have received. Without diligence and self-discipline it is impossible to remain upon the path, for one can be easily distracted by desires and convinced by the conventional wisdom of an unenlightened society that there is no harm in such distractions. All Wisdom Traditions speak of the damage that can be done to one who knows, yet betrays what they know in their own heart.

The first instance of unreceptiveness is on account of dark and hostile forces or what are often called "demonic forces"; the second and third situations are due to forces of admixture, that is to say, forces that are neither Divine nor anti-divine, good nor evil, but rather neutral in nature. Since two states of nonreceptivity are mentioned on account of forces of admixture, it indicates that such forces may prove the most difficult to overcome and perhaps the most challenging to the Gnostic initiate by the very fact that they are not obviously opposed to the Divine or evil and because they are related to things unenlightened societies condone and encourage. Thus more aspirants will fall to the forces of admixture than to the dark and hostile forces. It is for this reason that many among the tzaddikim do not distinguish in their teachings between forces of darkness and forces of admixture. To their disciples, the effect of either is fundamentally the same.

"And others fell on good soil and it produced good fruit: it bore sixty per measure and a hundred and twenty per measure." This is the situation of the person who is receptive, not only receiving for oneself alone but for the sake of being able to share and impart with others what has been received. Teachings and initiations are not fully received until they are integrated and our reception is not complete until we are able to share and impart these teachings with others. Sharing and imparting the Light received is an integral part of receiving it, and we ourselves are received as we receive others in the Spirit of the Messiah.

Here, we discover that we are all called to the divine labor of the great work and that we receive the Light-transmission only to the degree that we integrate it into ourselves and facilitate its extension beyond ourselves, in one way or another, helping to share and impart it with others. This is the true balance to reception and likewise the reflection of God and the Godhead, the All-Giver.

VERSE 10

Jesus said, "I have cast fire upon the world, and see, I am guarding it until it blazes."

The Master comes with a holy fire, a fire-consuming fire, making all like unto itself, Divine. The Master imparts the fire, kindles the fire, and tends the holy fire until it blazes and transforms the disciple. The disciple, too, once receiving the holy fire, must kindle and tend it until it blazes, the Master and disciple acting together so that initiation comes to fruition.

Now rightly, it is said that, without the blessing and guardianship of an adept or master, whatever spiritual practice you might take up is not fully alive and empowered, and thus cannot develop beyond a certain degree and come to fruition. The master generates and imparts substantial spiritual energy-intelligence, energy on the one hand that the disciple needs to actually fuel spiritual practice and, on the other hand, a field of energy that serves as a protection against other forces that would hinder or obstruct. Fire is an appropriate symbol of this substantial spiritual power, a power that transforms and illuminates and, indeed, serves to protect.

There is a holy continuum adepts or masters tend that empowers the continuum of spiritual practice and spiritual living among their disciples and at the same time blesses and protects those they have received as disciples. Once such a connection is actually formed, it remains until it is brought to fruition or completion, the actual completion occurring when the disciple imparts the initiation to another person. Here, the Master speaks of this secret continuum. In this way, passing from one to another, the whole world is set on fire with the Word of the Lord.

The Master is also speaking of something more, for Yeshua Messiah is an incarnation of the great World Teacher. More than a prophet, he is Messiah, and he brings into the world a new Divine consciousness-force along with a new dimension of teachings and initiations corresponding to this Supernal Light-force. Embodying this Divine consciousness-force, he transmits it to his immediate disciples and, through his disciples, to the larger collective of humanity and the world, initiating a Light-transmission that passes from one generation to another through the succession of apostles, the initiates who hold the secret keys of the mysteries that the Master taught and who embody something of the Light-force he brought into the world.

The nature of this supernal consciousness-force is akin to "fire" in that it transforms and illuminates all that it touches. It illuminates and transforms every level of consciousness into the likeness or image of itself. To describe this holy fire today, we would speak of it as a spiritual nuclear fire, a secret Divine energy or light that is hidden within the center of everything, within the center of every particle of matter, and that when fully actualized and released can radically transform, not only consciousness, but matter itself. The self-radiance of the Transfiguration and the demonstration of the resurrection body reveal something of the nature and transforming power of this spiritual consciousness-force.

Now, indeed, the person of the perfect Master has departed the world, yet his presence and power remain, the Holy Spirit with which the Lord initiated and ordained the apostles. The Divine presence and power lives and moves among us today in the secret apostolic succession within certain esoteric orders, and wherever Grace manifests it, as in the case of St. Paul. Likewise, the Lord is present wherever his name is spoken with understanding, and so, indeed, the Master continues to cast fire upon the world and to guard it until it blazes.

In these words, there is a prophecy of the transformation of humanity and the world by this Supernal Light-force of Messianic consciousness. While some would think in terms of a rapid and radical change, long before the appearance of such a quantum leap in evolution, the transformation is being worked out on invisible and hidden levels as nature slowly savors her process of development through ever more refined and higher forms of life. A radical change occurs on a perceptible level only when the ground and conditions for it are prepared. When, where, and how this great transformation will happen is not known; yet according to the prophets and the Word of the Lord, it is certain that the great transformation will take place.

That the Master is speaking of himself as transmitting and guarding this spiritual power until it comes to fruition in the great transformation or resurrection of the world indicates the duty of the faithful and all initiates to labor toward this greater advent of the Second Coming—hence, active engagement in the great work. For this holy fire to blaze, many must embody it and bring it into the world full force. You must give the Lord a body and life to accomplish the great transformation. What the Master does, the disciple must also do, and the Lord has promised that his disciples shall do even greater things than they have seen or heard him do. This is the very essence of a mystical and Gnostic Christianity, that you also must embody the Spirit of the Messiah and labor to bring about the Second Coming in your own lifetime.

In this verse is the secret teaching of the soul of the Messiah coming forth from the universe of Adam Kadmon, the primordial human being, and passing through the universe of Atzilut, bringing forth something of the fire of Atzilut with him. Why would this be necessary for redemption? To burn away the husks and liberate the holy sparks and so restore the body of Adam Kadmon to its primordial state, and more than to restore the image of the Lord, to recreate the holy body of the primordial human being according to the image of the Lord revealed in a new heaven and new earth. Bear in mind that the Master ministered not only upon the earth and in the heavens, but descended also through the gates of hades to liberate souls bound in the hells. What is new about the heaven and earth transformed by the Supernal Lightforce or Messianic consciousness? Hell and demonic powers no longer exist, for even Darkness realizes the Light hidden within it.

VERSE 11

Jesus said, "This heaven will pass away, and the one above it will pass away. The dead are not alive, and the living will not die. In the days when you consumed what is dead, you made it what is alive. When you come to dwell in the light, what will you do? On the day when you were one you became two. But when you become two, what will you do?"

What is that which does not change? I tell you, it is the essence of change, change itself. The nature of God (the Creator) is to create. The activity of Creation is change or transformation. Thus, it may correctly be said that the nature of God is constant change. Therefore, rightly is God called the Almighty Living God.

God is that which was, is, and forever shall be. From this, some have taught that God never changes, forever remaining the same, and in a certain sense they are correct. In the view of eternity, there is no such thing as past, present, and future. There is only the now. Everything is now, always.

Likewise, in eternity, there is no such thing as change. Everything is always the same. All is at one with the Holy One of Being. Yet timeless-eternity generates time-eternity, being generates becoming. God is infinite and eternal Being; yet God is the ever-becoming of all that was, is, or shall be. God is not only changeless, God is constantly changing. God is ever coming into being, without beginning or end.

"This heaven shall pass away, and the heaven above it will pass away." If this is true of the heavens, then it is equally true of everything else in Creation. Everything shall pass away, everything is in flux, everything is changing and will change—even the heavens or higher states of awareness change. This is the truth of creative evolution. With each emergence of a higher state of consciousness, a new heaven and new earth come into being, the former heaven and earth transforming into a new realm of manifestation. There is no end in sight to this process, for our teachers tell us that, following the attainment of Messianic consciousness, evolution continues toward ever more refined and higher states of consciousness-being, although indeed such states are far beyond our present capacity to imagine or comprehend. Thus we understand that seeking to live forever, even in the highest heavenly state, is a desire founded upon ignorance and inherently deluded. The very truth and nature of reality and our very own consciousness-being is different than that. God is quite different than we think!

"The dead are not alive, and the living will not die." If I know through direct experience the inner and more subtle and sublime dimensions of reality, and, yet more, I realize the bornless nature of my spirit, I realize the essence of my being in the Holy One of Being. Therefore, I know what we call death is but a shift of consciousness to another state of existence, and surely there is no such thing as death for me. I realize death has never existed! If I have not yet awakened and generated a conscious continuity of self-awareness throughout all states of existence, whether waking consciousness, dream, sleep, or death and the afterlife, then am I as yet truly alive?

I tell you, until you awaken fully in the Spirit of the Messiah, it is as though you are dead while in life. One who is awake is truly alive, and knowing the only way to live, there is no such thing as death. The one who dies was never alive, and the one who is alive will never die. In ignorance, we believe we are the one who dies; yet in truth, we are the one who was never born and therefore never dies. The bornless one is the Christ-self within us.

"In the days when you consumed what is dead, you made it what is alive." If you are alive in the Spirit of the Messiah, whatever you receive or consume you uplift and bring into Life. This is the meaning of the blessings and thanksgiving the initiate performs over the meal. Purified, consecrated, and consumed, the holy sparks contained in the food are restored to the body of Adam Kadmon, the primordial human being, and so redeemed in the soul of the Messiah, attached through you to Christ. As long as we live in this world, this is a central part of our sacred mission, to uplift the sparks in all that we do, in every way we can imagine.

Now, here too, is a most subtle teaching on the rite of the Holy Eucharist, for in eating what is alive, the dead are brought to life! In this supper, we receive the resurrection, and receiving it, we are empowered in the Spirit of the Messiah to share and give this eternal life. Perhaps in contemplation and meditation, the Holy Spirit will tell you more about this.

"When you dwell in the Light, what will you do?" This is a trick question, for you will do nothing! When you come to dwell in the Light, it is the Lord and his Holy Spirit that will do and accomplish everything. Of yourself, you will no longer do anything. Yet, dwelling in the Light, surely it will be your impulse to extend and share that Light, on account of love and compassion, although it will be Grace that accomplishes this desire. But do not be deceived! I have not given an answer to this question, nor shall I give an answer for the next question. No one can give you the answer. To such a question, there are many answers, and a special answer within yourself that belongs to no other person but you. Within your own reflections, you will find a greater answer than anyone could possibly give you, and more, you will find many layers of answers if you probe deeply.

"On the day when you were one, you became two. When you become two, what will you do?" Yes, indeed, what will you do? Will you "be fruitful and multiply," or will you seek to become one again? Are these two choices mutually exclusive or can both occur at one and the same time? You are presently divided; you are two. What are you going to do? Perhaps a secret key lies within stopping doing altogether; hence not doing, but only you can know and say what you will do or will not do. The Lord invites you to follow him, but whether or not you accept the invitation is up to you and only you.

VERSE 12

The disciples said to Jesus, "We know you will depart from us. Who is to be our leader?"

Jesus said to them, "Wherever you are, you are to go to James the righteous, for whose sake heaven and earth came into being."

The Master chooses the one who is to succeed himself as the teacher and guide of the assembly of the elect. In this case, it is St. James the Lord chooses, along with St. Peter, as teacher and guide of the general assembly. Yet among the apostles, each is given a sacred task and mission according to the nature of teachings and initiations he or she has received. Among the apostles there are those who are ordained to impart the outer teachings and initiations, those who are ordained to impart the inner teachings and initiations, and those to whom are entrusted the inmost secret wisdom. Every disciple receives teachings and initiations according to their capacity to receive and according to the development of their soul. Every apostle, moreover, is given a sacred task and mission according to the level of their initiation and attainment. Tradition tells us that the outer assembly leadership was given to St. James and St. Peter, while leadership of the inner circle was given to St. John and Mother Mary. To St. Mary Magdalene was given the sacred trust of the inmost secret wisdom, she being the apostle of the apostles, the incarnation of Sophia, and consort of Logos.

Here we understand the perfect Master as tau of a Mystery school, the holy tzaddik of a mystical order, for the incarnation of the Messiah is not the institution of a new religion. Rather, it is the revelation of the keys of the mysteries and transmission of the Light-force of the supernal consciousness that the Messiah embodied. The Master is the initiator of a stream of the Light-transmission and founder of a mystical and esoteric order bearing the keys of the mysteries and the Light-transmission in the world. Hence, not only by faith, but also through actively engaging in the divine labor and through knowledge (gnosis), we are awakened and redeemed. Faith is the beginning of salvation; gnosis is the fruition of salvation. Faith is accounted as righteousness; gnosis seeks the aim of perfection.

According to the different ordinations of the apostles, the one Light-transmission in the Master becomes many rays, as though light passing through a prism. Thus, not only is there the holy threefold order of Melchizedek embodied by the Master, as we read of in the Epistle to the Hebrews, but several mystical orders under the guidance of one holy order. The Light is manifest in different forms and levels of intensity so that everyone ready and willing might receive something of that holy illumination. This, of course, reflects the function of the holy Sefirot that span the five universes, which elsewhere the Lord speaks of as the five trees in paradise reserved for the faithful and elect. All of this is alluded to in this verse.

One might inquire, "What does it mean when the Lord says 'heaven and earth came into being for the sake of James the righteous'?" Let it be said that, in Genesis, there is no mention of God creating hell. It is written that God created only the heavens and the earth. God does not create hell; rather, dark and hostile forces and the evil inclination in humankind creates hell. While we might speak of ignorance and Darkness as a secret operation of the Holy Spirit, nevertheless, hell is the product of separation from the Lord our God, created not by God but by the delusions of ignorance and forgetfulness.

Here, the Master is not speaking of St. James alone, but of all the holy and righteous ones, all the tzaddikim and maggidim. The heavens and the earth and the whole of creation are the matrix through which souls or consciousness-being evolves. Thus, the Divine intention in

evolution is the purpose of Creation, of the heavens and the earth—
the development and evolution of the supernal and Divine human
being. It was for this purpose that Creation came into being, Creation
being the womb of God birthing the Spiritual Sun, the soul of the
Messiah. Whoever embodies something of this Holy Spirit and heavenly soul, it is as though for their own sake heaven and earth came
into being.

VERSE 13

Jesus said to his disciples, "Compare me to someone and tell me whom I am like."

Simon Peter said to him, "You are like a righteous angel."
Matthew said to him, "You are like a wise philosopher."

Thomas said to him, "Master, my mouth is wholly incapable of saying whom you are like."

Jesus said, "I am not your master. Because you have drunk, you have become intoxicated from the bubbling spring which I have measured out."

And he took him and withdrew and told him three things. When Thomas returned to his companions, they asked him, "What did Jesus say to you?"

Thomas said to them, "If I tell you one of the things which he told me, you will pick up stones and throw them at me; a fire will come out of the stones and burn you up."

How you view an apostle of God determines the nature of the blessing you receive. If you view the apostle as an ordinary person like yourself, then you will receive the blessing of an ordinary person. If you believe the apostle is a sage, you will receive the blessing of a sage. If you perceive the apostle as a maggid, then you will receive the blessing of a maggid. Yet, if you realize the Spirit of the Messiah manifesting to you as the apostle and have faith in the Divine presence and power within and around the apostle, you will receive teachings and initiations from the soul of the Messiah itself. It is the one who is receiving who determines the nature of the blessing received. One can only receive what he or she has a capacity to receive. To receive more of the Divine power than you have a willingness and capacity for is to be injured spiritually!

Which levels of teachings and initiations are received depends entirely upon your relationship with the teacher and your view of them. The more psychically and spiritually intimate your relationship, and the more you are able to perceive and embrace your teacher as he or she truly is, the greater the transmission of teachings and initiations. Never is it the teacher who limits what can be shared and imparted. Rather, it is the capacity of the student or disciple that places a limit upon the love of a master—that is, a limit upon the Light-transmission.

Now, truly, one must be a student and companion before one can be a disciple. A true and faithful disciple is a rare and precious thing. Some masters never find one, others find only one or perhaps two, while only on rare occasions does a master live who finds several or many. Many may think they are disciples, but few are truly disciples, for a disciple is a most intimate lover of the Beloved and, by the nature of their love, incapable of thinking of oneself as separate from the master, let alone the Beloved. Such love and devotion are rare in this world.

To have a master is to serve the Master and accomplish the Master's divine labor. No longer does one live for oneself but for the sake of heaven. One lives for the Lord. It is a mystical death and transformation of oneself into the image of the Lord, an intimate embrace from which one will return—never to be the same. There is knowledge, understanding, and wisdom in this embrace, as well as Divine power. Those who enter the bridal chamber never depart once entering, for they are no more. The Beloved has come to manifest as them. "I," "me," and "mine" do not exist in the bridal chamber. There is only the Beloved. When you behold only the Beloved, then you and the Beloved will be one.

What transpires in a secret discourse or in an initiation cannot be spoken of outside of the sacred moment. It is secret. First, it is secret so that the experience is not spoiled or contaminated. The disciple keeps it pure by not speaking of it. To speak of it to others is to open the experience to other outside forces and also to dissipate the spiritual power imparted. Rather, it must be kept to oneself until it is integrated and brought to fruition, or one could potentially lose the power of the master's blessing altogether. Second, just as the experience and energy needs to be protected as one would an infant, one must also protect those who would seek to receive before they are ready to receive, for spiritual knowledge and power given to an immature soul can cause great harm. Spiritual or mystical knowledge and power can be misused. Also, it can be overwhelming. Only one who is an adept or master, an apostle, can discern in Spirit what teachings and initiations an individual can receive and, further, guide and protect that individual in the Way. Thus the inmost wisdom and initiations are always kept in secrecy, spoken only to those who know the mystery already.

Here, there is another indication of the very real and substantial spiritual power the Master imparts. Fire coming from within stones might sound fanciful to those not having entered into mystical experience or having no knowledge of the magical arts, but for one who has had some experience, for the initiate, these words seem quite normal and convey a secret meaning revealing the nature of the teaching that Thomas received from the Master.

This verse, however, does not intend revelation of the secret teaching and initiation given. Rather, it is a teaching on discipleship and how one may pass from the outer to the inner and secret levels of the teachings, as well as the importance Yeshua placed upon initiation. All of the Master's teachings were based upon initiations or shared experiences through which faith bore the fruit of Gnosis. It is this awareness, more than anything else, that the verse is intended to convey.

VERSE 14

Jesus said to them, "If you fast, you will give rise to sin for yourself, and if you pray, you will be condemned, and if you give alms, you will do harm to your spirits. When you go into any land and walk about in the districts, if they receive you, eat what they will set before you, and heal the sick among them. For what goes into your mouth will not defile you, but that which issues from your mouth it is that which will defile you."

What does it mean that harm will come to you if you fast or pray or give charity? Surely, it makes you a good person if you engage in spiritual practice and do such things as these. Yet, indeed, if you are doing such things from self-cherishing or egotism, or to appear as a good and righteous person, then truly these things are harmful to your spirit because they are a lie! In truth, it does not matter how you appear to others but how you appear to the Lord, how you actually are. Regardless of what sort of activity you might outwardly engage in, unless your heart is good and bright and your mind is clear, there is no benefit for your soul and spirit. Yet equally true, if your heart is good, your mind clear, and you are centered inwardly in Christ, then all that you do will benefit your soul and spirit, and it will be as though God itself is doing it.

It is a question of living within, centered in the Christ-Spirit. If I live centered in the Christ-Spirit, then no longer am I the doer of any action. Rather, it is the Spirit of the Messiah in me, the Holy Spirit, that is the doer and that accomplishes everything that needs to be done. Whether it is the spiritual life in daily living, in prayer or meditation, in sacred ritual or spiritual study and contemplation, in active compassion and charity, or whatever activity I might engage in, that action is only as powerful and beneficial as the degree to which the Spirit of the Messiah is in it and accomplishes it. Only my Neshamah, my heavenly soul, and the Christ-self that indwells it, knows how to study and contemplate the secret wisdom, or how to fast and pray and meditate, or how to accomplish what is good. The outer person is but a shell, devoid of the Christ-self.

Also, it must be said that spiritual practice, however advanced and great the practice may be, has no true meaning or transforming power unless it is integrated into daily living and a spiritual life. Although I may practice a great deal and give freely to charity and appear to myself as a righteous and spiritual person, unless inwardly I live in the Spirit and Truth and I live according to the Truth and Light each day, my spiritual practice is worthless and perhaps even harmful to my spirit.

What I will tell you now may be shocking. It does not matter whether you eat meat or do not eat meat, whether you eat pork or do not eat pork, whether you drink alcohol or do not drink alcohol, whether you smoke or do not smoke. It does not matter to God whether you do or do not do any of these things. Moderation is the rule of health and happiness, but these things will not bring you closer to God or take you further away from God than you already are. You could dress in white, refrain from eating meat, drinking and smoking, yet inwardly, if you were far from God, you would remain in your exile. The opposite could equally be true, for one who lives conscious of the Sacred Unity could do all of these things and never be separate from the Lord. It is not any outward appearance or activity that brings you nearer to God. It is an inward state, the state of your mind and heart that matters.

This awareness is certainly not license for hedonism nor a suggestion that the aspirant should not engage in spiritual practice and spiritual living—rather it is quite the opposite. More to the point, however, it is the inward state and inner intention behind any action that determines the reality and value of the action itself. This is an essential realization every spiritual practitioner must come to as they mature in the Divine Life.

That the Master mentions healing the sick reflects the substantial spiritual power the disciple bears and the necessity that it is freely used to benefit others. It also indicates the holy Sefirah Tiferet, the Christ-center on the Tree of Life that represents the inner self and a balanced and harmonious inner and outer life.

The mention of food or offerings given and healings performed indicates the necessity of the desire to receive and desire to impart acting together to form a circuit of transmission. Unless we receive, we cannot give; unless we give, we cannot receive. This is a simple truth regarding the operation of Divine Grace that freely flows only when there is a desire to receive for the sake of sharing and giving to others. The holy Shekinah cannot rest upon a depressed person; equally, she cannot be the companion of a selfish person. One must be willing to give so that she might give through oneself. Give what you want to receive and you will find that, in giving it, you have received it. Receive freely and give freely and you will find a constant flow of Divine Grace.

VERSE 15

Jesus said, "When you see one who was not born of woman, prostrate yourselves on your faces and worship him. That one is your father."

What does it mean that someone is your father or your mother to whom you are not connected by blood? Truly, more than one who is your parent by physical birth, the apostle of God who becomes your spiritual teacher and guide is your holy father or mother, that is to say the parent of your rebirth in the Holy Spirit. Surely, the teacher is more than a brother or sister, for they have sojourned the path to enlightenment before any other companion in the assembly was born in the Spirit. The teacher knows most intimately the origin of your holy birth, as would any parent. Just as your teacher's holy tzaddik is your grandfather or grandmother, so your teacher is the holy father or holy mother of your soul.

Now what does it mean to speak of "one who was not born of woman"? Surely there is no one who lives who was not born of a woman's womb. Yet, it is not the physical and material body of which the Master is speaking, but rather the spirit and the soul. Just because one is born into a physical body and incarnate in the world does not mean that the spirit and soul has been brought forward and embodied. For that, there must be a rebirth from the womb of Mother Wisdom, a rebirth or awakening in the Holy Spirit, and she, not a woman, is the Holy Mother of the prophet or apostle of God. God, itself, is the true Father-Mother of the holy tzaddik. So the Lord called the Lord God "Abba," which means father or daddy.

How should it be that we should bow down and worship another human being? Indeed, it is unacceptable that we should worship any man or woman, for as the Lord himself has said, no man or woman is good, but only the Lord God in heaven is good. That is to say, only God is the Lord our God. No, it is not the human that the Lord tells us to submit ourselves to and worship, but rather the Spirit of the Messiah or Spirit of the prophets, which is the living Spirit of God embodied in the holy tzaddik. It is the holy spark of the soul of the Messiah in the tzaddik that we bow before and worship. In doing so, we open and surrender ourselves to that holy spark or Christ-Spirit within ourselves, and so we live according to the Way of the One Anointed in the Supernal Light.

The question becomes, how shall we recognize our spiritual father or spiritual mother? If we see a holy one, how shall we know to bow down before them and worship the Spirit of holiness? For the holy ones look like everyone else, like any ordinary person! How will we recognize and know them, let alone submit ourselves to their spiritual guidance and advice? Truly, most ordinary people cannot see and recognize an adept or master. Their souls do not yet have the necessary level of refinement and evolution. Even among those whose souls are on the threshold of awakening, most are ensnared and distracted by the web of illusion and too intoxicated by self-cherishing to look and see in this way. But there is more than the development of the soul involved in such recognition, for it is Divine Grace that allows recognition, the Holy Spirit herself who sees and recognizes and so establishes a connection. Were it not for Grace surely not one of us would be able to recognize a holy tzaddik, as it is by no outward standard that they are known, only inwardly through the knowledge of the Spirit.

The meeting of your holy tzaddik is a most sacred moment. In that instant, holy sparks are exchanged and a covenant spontaneously comes into being. It is like the instant of falling in love, although indeed something yet more subtle and sublime and often passing unnoticed. At certain times it may be easily mistaken for falling in love, as sometimes the connection and contact is so very strong that emotions immediately respond in the only way familiar. Nevertheless, it is the moment of a lifetime, and, indeed, a moment that we might have waited many lifetimes to enter. There, before us, is our gate to initiation, an everlasting door to enlightenment and liberation.

While the outer person or superficial consciousness cannot recognize our holy tzaddik, something deep within us does. If we are wise, we follow that intuitive sense and seek teachings and initiations from the holy one we have met. Receiving teachings and following them is what it means to prostrate oneself before the holy tzaddik. Receiving initiation and living according to that Truth and Light revealed in one's experience is what it means to worship the Divine presence of the Master. It is an opening and surrendering of oneself in faith and aspiration, a dynamic activity of a desire to receive in the disciple that stirs the desire to impart in the master and co-create the conditions necessary for Grace to move and initiation to transpire. Surely, this is a true bowing before and worship of the tzaddikim and is what the perfect Master calls each of us to do in the presence of our holy tzaddik. If I do not bow before and worship the living presence in this way, it is impossible for me to be a follower of the Spirit of the Messiah.

Such meetings are rare. It is very rare to find a living tzaddik in this world. Typically, there is only one spiritual master for us, although we might have many teachers. It is important not to lose track of the holy one we meet, for it may well be that we will not meet another, or that, if we do, we will find that we have no connection with another tzaddik, only the tzaddik given to us in Spirit.

VERSE 16

Jesus said, "Men think, perhaps, that it is peace which I have come to cast upon the world. They do not know that it is dissension which I have come to cast upon the earth: fire, sword and war. For there will be five in a house: three will be against two, and two against three, the father against the son, and the son against the father. And they will stand solitary."

Our teachers ask, "Does the Lord bring anarchy?" They answer, "Certainly not!" The world is already a place of anarchy, countless spiritual forces in conflict with one another, and countless wills acting in ignorance and in opposition to the Divine Will. It is a world of anarchy in which we live, and in truth, you are the world and the world is you, this world reflecting the anarchy of the fragmented consciousness of the human being in the bondage of ignorance.

Now, of a certainty, one who takes up God's Will shall find oneself in conflict with the world and the spiritual forces that play behind what transpires in the world. Before the resurrection of oneself and of the world in unification, there must first be a division made. One must separate oneself from the world, so that no longer is one of the world, but rather one is of the Holy Spirit while living in the world. Something holy is something set apart, and the holy of holies is the reunion in awakening, the blessing of the bridal chamber where there is only the Beloved.

The current of the world goes one way and the current of the Will of God the other. The unenlightened go one direction; the holy ones go another. Yet, although there are two paths, there is one Divine mind, one consciousness-force. It is the same consciousness-force that manifests as ignorance and as true Gnosis. The nature and essence of all being is the same, whether awakened or unawakened, clear or clouded. If you go with the current of society and conventional wisdom, you will naturally be opposed to the Wisdom and Word of God. Until humanity and the world dwells in Messianic consciousness, it can be no other way. For this reason, we are taught that "one cannot serve two masters"; one cannot serve God and the world at the same time, for you will either love one and hate the other, or love one and betray the other. First, there must be a division made. You must choose before gnosis of Spirit and matter are united within you.

The world is ignorant of the unity of heaven and earth, Spirit and matter. Human society, as yet, lives according to this ignorance, unaware that everyone exists in Sacred Unity and that one and all are intimately interdependent and interconnected. On account of this, one tends to live as though in an isolated and separate self-existence, although quite clearly that is not the case, and against the one who becomes aware of the Sacred Unity, the children of Darkness must rebel. In truth, these children are intoxicated and do not know any better.

As long as ignorance and falsehood reign supreme in the world and the world exists under the dominion of dark and hostile forces and forces of impurity and admixture, can you go along with the world and serve the Will of God? As long as any soul is yet held in bondage to the veil of forgetfulness and terror and death, can I withhold myself from the strife and battle for the advent of a greater good? Can one who is in any degree awake in the Spirit of God sit idle while compassion is lacking and injustice dominates? No, indeed. To remove oneself from the conflict and struggle of conscious evolution cannot in any way be called righteous! The Lord calls the elect to become righteous warriors and to dare to struggle for psychic and spiritual evolution, to struggle to fulfill the Divine plan on earth.

Not to a mortal combat for petty desires and vain spoils of war does the Lord call us to battle and, as St. Paul informs us, not "against

flesh and blood." We are called to a holy war against the rulers, authorities, and principalities of spiritual forces in this present ignorance
and darkness, against cosmic forces established in celestial places. Yet
these forces inhabit flesh and blood. They are incapable of acting
upon the material plane, save through the agency of physical living
beings, more often than not human beings. So, following the Christ-
Spirit and walking in the Way of the Light, before there is a greater
peace, there shall be strife and struggle and war. However, the sword
in the hand of the righteous warrior is Truth, the fire is the power of
the Holy Spirit. Living according to the Spirit and Truth, we bring
forth the Divine powers to bear upon the cosmic forces of ignorance
and falsehood.

Here, for the sake of understanding, it must be said that even the
force of ignorance and darkness is a secret operation of the Holy Spirit of God. There is nothing that exists apart from God and nothing that
exists in which something of God does not dwell. Although ever beyond Creation, God is ever within all of Creation and every being-
force or creature. Hence, resolution of the great conflict is not so much
the destruction of the heart of evil, but rather the release of the Light
that secretly exists within it. So we are called to battle significantly differently than the wars human beings wage upon one another; it is a
struggle toward uplifting the sparks of holiness into unification. First,
however, one must discern between good and evil, ignorance and true
knowledge, and understand how to purify all that is admixed. Only in
this way can one consciously entertain the conflict and perform the
spiritual alchemy necessary for the great transformation.

There is an inner level of wisdom in this verse. It speaks of entering
the mystical path and receiving teachings and initiations into the hidden wisdom. Many would come to the path seeking peace and happiness according to mortal terms, thinking that spiritual practice and
spiritual living will swiftly fulfill this or that egoistic desire or will
bring instant peace and good fortune. While, for some, peace and joy
swiftly follow their entrance and good fortune seems to abound, more
often than not, that is not the case at all. Before a greater peace, joy,
or attainment, trial and tribulation come and, in some cases, what
might seem to be the greatest misfortune of all. Moreover, preceding

any initiation, there is typically a certain ordeal, for a mystical death precedes every rebirth in the Spirit. But there is more to be said as to the reason for this.

The soul has passed through many lives before the present life and may well have engendered a great deal of negative karma or the accumulated effects of sin. Before a further advancement of the soul in evolution, these things must manifest to be worked out, but now with the guidance and help of a spiritual teacher and, yet more, the Grace of God in the form of the Holy Spirit. Quite simply, there are things to be finished, cycles to be completed. Therefore, trials and tribulations reflecting these things often arise swiftly as one receives teachings and initiations, so that whatever hindrances or obstructions or impurities exist might be dissolved or transformed so that there might be purification. It is for this reason that the "confession of sin" precedes the rite of baptism, so that, in the first initiation of the tradition, one might purify oneself of former ignorance and sin. The confession of sin, of course, esoterically, is simply the awareness of the ignorance and negativity that binds us, which is necessary for us to dissolve it. This confession is inward, not outward, basically speaking. There is also another aspect to this purification.

Along with the negative energy-intelligences accumulated by former actions and habits of behavior, there are also distinct connections formed to the klippot, the cosmic forces of ignorance and falsehood. Such connections must also be dissolved or transformed and, until they are, such negative beings-forces continue to have much power to hinder or obstruct the soul's development and evolution. Therefore, upon entering the path and at various points along the way, these beings-forces assault the aspirant, attempting to do everything possible to prevent them from the attainment of Christ-consciousness. It may be that one's "good fortune" before entering the path came not from the Divine powers but from forces of admixture or even dark and hostile forces, in which case consecrating oneself to the Holy One of Being will first mean a cessation of the alleged good fortune.

You are in this world for the sake of the struggle of the soul's evolution, to become truly human and more than human. In a manner of speaking, you must understand that you have not come into the world to cater to petty desires, nor for the sake of rest or repose, but for the struggle of conscious evolution and the divine labor of God's intention upon the earth. That is not to say that a secret center of repose and joy is not to be found within you in this life, but that only by finding it amid the struggle and conflicts in this life will you possess that Christ-center in the afterlife. By nature, this is a place of work upon oneself and humanity, a place of planting and cultivating good seeds toward harvest, a place for a change in consciousness and self-realization. It is truly not yet time for us to rest. That time shall come soon enough. Now we are called to struggle and attain dominion spiritually, so that, according to God's Will, like Yeshua Messiah, we might become the masters of our destiny, no longer held captive by cosmic forces of ignorance. The Master is saying that it is time to fight for a greater good if we wish to see the all-good manifest in the world.

As one sage has asked, "If not now, when?"

Just for contemplation's sake, it might be pointed out that the "five in a house" in conflict are the senses and also the levels of consciousness within each person. In addition, it indicates a certain point of division or separation in the holy vessels to be mended, an abyss between the two upper worlds and three lower worlds, between Atzilut and Beriyah.

VERSE 17

Jesus said, "I shall give you what no eye has seen and what
no ear has heard and what no hand has touched and what
has never occurred to the human mind."

The preacher has said, "There is nothing new under the
sun." Therefore, either this secret is hidden right here
and now or it is something "beyond the sun" that the Lord
has brought down. In truth, it is both hidden here in every
particle of matter and beyond the sun. Did you know that
your body is literally made of stardust?

There is a Supernal Light-force of which the stars and matter in their inmost essence are the physical reflection and material expression. The Light we behold in the perfect Master is
a spiritual nuclear force having the power to transform everything it touches, but the true meaning of this escapes mental
concepts and human imagination, for, by its very nature, the
supernal consciousness-force is supramental, that is to say,
wholly beyond the mind or mental being and its concepts. It
has never occurred to the human mind and can never occur to
a mental being. It is only revealed in the experience of the
supramental state or supernal consciousness; hence, it is only
known to itself in full. Among the Gnostics, it has been called
the "Perfect Thunder Mind," although it is No-Mind. Such is
the nature of Messianic consciousness.

How shall I speak conceptually of what transcends all concepts? If I were able to speak about it, but you did not even

know the clear radiant nature of the ordinary mind, how would you understand and believe me if I spoke to you of this heavenly mind that is No-Mind, that is pure primordial awareness?

If I say to you that there is no thought in it at all, it will seem as if it were the mind of an alien God, or perhaps be confused with a state of dull stupidity that lacks intelligence. In fact, this Gnosis mind beyond mind has no need for thought. It is a consciousness of pure awareness that operates from a silent will. It brings forth everything from within itself and knows everything directly within itself, being a non-dual, gnostic awareness. There is no duality in it whatsoever, so that the individual and the universal exist in perfect unity with the transcendental. Yet, neither the individual nor universal is in any way lost; all exists as it is in Sacred Unity. Rather than the drop of saltwater poured back into the ocean, it is as though the ocean pours through the drop of saltwater, so that the individual and universal are perfectly self-aware as one self that is completely selfless. Such perfect peace and divine joy is this Christ-consciousness. No words can describe it nor human mind conceive it. It is completely beyond mental being, although mental being is a manifestation of this one supernal consciousness-force, and every gradation of consciousness-being is an expression and operation of this one consciousness-being, the Holy One of Being, who human beings call enlightenment or God. The perfect Master reveals our Divine destiny. It is the intention of God that we become more than human. The very nature of the great work is to strive and labor to become more than human—to become Christ-like or God-like.

In order to consciously labor to evolve toward the image of the Lord, that Divine image must be revealed to us. You cannot direct the creative power that is in you to act with God as a conscious co-creator of your Divine destiny unless the image of your potential and future self is revealed to you. You cannot be and become what is not seeded in your creative imagination. This must be a Divine vision, a direct experience, so that, to some degree, you have a noble ideal by which to shape yourself. You must receive initiation, and receiving initiation, you must then strive to shape yourself according to that Truth and Light revealed in your experience.

Here is a secret: your "future self," the Christ-self, is your present and real self! The Lord has shown you your own inner or higher self, and, truly, the Lord is that self which is No-Self. Not only are you to become Christ-like; you are to become Christ, the only-begotten Spiritual Sun of God. It is the nature of the Messiah, the inmost Spirit of the Messiah, that Lord Yeshua reveals, and it is this Supernal Light that passes through the apostolic succession into this present generation.

This manifestation of the Holy Spirit that moves through the succession of apostles was not manifest in the succession of the prophets. Only the holy Shekinah below rested upon the prophets, but in Yeshua Messiah, the holy Shekinah above and below rested upon him and worked within and through him to reveal and transmit herself. Through the mystery drama we know Mother Mary as the personification of the upper Shekinah, and St. Mary Magdalene, the consort of the Master, as the personification of the Shekinah below. Both Mother-Sister and Daughter-Sister Wisdom lived and moved in union with the Son-Brother Logos, revealing the Divine fullness of the heavenly Father-Mother, and the One-Without-End.

What is the meaning of this saying? The Lord has a secret and has told you that he has a secret so that you might seek to know the secret. After all, if you did not know there was a secret or mystery, how would you seek it, let alone find it?

VERSE 18

The disciples said to Jesus, "Tell us how our end will be."

Jesus said, "Have you discovered, then, the beginning, that you should look for the end? For where the beginning is, there will the end be. Blessed is he who will take his place in the beginning; he will know the end and will not experience death."

What is the "beginning" in which the end will be found? Surely, it is the intention of God in Creation; for the beginning of Creation is the holy thought or intention from which everything emerges according to the Word and Wisdom of God Most High. Therefore, to understand the end or fruition of creation, you must realize the beginning; that is to say, the Will of God in Creation and the Will of God in your soul. For it is that Divine Will that will ultimately be your end.

Now our teachers tell us that the holy intention of God in Creation was and is the manifestation of the Divine human being, the whole of Creation having the aim of bringing into manifestation the soul of the Messiah. The first holy thought of God is the image of Godself in the form of Adam Kadmon, the primordial human being. From this holy thought and image, Adam Ha-Rishon, the first human being, was created. The first also being the last, the "end" is the Divine human being manifest in the image of the Lord in conscious unity with the Lord God; hence awakened.

There is involution in the process of Creation for the sake of evolution, involution proceeding by gradation and therefore evolution also proceeding by gradation. In the beginning, the first human being is unaware and unconscious of the Sacred Unity and thus must "fall from Grace," or be involved in the process of Creation in order to consciously evolve individuality and self-awareness and realize a conscious unity with the Lord God; hence to awaken from primordial sleep or unconsciousness. Creation, then, having its source and issuance in God, is the progressive self-expression and actualization of the infinite and eternal potential of God, the Divine potential being exhaustless. Therefore, while we might speak of awakening as the "end," in truth, the Divine potential is exhaustless or limitless (Ain Sof), and there is no end in sight. Quite simply, there is no end to creative evolution. For that matter, if you go seeking the beginning you will find no beginning.

In truth, Creation is a beginningless continuum of coming into being, the source and ground of which is the One-Without-End, the Holy One of Being. Such is the nature of the reality-truth-continuum; it is without beginning or end. It is this gnosis that constitutes the holy order of Melchizedek. Of the initiates of this holy order, it is said they are without genealogy, having neither beginning of days nor end of life, but abide in conscious union with God Most High as holy priest-kings forever. Hence, this verse contains the secret of entrance into the holy order of Melchizedek, indicating the central key to the mysteries the initiates of that order possess.

The Master is speaking of the inmost secret key of the mysteries. This key is reflected in the knowledge displayed by the author of the Epistle to the Hebrews, a letter written not to the outer assembly of the elect but to the inner assembly, so that, having entered into the sanctuary of the Rose Cross, they might also enter into the inmost secret assembly of the threefold holy order of Melchizedek. In association with this verse, the Epistle to the Hebrews provides a good source for contemplation.

Understand the beginning as the intention of God in Creation. Taking one's place in the beginning means not only the attainment of self-realization, but also acting as a conscious agent of God's Will in humanity and on earth. One who enters into the realization of the Christ-self, like Yeshua Messiah, becomes an embodiment of the Living Word and conscious co-creator with the Lord God. It is for this reason that the Master informs us that we will potentially do even greater things than we have seen him do. The Holy Spirit will manifest uniquely in each individual soul that awakens in Christ and she will accomplish far more than already accomplished. There is as yet the resurrection of the world to be accomplished and the Spirit of Truth in the apostolic succession labors to this end-which-is-naught. While, indeed, this is a teaching of entering into the perfect repose and delight of the bridal chamber, it is also a call to enlightened action.

Now gnostic masters speak of the beginning in another way, saying that the beginning is the clear Light that is the very nature of our consciousness and being, the very essence and presence of God in the inmost part of our soul. Reading Genesis, we hear the first utterance of God as the Holy Word: Let there be Light! This Light comes before all else, even the sun, moon, planets, and stars. It is not any light known, but rather is a hidden and transparent Light, the holy Light, as it were, before the point of the beginning. That Supernal Light is, in fact, the Spirit of the Messiah. Of this Light, the prophet tells us, the Lord formed the Light and created the Darkness. "Formed" means that this Light was revealed but not created. Hence, this Light is without beginning or end. Indeed, it is the bornless Spirit, the Spirit of Messiah.

This Light is the Light of awareness. It is the pure, pristine, primordial awareness that is the very nature of all consciousness-being, the inmost essence of your consciousness-being or soul on every level, even the ignorant and ordinary level of consciousness. To realize this clear Light nature of consciousness is to attain enlightenment and liberation; liberation from bondage to ignorance and death. Death is the devil of forgetfulness, which breaks the continuity of conscious existence. Remembering the Christ-self, you will awaken and never forget again.

In closing, I will tell you an open secret: That which holds you in bondage is that which will set you free!

VERSE 19

Jesus said, "Blessed is he who came into being before he came into being. If you become my disciples and listen to my words, these stones will minister to you. For there are five trees for you in Paradise which remain undisturbed summer and winter and whose leaves do not fall. Whoever becomes acquainted with them will not experience death."

B lessed is he who came into being before he came into being. The Lord is speaking of himself and of all the enlightened and righteous ones who incarnate to accomplish God's Will on earth and to guide and uplift humanity toward its Divine destiny. They are messengers of the Lord, spiritual teachers and guides, holy souls that have previously awakened to one or another degree and who continue to incarnate in humanity out of love and compassion in order to uplift the holy sparks and enlighten and liberate souls from the power of ignorance. They are, indeed, blessed and a blessing, worthy of all praise and honor. It is a priceless gift to encounter and meet one of these tzaddikim in life, and the wise who encounter them listen to them and follow their teachings, becoming disciples or companions of the master.

To *listen* means to open and surrender oneself, to practice and live according to the holy teachings, and to establish the conditions necessary to receive initiation. The secret wisdom may be openly spoken to many, but only those who listen and hear will receive initiation and be *saved*—that is to say, attain a degree of self-realization. One must practice and live according to the Spirit and Truth in order to awaken and set oneself free. The initiate will tell you that there is no other way to live, no other way to eternal life. Every other way is as though being in a deep slumber of strange and fitful dreams or in a living death of which death itself is the lord and fruit.

Now for those who listen and hear, there will be a radical change in consciousness. Upon entering into the mystical path and involving oneself in it through actual spiritual practice and spiritual living, the inner dimensions will open and one will discover God constantly speaking to one's secret and undying soul in every circumstance, situation and event of life, the whole of life being filled with the Divine presence and power. The disciple will discover the kingdom of heaven within and all around. Even in the most ordinary thing, the Holy Spirit will minister to the soul and self. The world is alive and full with the holy Shekinah; the Living Word and Wisdom of God are to be found within everyone and everything. The Spirit of God indwells Creation, as much as transcending it altogether. Realizing this you will truly live and move, and consciously have your being in God, knowing the Spirit of God indwelling you, and even rocks will speak the Word of the Lord to you.

But what if I told you that stones do speak as heavenly angels, all manner of Divine spirits and angels, from spirits of the prophets and sages to great angels? What if I told you that hosts of angels constantly minister to the holy ones, the Divine powers continually coming and going from their presence? Does it sound too fantastic? I will tell you this, what the Lord has in store for you is fantastic. It is unbelievable, awesome, and wonderful! It is incredible, absolutely incredible!

So let me tell you more. If you don't believe me, it won't matter anyway. But if you are blessed to believe me, perhaps it will set you to seeking, so that you might find and know yourself and therefore receive far greater blessings than anyone could ever possibly bestow, blessings straight from the Lord God itself!

Not only can we speak of the Divine powers that serve and minister to the elect, but the tzaddikim become aware of other worlds in the inner dimensions, worlds within worlds and worlds beyond. Each world is as "real" as this material world and those nearer to God are perhaps more real in experience. Not only does the initiate commune with the presence of the Lord and the Divine beings-forces. The initiate enters into other worlds and brings blessings back. Indeed, as St. Paul tells, oftentimes the apostles of God are taken up into the heavens while yet in this life, just as the prophets before them, and they return bearing gifts of the Holy Spirit and a Divine vision or message, whether for themselves or for the people of the book. The holy Master is teaching and initiating his disciples into these mysteries, imparting the secret keys of the mysteries to them.

It must be understood that such holy things are not taught openly but in secret, never in public, only in private, and only to a true and faithful disciple and one who has already had something of the experience and therefore knows already. Only a disciple can receive such precious gifts in Spirit. Only a disciple is involved so deeply in the holy covenant with the master as to share in such mystical experiences. The outsider cannot receive such things, only one who has become an insider and, yet more, a lover of the mystery and the Beloved.

I will share another secret with you. It is unbelievable, but nevertheless valuable. Although great angels are sent with messages for the holy tzaddik, they always are delighted when sent by the Lord into the presence of a holy one who bears the presence. While it is their mission to help the tzaddik in the Divine labor, the angels go also to learn secret wisdom from the tzaddikim and, like the disciples of the holy tzaddik, receive secret teachings and initiations.

All of these things that I have shared are not really so secret. The greater secret lies in the meaning of the five trees in paradise and the nature of acquaintance with them. These five trees are the holy Sefirot in the five worlds or universes, hence "Jacob's Ladder" or the "Palace of Lights." They are the spiritual flows of the Divine powers in the universes of Adam Kadmon, Atzilut, Beriyah, Yetzirah and Asiyah. Acquaintance with these holy trees, the Tree of Life that spans five infinite universes, is the spiritual experience of the Sefirot through binding oneself to them and binding them to oneself. Hence, the Master is teaching his disciples of Merkavah, the ascent and descent of the soul through the Ladder of Lights and, yet more, is imparting the secret keys to mysteries never before disclosed, namely ascent into Atzilut and into the universe of Adam Kadmon. No prophet had ever passed so far in ascent before, nor had any master ever held the keys of these holy mysteries. They are known only to the soul of the Messiah.

"These stones will minister to you." Yes, with such gnosis, one would realize the Supernal Light of Keter secretly hidden in every particle of matter and would possess the knowledge to actualize and release this spiritual nuclear energy. This same truth is reflected in the earlier verse when Thomas speaks of stones thrown at him, from which fire would come and burn up those who threw the stones. It is an allusion to this secret spiritual power of Messianic consciousness.

There is a spiritual power the Lord has in store for us that is far greater than we can imagine as mental beings. This Divine presence and power is now active upon the earth, working in secret among us to bring about the great transformation. Living and moving among us are individuals who embody something of this Light-force, and they transmit this holy Light to those who are ready and willing to receive it. This is the nature of the succession of apostles in the lineage of Yeshua and Magdalene, the divine labor of the great work.

This is a verse of crazy Wisdom. May you become so mad with Divine passion as to receive such Wisdom and embody the Light of Messiah! Amen.

VERSE 20

The disciples said to Jesus, "Tell us what the kingdom of heaven is like."

He said to them, "It is like a mustard seed. It is the smallest of all seeds. But when it falls on tilled soil, it produces a great plant and becomes a shelter for the birds of the sky."

Perhaps now the Lord might say, "It is like a quantum leap. A quantum leap is the smallest movement, not really moving at all. But when it happens under the right conditions, it produces the most radical change in consciousness and reality, so that the reality of one's experience is not at all the same and one's knowledge vastly increases." Yes, perhaps he might say this or, perhaps again, he might use the analogy of the nucleus of an atom. Nevertheless, he is speaking of the smallest thing that produces the largest transformation, saying the nature of the kingdom of heaven is like that, the smallest thing, which is the most powerful thing.

Here, once again, we have an allusion to a spiritual nuclear force that bears a most radical power to transform, the very power of Keter everywhere in Creation secretly waiting to be realized and actualized. The Master alludes to this Supernal Light-force again and again in his teachings. It is the heart of the Divine presence and power we behold in him.

Now planting of a seed always holds the meaning of initiation. In this context, the Master is speaking of an initiation from which the Tree of Life grows and provides shelter for souls of righteous and angelic beings. When one receives initiation and instruction on how to bind the holy Sefirot to oneself, so that these streams of spiritual power are established in one's aura and subtle body, one experiences directly something of the kingdom of heaven, and angelic beings will frequent the environment of the initiate. What this means is that you have the ability to manifest the kingdom of heaven at any time—you merely need to learn how to shift to a higher state of consciousness.

A shift in consciousness is, most truly, the smallest movement. Like the mustard seed it is the slightest of things, yet the affect/effect is incredible! The whole magical display of reality can completely transform in an instant. One becomes aware of the presence of God everywhere in everything, and becomes conscious of countless worlds and countless beings-forces occupying the same space at the same time in a vast matrix that is completely interconnected. Now, here, I'm not proposing to say what the experience of the kingdom of heaven is, but rather attempting to give some glimpse of what one aspect of the experience might be. And I tell you, this tiny taste or suggestion is nothing compared to the actual experience, nothing at all. It is something far more, and it is contained in the most ordinary level of reality. It is so ordinary and so close, no one notices the key to heaven's gate!

In truth, it can be said that the first heaven is the awareness of the presence of God everywhere in this very life, an awareness of the living presence in everyone and everything, which, of course, comes from the awareness of the Divine presence in you. This level of awareness itself is what it means to enter into Malkut, the kingdom of the Tree of Life. Any moment this awareness is present, one is experiencing Malkut. It is the slightest change in levels of awareness, yet the change in one's view of life is radical. Such awareness is a direct manifestation of faith, a level of gnosis which is the fruit of faith.

The seed of faith sown in the mind, heart, and life, purified and consecrated to the Divine Life, will naturally lead to this level of awareness, and yet higher levels of awareness. But the desire for heaven cannot compete with all manner of base and petty desires, nor come to fruit amid insecurity and fear. Such impurities, hindrances, and obstructions must be progressively rooted out, so that your faith might grow and the Holy Spirit might do her work in you. Everything that in any way hinders or obstructs the Spirit's work must be either cut away or transformed. Hence, the soil of consciousness must be tilled to allow the seed of faith to take root and come to fruition in some degree of gnosis or higher awareness.

A great deal could be said of the experience of higher states of awareness and the inner dimensions, but these are things best discovered and learned through one's own experience. Voyeurism in spirituality never results in attainment, thus spiritual practice and spiritual living are called for from each aspirant. The fruits of experience will accord with one's labor in the field of one's own consciousness, but it must be said that whenever the right conditions in consciousness are manifest, Divine Grace immediately flows and acts to impart all blessings.

VERSE 21

Mary said to Jesus, "Whom are your disciples like?"

He said, "They are like children who have settled in a field which is not theirs. When the owners of the field come, they will say, 'Let us have back our field.' They (will) undress in their presence in order to let them have back their field and to give it back to them. Therefore I say, if the owner of a house knows that the thief is coming, he will begin his vigil before he comes and will not let him dig through into his house of his domain to carry away his goods. You, then, be on your guard against the world. Arm yourselves with great strength lest robbers find a way to come to you, for the difficulty which you expect will (surely) materialize. Let there be among you a man of understanding. When the grain ripened, he came quickly with his sickle in his hand and reaped it. Whoever has ears to hear, let him hear."

Not only must disciples recognize the Divine presence and power in the apostle of God who is their holy tzaddik, but they must recognize their inner connection to the apostle, that within them is the same Divine presence and power awakening, and so *hear* the call of the Holy Spirit to the great work of redemption. The disciple is a child of Light in whom the Light is awakening. In this knowledge is the beginning of enlightenment and liberation. The disciple has humility in the presence of the master and also has divine pride, knowing him- or herself as a brother or sister of the Son of God and seeking to identify with the Christ-self within.

Entering into the continuum of the Light-transmission you must know who you are. No longer can you live according to a limited self-identity with superficial consciousness and mortal name and form. Rather, you must dissolve this ignorant self-identification and instead generate a new self-identity with fully evolved and enlightened being— hence a new self in Christ.

The gnostic initiate does not wait upon the Second Coming of Christ, continuing to live in ignorance. In faith, the initiate seeks knowledge of Christ within, labors actively to bring the Christ-self forward, and lives according to that Truth and Light revealed. To gnostic initiates, the attainment, the image of the Lord, is the path. Practicing and living the attainment, they bring forth the fruit of the attainment and so embody something of the Christ-Spirit.

Now what does this mean? It means they understand the way of holy meditation through which they unite themselves with the Spirit of the Messiah, merging their heart with the enlightened heart of the Master, their mind with the gnosis mind of the Master, their soul with the Soul of the Messiah, and their life with the holy name of the Anointed One. Entering into mystical union with the Lord, they seek to extend the Light into the world and to labor for the redemption of the sparks, living in the world as the Lord himself.

How shall you practice this mystical union? To enter into such a continuum of spiritual practice, you must be received by an apostle of God and so receive teachings, instruction, and initiation. The way is different for each soul and so the way for you cannot be written in a book. Only a living tzaddik can guide you in this way. Yet, surely, the interior church and college of the Holy Ghost is open to anyone who desires to enter. Therefore, such a practice can be shared in a general form. If practiced with faith, this practice may establish the conditions necessary for an apostle to come to you.

Gather your consciousness inward behind your heart, as though into a Spiritual Sun shining there. Let your attention be directed inward and upward and so attune yourself to the Divine presence and power. Then envision the glorified image of the Lord magically appearing in the space before you, his body formed of translucent light. Let yourself see, feel, and experience the presence of the Lord as fully as you can. Open your mind and heart to the Holy One of Being. Holding the image of the Lord in your mind, pray to the Lord for a blessing, for his Grace to pour out upon you. See the Lord answer your prayer. See light streaming from his sacred heart and body pouring over you and into you, transforming your own body into a Body of Light. As your body becomes a Body of Light, intone the holy name of Yeshua Messiah. While you chant the holy name, see your body rise, dissolve into fluid light, and pour into his resurrection body, merging yourself completely with the image of the Lord. When you stop the chant, abide in the state of union as long as you can. Then let the Lord be praised and the blessing received be grounded in your own body and environment. Practice walking in the world with this awareness.

This is a practice that is good for conscious living and conscious dying. It is a practice our teachers would give to anyone willing to practice it and so it is given here to you, with the prayer it might bring knowledge of the Lord and good fruits. In this way, you might gain insight into the nature and way of a mystical union, although, indeed, such a practice is but one part of the way.

The power of this practice is that it is a practice of the Truth of yourself and, over time, leads to the realization of that Spirit and Truth. You are not a spirit of this world, as in ignorance you might believe. Rather, you are a child of the Light, a bornless spirit of the world of Supernal Light. The ignorance from which you suffer is a forgetfulness of who and what you are. Spiritual practice is remembering and awakening and so setting yourself free. The disciple is one who is awakening, just as the master is one who is awake. The disciple is a child of the Light, a brother or sister of the Son of God; hence a son or daughter of the Living God.

Now listen carefully. If you practice and realize this Truth, you will not experience death. On that day of reckoning, you will simply undress, shedding the material body, the garment of this world, and put on a new garment, the Body of Light. In joy, you will leave the world to the powers of the world. Entering into the world of Supernal Light, you will enter into perfect peace. Yet, there is a further secret to this attainment. Those who realize the Christ-self in life know the world of Supernal Light within and all around them, here and now. Resurrection is not an attainment in death but rather an attainment in life. Therefore, even before the enactment of the mystery of crucifixion and resurrection, our Lord and Savior could proclaim, "I am the resurrection and life."

Who is the thief that would steal the Divine Life from you? It is ignorance and forgetfulness and the cosmic forces that support the Darkness that has dominion over this world. While in this world, you must be on your guard and not be distracted, lest you fall asleep, lose yourself in forgetfulness again, and so fail to awaken and set yourself free. Indeed! You must keep a constant vigil, a constant continuum of spiritual practice and spiritual living. Such a holy continuum consists of study and contemplation of the Holy Scriptures and spiritual teachings, most especially those of the secret wisdom, mystical prayer and meditation, sacred ritual and actively living the Divine Life. All of this is what is meant by living from within.

Just as much a labor for enlightenment and liberation for yourself, you must labor to extend the Light to others. There is ultimately no such thing as personal salvation. We are all interconnected and interdependent and love and compassion does not allow only personal salvation. Our salvation is a self-transcendence, not a personal and egoistic deliverance. As long as any living soul is bound to ignorance and the holy sparks remain trapped in klippot, the body of Adam Kadmon is as yet incomplete in redemption, which is to say, the mystical body of the Messiah is missing some part of itself. Not only are you called to labor for the fruition and harvest of your soul, you are called as a laborer in the field for the greater harvest of souls. It is such a holy vigil or continuum that gives "great strength," the spiritual powers of a righteous warrior or holy tzaddik.

VERSE 22

Jesus saw infants being suckled. He said to his disciples, "These infants being suckled are like those who enter the kingdom."

They said to him, "Shall we then, as children, enter the kingdom?"

Jesus said to them, "When you make the two one, and when you make the inside like the outside and the outside like the inside, and the above like the below, and when you make the male and the female one and the same, so that the male be not male nor the female female; and when you fashion eyes in place of an eye, and a hand in place of a hand, and a foot in place of a foot, and a likeness in place of a likeness; then you will enter [the kingdom]."

What does it mean to be as a little child? It means to look and see with eyes of wonder, experiencing everything as for the first time every time. So, too, it means a playful and creative way, a path of enjoyment and delight in each moment, living in the moment as the child lives, not in the past nor in the future. It means that it is always in the present moment that you will find yourself and find eternal life and God.

What does it mean to be as an infant? It means you cleave unto God, as though suckling at your Holy Mother's breast, in such a way that you and the Divine are one and the same and there is no division between you and the Beloved. You are the Beloved and the Beloved is you.

"When you make the two one." The two are Nefesh Behamit and Nefesh Elokit, the bestial part of the vital soul and the godly part, which must be brought into harmony and united. This is an attunement of one's desire energy or vital energy to Ruach, which is able to receive the influences of Neshamah, the heavenly part of the soul and higher self. Unless the vital soul is unified and attuned to the spiritual flows of the Divine power, it cannot receive Neshamah's influence nor the guidance of the Holy Spirit, and it remains unaware of the living presence of God.

"When you make the inside like the outside and the outside like the inside." The outer superficial consciousness must be shaped upon the pattern of the inner self, so that the outer self and inner self are integrated and harmonious, completely reflecting each other. Your thoughts, feelings and emotions, words and deeds must follow the way of the inner self or Christ-self, so that, indeed, you are the Holy One. This is the meaning of "righteousness," being rightly ordered according to the image of the Lord or the Christ-self.

"When you make the above like the below." Here we should expect the Master to say, "When you make the below like the above." Perhaps there is a mistake in passing on the words of the Master here, but, nevertheless, there is a profound truth in these words, for it is our aim to bring heaven upon the earth, thus making the "above like the below." Likewise, there is the suggestion that one is to bring down something from above—the Neshamah and the Supernal Light-force within it. You are to actively aspire to embody Christ-consciousness and to the degree that you do you will experience the kingdom.

"When you make the male and the female one and the same, so that the male be not male nor the female female." First, the Master is speaking about the desire to receive (female) and the desire to impart (male). Hence, to make the male and the female one and the same means to develop the desire to receive for the sake of imparting, so that one is perfectly transparent to the Holy Spirit. Receiving so that you might impart is a complete self-transcendence. Not only do you become like the Holy One, but the Holy One comes to manifest as you. In this instant, you become the flow of Divine Grace, the Divine presence and power living and moving in the world.

On another level, there is a secret here. If you are female in Asiyah, then in Yetzirah you are male, in Beriyah female, in Atzilut male, and in the world of Adam Kadmon you are neither male nor female. The reverse is true for the person incarnate as a man. Thus, there is the suggestion of linking these levels of consciousness, and the spiritual flows associated with them and shaping them, into the image of the Lord above, an image that contains within itself all opposites in perfect union, including the male and female. Hence, in the prophets, we hear of the presence or angel of the Lord that sits upon the celestial throne appearing as a Divine human being. While we may speak of this in terms of the spiritual experience and state of enlightenment, it is also a prophecy that life on earth is seeking to accomplish, our present state being a transitional state moving toward that Divine intention.

This speaks of the holy mystery of sanctification in the union of husband and wife. Performed with love and mystical knowledge of sexuality, this union brings about a union above and below between the Holy One and the Shekinah. It is a secret mystery enacted perfectly by Lord Yeshua and Mary Magdalene. It is also reflected in the relationship of Joseph and Mother Mary, whose union brought into the world the soul of the Master who would embody the soul of the Messiah.

"Eye in place of the eye" indicates the enlightened view of a higher level of awareness associated with the center in the head, the first center associated with a conscious union with God or God-consciousness. "A hand in place of a hand" indicates action founded upon this enlightened view. "A foot in place of a foot" indicates directing one's whole life according to this true Gnosis. "A likeness in place of a likeness" is the development of the solar body or Body of Light (body of the resurrection) that is naturally and spontaneously generated through such spiritual practice and spiritual living. Fundamentally, the Master says that you enter into the kingdom when you live according to the Spirit and Truth, and so embody the holy kingdom.

While the foolish would wait upon the kingdom to come, the wise labor to bring the kingdom of God on earth in their lifetimes. Indeed, there are those who experience the kingdom of heaven while yet in this life. May you be "wise as serpents" and so act to transform yourself and the world!

VERSE 23

Jesus said, "I shall choose you, one out of a thousand, and two out of ten thousand, and they shall stand as a single one."

I tell you, it is not the disciple who chooses the master, but the master who chooses the disciple. The holy tzaddik is like the farmer who passes through the vineyard and selects only the ripe fruit from the vine of life. Only the grapes that are ripe and mature will make the finest wine of the Beloved. Those that are unripe, the holy tzaddik will not pick but will leave them on the vine until they ripen.

Truly, only the mature soul, having a certain level of development and evolution, can become a disciple of an apostle of God. We may speak of ten levels of soul evolution in present humanity, and only when approaching the fourth level is a soul ready to enter into a Mystery school or mystical order to receive teachings and initiations of the secret wisdom. It may be one in a thousand that will enter, and two in ten thousand that will attain and bear fruit, that is to say, become an apostle of the Lord imparting the Light-transmission. "Only by going to school," as one mystical teacher once said, "can you enter into the fourth level and pass beyond to the inner levels of the soul's destiny. One must receive teachings and initiation, and have guidance and protection along the way."

In all Wisdom Traditions, the mystical order has an outer and an inner circle. There is a spiritual fellowship that forms a link between the order and the world. There is an outer order of students and practitioners and an inner order of disciples and adepts. Within and behind this magical display is a secret and invisible order of the Holy Spirit. So it was, and is, in the sacred circle formed about the Master. "One in a thousand" indicates those called to initiation of the outer order and "two in ten thousand" those called into discipleship and initiation into the inner order; yet the fellowship and holy order form one mystical body of Christ, united as one mind, heart, and body, knit together in the bonds of love and knowledge.

It is only when one understands the transmigration of the soul through countless lives that one will come to realize that the soul-being progresses through various stages of evolution, and that within humanity several different levels of development are present. Likewise, one will understand why the tzaddikim and maggidim do not try to *save* the multitude or masses of humanity, but rather labor to teach and initiate only those who are ripe and mature—hence, only a few. The multitude are not yet ripe on the Tree of Life, but must continue the rounds of life, death, and rebirth so that they might ripen and mature under the sun before passing into the Light, the secret Sun within the Sun of Life. Therefore, those who are ripe for the harvest are rightly called the chosen ones or elect.

Now, it must be said that, by the very fact that you are reading this and considering these esoteric teachings in your mind and heart, you are approaching the fourth stage of the soul's evolution or have come to labor in one of the stages beyond it. The very impulse to seek in the mystical and esoteric dimensions is the call of the Holy Spirit within a deeper part of yourself that is awakening. Hearing the call, it is your choice whether to answer the call or not. Answering the call means seeking to receive teachings and initiation and to actively practice the Way—hence, to pass through the gate of initiation.

In this context, the Lord has spoken, saying, "Many are called, but few are chosen." Many will encounter an adept or master of the Light-transmission, but few will choose to follow the tzaddik through the gates of initiation. What one does or does not do, whether one actively answers the call of Spirit or not, is the fundamental test of the ripeness or maturity of the soul, from which the response of the tzaddik naturally follows. Once having made its first contact with the continuum of the Light-transmission, the soul begins to form a link with the soul of the tzaddik or maggid, and continues through various lives, here and there making contact, until at last the soul is able to enter the path. Then the soul sojourns the path from one life to another until awakening and liberation. This, in essence, is the journey of every soul through the endless rounds of transmigration, the purpose and meaning of which is conscious evolution and awakening— the attainment of Messianic consciousness. It is the journey of the individual as well as the collective soul of humanity.

This evolution is reflected in the various levels of covenants between the chosen ones and God in the Holy Scriptures. In the Scriptures, we see five manifestations of the holy covenant continuum: one with Noah, one with the patriarchs and matriarchs, one with the children of Israel at Mount Sinai, one with Israel at Moab before entrance into the Holy Land, and one promised in the prophets that is manifest in Yeshua Messiah. Likewise, we see this evolution in the three holy covenants redeeming the three branches of the seed of Abraham, namely, the Light-transmission passing through Moses, the Light-transmission passing through Yeshua, and the Light transmission passing through Mohammed (Judaism, Christianity, and Islam).

Here, Lord Yeshua is giving instruction on the evolution of the soul and its progress to maturation, and on discipleship in the Way. Anything so rare is precious and, indeed, priceless. It would seem the disciple must know this in order to be a true or faithful disciple, lest things of less value easily distract and carry the would-be disciple swiftly away. The good news is that the tides of lives will eventually bring the soul back to the gate, and in one life or another, the soul will cross through to the other side. The bad news is that it could be a long while before the tides turn. This is the simple Truth.

VERSE 24

His disciples said to him, "Show us the place where you are,
since it is necessary for us to seek it."

He said to them, "Whoever has ears, let him hear. There is
light within a man of light, and he lights up the whole world.
If he does not shine, he is darkness."

Here, the Lord speaks of the interior life, living from within one's Godly soul (Nefesh Elokit) and the Christ-Self, which naturally brings forth the Light of God into one's life, so that oneself, one's environment, and one's life are the extension of that Divine illumination. In effect, the Lord says, "I am within you, and when you contact the Christ-Spirit in you and bring your Godly soul forward, you will know the place where I am, for I am wherever you are."

As one beloved saint proclaimed, "Why do you seek your Lord outside of you? For as the fragrance abides in the flower and your reflection abides in the mirror, so does your Holy Lord abide within you." Truly, this is the most wonderful news, for we know where to seek the Lord and how to enter into communion with God, and so the Way is opened before us. We need only turn our attention inward and Godward to enter into the holy sanctuary and meet with the Beloved.

At this point, it must be said that, in receiving teachings and initiations of the secret wisdom, we are not actually receiving something from outside ourselves nor anything we do not already possess inwardly. Rather, it is an education in the truest possible sense—a drawing out of what is within. Until we are educated, that is to say, until we draw out that which is within ourselves, we remain in bondage to ignorance. Our liberation is simply the recognition and realization of the Light that is within and living in such a way as to let that Holy Light shine forth.

This is a beautiful, simple, and direct verse, so it seems to me the less commentary the better. Understanding the context, it speaks for itself. The Spirit of the Messiah is within you, within everyone you meet.

VERSE 25

Jesus said, "Love your brother like your soul, guard him like the pupil of your eye."

How deep is the nature of the spiritual love the elect seek to cultivate in their fellowship? It is a love and compassion so deep that one holds the interests and welfare of one's spiritual companions equal to one's own self-interest, as though the needs and well-being of one's brothers and sisters were one's very own needs and well-being. Anything less is no different than the way all ordinary people live in an unenlightened society. In striving toward an enlightened society, we are called to live according to a higher state of awareness and to practice living this higher awareness in our spiritual community, so that, being empowered by love and compassion, we might be able to extend that Light of awareness beyond the boundaries of our spiritual community into the greater community and world.

I have previously discussed the various levels of development and evolution of the soul-being. When speaking of entering into the fourth level, the level of the heart center, it is through the cultivation of spiritual and, ultimately, unconditional love that one enters this level and passes through it to the next stage of the soul's coming into being in the image of the Lord. Such love may be regarded as the gate to the path of enlightenment, the foundation of the mystical journey to conscious union with God.

Here, the Master speaks of this love in terms that are quite clear. Practice loving your brothers and sisters as you do your very own soul and self until, at last, such love is a subconscious endowment to you or your second nature. What does it mean to have this love as a subconscious endowment? How swiftly do you blink or close your eye when there is danger of harm to it? So swiftly that thought is not even involved. It seems to happen automatically with no need of thought at all, and surely no debate as to whether or not you will take action. When compassion and love are spontaneous in this way, you have the love in you of which Lord Yeshua is speaking.

Now this Divine fullness of love is not complete until the soul enters into the sixth stage of development, for the perfection of such love comes with a conscious unity with God and that unification brings the awareness of the Sacred Unity you share with everyone and everything in creation. Only this higher awareness fully embodied would allow the perfect fruition of this spiritual love as we see in the perfect Master himself. How limitless is the love and compassion of the perfect Master? Such is his love that he freely gave his life, the most precious thing he had to offer, for the sake of the awakening and liberation of his spiritual companions, his disciples then and now and in the future. Through death, he revealed the Supernal Light and eternal life.

Not only is love being spoken of here, but since this gospel already addressed the state of the Master and disciples, and the reception of teachings and initiations of the secret wisdom, now the Master addresses the need for spiritual community and spiritual fellowship. It is spiritual love that binds one to one's holy tzaddik and to one's spiritual companions, so that the sacred circle united with the mystical body of Christ acts with one mind, heart, and life to accomplish the great work. As much as the holy tzaddik and the teachings and initiations, the spiritual community is also a holy sanctuary for the soul and a necessary development and evolution of the soul-being. Just as without a spiritual teacher, and reception of teachings and initiations, we cannot typically venture and advance very far upon the path. Likewise, without spiritual community and fellowship, our spiritual growth and evolution would be distinctly limited. A loving spiritual fellowship is needed for our growth.

Here I will share a secret with you. The assembly of companions that forms around a holy sage and apostle or prophet of God determines the degree to which the Divine can be revealed and the Light extended into the world. The holy tzaddik can reveal the inner and secret wisdom and perform miracles with the magic-power only in an atmosphere of faith, hope, and love. Faith is the intuition of an experience not yet had, hope the active aspiration to attainment of that spiritual experience, and love the active power in the human spirit that allows God's Holy Spirit to freely act. If you wish to look and see this, then you might study and contemplate the Divine revelation at Mount Sinai. In that event, God first reveals the secret wisdom to the prophet, that he might impart it to the children of Israel openly. But faith, hope, and love were lacking in the assembly, the inner covenant was shattered, and only a veiled and outer revelation was given. The inner teachings were kept in secret, unspoken save to a few close disciples. Indeed, it is said that, had the assembly maintained the proper atmosphere at Sinai, the soul of the Messiah would have entered into the world at that time. There and then would have been the advent of Messianic consciousness on earth. So it is in every generation. When a large enough assembly of righteous souls are ready and willing to act together in the bonds of love, the advent of Messianic consciousness or the Second Coming will be at hand.

There are two commandments given to us by the Master, which are the very essence and light of the Holy Torah: To love the Lord our God with all our heart and all our soul, and all our mind and all our strength; and just as we love the Lord God, to love our neighbors as ourselves. Now, as creatures of form, it is almost impossible to leap into the love of God, who is formless, invisible, and hidden. To love God at the outset is a very difficult thing. Likewise, to love all people as we love ourselves—friends, strangers, and enemies alike—is unlikely to be our first step in love. Thus, the Master gives us steps of spiritual practice toward such love. Although we cannot see God directly, we can see the sons and daughters of the Living God, our holy tzaddik and spiritual companions. We can begin to cultivate our love and compassion with those we can see.

Likewise, although at the outset it would be almost impossible for us to love all people equally, actually experiencing love for the stranger and enemy as we do for ourselves, we can begin with the whole of our spiritual community. Having established a strong love of our spiritual brothers and sisters, we can extend it from there. If we cannot love our spiritual companions as we love ourselves, surely then we are missing the mark of the two holy commandments the Lord has given us. Indeed, as St. John informs us, if we say we are of the Light, yet hatred remains in us or an imperfection in our capacity to love, then something of the Darkness remains in us and we are not yet wholly of the Light.

In closing, I would share this with you. If you wish to be loved, then be loving, for it is in being loving that the depth of love is experienced. It might rightly be said that the unloving person, although he or she is loved most deeply, is incapable of receiving that love. Not knowing love within oneself, one cannot recognize one's love manifest. Be loving and you will experience the fullness of love; the Lord's love will fill you to overflowing and will become a great power in you. The activity of love is its own blessing. In truth, there is no greater spiritual or magical power than love.

VERSE 26

Jesus said, "You see the mote in your brother's eye, but you do not see the beam in your own eye. When you cast the beam out of your own eye, then you will see clearly to cast the mote from your brother's eye."

If you want to draw near unto the Lord your God and enter into direct experience of the Holy One of Being, you must purify yourself and consecrate yourself to the Holy One. You must learn to abide in a state of purity. Indeed, you cannot draw near unto God without self-purification. For this reason, before the prophet ascended the holy mountain to receive the divine revelation, the Lord gave instructions that the people should prepare for his ascent by passing three days in a state of ritual purity. Now the people were not called to ascend the holy mountain, but merely to be as near to the source of revelation as the base of the mountain and to create the conditions proper for the prophet's ascent. If self-purification is necessary in order to receive an indirect revelation of the glory of the Lord, how much more essential is self-purification for the mystical initiate who seeks to enter the prophetic states and to experience the glory of the Lord directly?

Here, the Master is speaking of self-purification as central to the great work. As long as there is a misdirection of your vital energy and consciousness, impurities, imperfections and obscurations, links to forces of admixture and dark and hostile powers, how shall you fully awaken in the Holy Spirit and set yourself free, let alone be able to strengthen and assist other souls to awaken and liberate themselves in Spirit? We might use the analogy of the prophet Moses. Before he could serve as God's messenger to liberate the children of Israel from slavery, he had first to liberate himself and venture through the wilderness to encounter the presence of the Lord. So it is with any sojourner upon the mystical path; one must purify and consecrate oneself to the Holy One of Being and actively perform the great work within oneself.

Self-purification is not only cutting off or transforming negativity found at the various levels of consciousness. Equally, it is the development of noble and Christ-like qualities. Having dissolved or transformed a manifestation of negativity to maintain the state of purity, one must put in its place the corresponding enlightened quality. For example, as in this verse, if you find yourself standing in judgment of others, which reflects severe self-judgment, then dissolving self-judgment, you must practice self-forgiveness and establish forgiveness in place of judgment. Two qualities essential to self-purification are forgiveness and love. In order to be empowered to forgive and love others, you must first manifest self-forgiveness and self-love so that you have forgiveness and love to give. While remaining judgmental and unloving of oneself and others, self-purification is not really possible.

The mystical path or path to enlightenment is first and foremost a work upon oneself. Only through this divine labor of conscious evolution within oneself can one actually give strength to others and eventually be able to render both visible and invisible assistance effectively. This is not advocating a falling in upon oneself nor another state of self-cherishing under the guise of spirituality, but rather proceeds from a fundamental understanding of the Sacred Unity underlying reality. The truth is that you are the world and the world is you. If you want to change the world, you must change yourself. Understanding this, you will realize that a radical change in the greater collective consciousness of humanity can only come about through a radical change in individual consciousness first. When a sufficient number of individuals embody a higher state of consciousness, then a similar change or transformation can take place in the larger collective. This basic truth is the secret wisdom behind the Lord calling a nation to be a "holy people," and when one nation alone could not accomplish the shift in consciousness, the Lord extended the call beyond the boundaries of a single nation, both through Jesus and Mohammed—although, indeed, it will be groups of people of one mind and heart and acting together that will be able to effect a radical transformation in the consciousness of humanity in the future. The foundation of this transformation will be individuals who have radically transformed their own consciousness.

The first three initiations of mystical Christianity place an emphasis upon the process of self-purification. The rite of baptism is specifically a ceremony of purification. It is a confession of a prior missing of the mark, the mystical death of that old self bound to sin, and putting on a new self in the Christ and the Holy Spirit. The rite of chrism (anointing) continues this process, the Darkness being transformed in the transmission of the Supernal Light, thus being a ceremony of purification and consecration. The Holy Eucharist completes the cycle, representing a spiritual alchemical transmutation or transformation, which is the fruit of self-purification.

Obviously, there is no fixed state of enlightenment and, as long as we live in this world, there is no end to the process of self-purification. It is an ongoing process at every stage of the path, hence an integral part of the actual enlightenment experience. The Lord himself has shown us this in the night of passion, for there, in the garden of Gethsemane, his prayer assumed the form of self-purification. If this is true of so great a Master, we know it is also true of ourselves. Thus we know that purification and consecration is an ongoing effort in the great work.

VERSE 27

Jesus said, "If you do not fast as regards the world, you will not find the kingdom. If you do not observe the Sabbath as a Sabbath, you will not see the father."

Here the Lord speaks of fasting with regard to the world— a fast, not starvation. You are in the material world and the Lord intends you to enjoy life to the fullest possible extent. This life, indeed, is a most precious gift, and the whole of life is sacred. Yet the sacredness of life is only manifest in a more complete way when you are Spirit-connected. Unless there are times that your attention is turned inward instead of outward, it is difficult, if not impossible, to know yourself and to maintain a Spirit-connection. Thus the Lord calls you to withdraw yourself from mundane activities at certain times so that you might entertain the supramundane dimensions of life and establish a Spirit-connection. The holy Shabbat is the central focus of those times one is to cease from mundane activities in order to seek the Spirit and Truth that is within and beyond.

Shabbat, itself, is a holy continuum of spiritual practice and spiritual living. It is a day of repose and joy, a day of celebration and worship of the Divine Life in Spirit and Truth. On this day, the elect dedicate themselves to holy discourse, study and contemplation of the Holy Scriptures, and esoteric wisdom, prayer, meditation, and sacred ceremony. Shabbat is

a fasting from the hyperactivity of the world to entertain a communion in the Spirit of God. One leaves the ways of mortal human society to engage in the enlightened society of the angels and the elect,
thus restoring one's soul.

When considering the nature of the holy Shabbat, our teachers tell
us that it is the space and time we make in our lives for the Lord and
the holy Shekinah. The Lord says to us, "If you do not honor the
Shabbat, you will not see God." Stated simply, if you do not make sufficient space and time to meet with God, then you will not "see" or
meet with God. Likewise, if all of your time and energy is invested
only in mundane and worldly matters, you will have neither the time
nor energy to find the kingdom of heaven. Here, in essence, the Master is speaking a basic truth. If you do not make the time-space-ener-
gy to seek the kingdom of heaven or to enter into a direct experience
of God, you won't be able to find or enter into the kingdom of heav-
en, nor will you directly experience the presence of God.

Now the Lord does not tell you what to do with this holy day
("holiday") or how to celebrate it. While a tzaddik may guide you to a
certain extent in how to keep the Shabbat, as will the spiritual community of which one is a member, ultimately you are called to follow
the inspiration of the Holy Spirit and to act as a co-creator of this day
of divine revelation.

Why is the Shabbat called a "Day of Divine Revelation"? Because it
is the fruition of Creation, and Creation itself is the self-expression
and revelation of God. When St. Paul was taken up into the third
heaven and secrets of the angelic world were revealed to him, the
masters teach that it happened on the holy Shabbat. Likewise, St.
John received the Book of Revelation on the Lord's day, when he was
in the Spirit. With everything to be done in the process of daily living
and all of the distractions of the world, if you do not make space and
time for the Spirit, when shall you be taken up in the Spirit of the
Lord to be shown hidden and secret things? As one sage has said, "If
not now, when?"

VERSE 28

*Jesus said, "I took my place in the midst of the world, and I
appeared to them in flesh. I found all of them intoxicated; I
found none of them thirsty. And my soul became afflicted for
the sons of men, because they are blind in their hearts and do
not have sight; for empty they came into the world, and
empty too they seek to leave the world. But for the moment
they are intoxicated. When they shake off their wine, then
they will repent."*

Entering into the repose and joy of the Holy Spirit and beholding the reality-truth-continuum from a higher order
of consciousness, every spiritual adept or master has shared
this vision of sorrow in seeing how greatly people suffer on
account of fundamental ignorance. Having awakened and realized the way of liberation themselves, knowing the presence
of God as near to all beings as their very breath, it is truly an
affliction within their soul to see others still in bondage to the
powers of ignorance and therefore suffering. Experiencing the
peace and joy of enlightenment and liberation, a conscious
unity with the Beloved, who would not be so deeply moved
by the continuation of other's suffering? Indeed, when the fullness of spiritual love and compassion dawns, one cannot help
but be moved to act and render assistance.

Perhaps one must understand how delighted and on fire
with the Holy Spirit the initiate is upon entering into

Messianic consciousness and directly experiencing something of the Supernal Light—so wonderful a blessing and so great a wealth that the mystics feel it will swiftly be received by all who hear and all who see the Divine presence that has come into manifestation. Yet bearing forth the Word and Wisdom of the Lord to the people and seeking to impart the Light-transmission, they find few, if any, willing to listen and hear, to look and see, and so receive the transmission of higher consciousness they embody. This is the meaning of the saying that the Word of the Lord is sweet in the prophet's mouth, but burns when swallowed and is bitter in the belly. Seeking, they find everyone drunk with the illusionary world and intoxicated with self-cherishing, desire, and hatred, unwilling or incapable of entering into the Light. Put bluntly, they find few are really interested!

Outside of such an experience, one can hardly imagine the mental-emotional turmoil and troubling of the soul that transpires on account of the vast contrast between the direct experience of Divine being-consciousness-delight and the dull and dense resistance of ignorance and forgetfulness in ordinary consciousness. It is a painful ordeal that is part of the coming into being of the prophets and apostles of God.

Now the word "intoxication," used by the Master, is a perfect analogy. In fact, it is quite wonderful, for he tells you that this ignorance and forgetfulness and the suffering that follows is not a permanent state. Rather, any time you are ready and willing to stop consuming the intoxicant, you can sober up and regain your intelligence and lucidity. He goes further, saying that eventually every soul will shake off the intoxicant and repent—that is to say, every soul will experience a spiritual conversion or radical change in consciousness.

Not only can you sober up—eventually you will—and when you do you will experience a transformation in consciousness! In the midst of great horror and darkness, the Lord offers hope!

Before you can seek sobriety, you must recognize that you are drunk and the negative affect/effect of the intoxication. You must see the sorrow and suffering drunkenness causes and how you become someone or something other than your true self. You must look and see clearly where selfishness, desire, and fear carry you, and realize the unhappiness and unhealthiness caused by it. Until a drunk is able to admit to being a drunk and able to see how it ruins one's life, he or she will not, actually cannot, attain sobriety. The same is true in terms of the intoxication of ignorance and darkness. Therefore, quite naturally, "confession of ignorance and sin" naturally precedes the holy baptism.

Without a true and strong awareness of ignorance and the illusory nature of the world, who will actually seek and find the kingdom of heaven or have any real desire for the Beloved? While one is deluded into believing anything in this world more valuable and important than the realization of Messianic consciousness, how could he or she actually desire and attain the awakening of the Christ-self? If things of the world are actually so fulfilling, why bother about God and all that? The only problem is that the joy gained from things of this world is temporary. Life and everything in this world is only a temporary condition. In truth, it is as though we are grabbing at dust and ashes, instead of the holy jewel of the Neshamah or heavenly soul. As the Master has said, "What does it profit you if you gain the whole world, but lose your immortal soul?" To the intoxicated individual, such words fall on deaf ears!

Now let it be said that the Spirit of the Lord is crying out in the wilderness of the world, saying, "Shake off the bitter dregs of your cheap wine and come to me and I will give you the finest delights of the Beloved. Awaken and set yourself free and you will see the world of Supernal Light within you and all around you! Come, let us entertain sobriety and put an end to sorrow and suffering. Let us rejoice in the indwelling Christ and extend the Light. Listen and hear, look and see. Worship the Lord in Spirit and Truth. Grace will receive you! Vehayah, amen."

VERSE 29

Jesus said, "If the flesh came into being because of spirit, it is a wonder. But if spirit came into being because of the body, it is a wonder of wonders. Indeed, I am amazed at how this great wealth has made its home in this poverty."

Life, itself, is a miracle. Creation is worthy of awe and wonder. The very fact that you and I are here, that we are experiencing this moment, that life, with intelligence and self-awareness, has evolved upon earth is an amazing and incredible thing. Who could imagine such potential of life on earth before life came into being upon the earth? Who can imagine the potential that will manifest in the future? It is all a secret operation of the Holy Spirit, and it is God who imagines and creates ever more refined and higher forms of life through the agency of Nature. Look and see Logos (the Word) and Sophia (the Wisdom) of God within yourself and all around you! It is truly amazing!

Amid countless billions of stars in an infinite universe, it is reasonable to assume that intelligent and self-aware life-forms have evolved in other worlds, just as we have come into being here on earth. It is even reasonable to assume that, out of innumerable worlds of intelligent life, more refined and higher forms of life have evolved, life-forms beyond our ability to comprehend. One need only see the multitude of life-forms here on earth to reasonably conclude how vast the spectrum of life-forms is in the material universe. Looking in this way at the starry night sky, surely awe and wonder of God, the Life-power, naturally and spontaneously dawns and Mother Wisdom speaks in one's soul.

To allow holy awe and wonder to emerge is to experience, to some degree, something of the presence of God in that very moment. The greater the intensity of awe and wonder, the more one enters and is entered by the living presence. Life and Nature herself is a gate into the Divine presence through which you may pass any time you wish—all you must do is allow yourself to be amazed.

In the eyes of a prophet or apostle of God, faith in God is an interesting idea. To the holy ones, God is self-evident in all of Creation, in everyone and everything, and both inwardly and outwardly, the holy tzaddik is experiencing God all of the time. In fact, so are you. If there is a difference it is only that, perhaps, you are unaware of what you are experiencing. Some individuals are so unaware that they would propose there is no such thing as God or an intelligent consciousness-force within and behind the Creation of the universe but rather that, from a void of ignorance, the energy-intelligence of life has emerged, and so suggest that the body gives rise to consciousness on account of some sort of random factor. If the idea of God seems amazing, then how amazing and unbelievable is all of this devoid of God? I tell you, it is absolutely unbelievable and unreasonable!

To speak of faith in God is something more than merely believing in the existence of God. Rather, it is belief with understanding in the ever-more you can be in the Spirit of God, the ever-becoming of yourself and the whole of creation, ever nearer and more like unto God itself. It is faith and hope in the infinite and exhaustless Divine potential—that all things are possible in God.

If one has seen something of the divine vision of the intention of God in humanity, then our present humanity does seem like a poverty in contrast to the Christ-like or God-like human being we are evolving toward. The potential in us of that Divine human being, the Messiah, is the wealth that dwells in our present poverty, that is to say, the gnosis hidden within our present ignorance.

Imagine, for a moment, a human being that is completely transformed on all levels of consciousness, with every level fully linked to every other level, a transformation even of the matter composing the physical body itself, which is the material level of consciousness, so that the human being becomes self-radiant like an angel. Yet more, imagine all duality dissolved, even the duality of gender, so that this person is even more angel-like. Imagine a state of consciousness that knows directly within itself all that it directs attention toward and that needs no thought but functions through pure awareness and accomplishes everything through a silent will, a will that is a manifestation of the Will of God. Yes, something above the angels, something Christ-like or God-like! Who can imagine it? It's too amazing and wonderful to imagine! Besides, it is beyond all imagination and thought as we understand it. It is supernal and supramental! How awesome! How wonderful! It really is so amazing!

VERSE 30

Jesus said, "Where there are three gods, they are gods. Where there are two or one, I am with him."

I f you walk in holiness, then you abide in holiness. If you walk with the Lord, then the Lord is with you. Wherever you go, that place is holy and the Lord is always with you. You are never alone. The holy Shekinah is your constant companion and the Word of the Lord indwells you. How beautiful is the covenant of those who worship God in Spirit and Truth! It is a covenant of the living presence.

If the Divine presence and power is present with one, how much more is the Divine power present when two or more are gathered together in the name of the Holy One? Two form the Pillars of Initiation; three form the Triangle of Manifestation or Evocation; four form the Foundation of the Temple of Light; five form the Fruit of the Holy Rites; six form the Image of Beauty; seven form the Dominion and Image of Perfection; eight form the Secret Covenant of a New Heaven and New Earth; nine form the Gate of the Mystery; and ten form the Mystical Body of the Holy One in Completion—the image of the Lord. Eleven is a number to remain in Dumah (silence), and twelve holds the Mystery of the Sacred Circle. Thirteen forms the Matrix of the Holy Tzaddik through which the Divine fullness is manifest. The ideal number is ten, not nine and not eleven, but one and zero. Let those who understand gather and bring forth the Divine powers of the mystical body in full!

It is good that the solitary and elect should gather together, united as a single body with one mind and heart, knit together in the bonds of love, and engaged in holy discourse, sacred ceremony, mystical prayer, and meditation, for being so united and acting together, they are a greater force for the Lord and are an extension of Light in the world. When a certain number of righteous persons act together in faith and gnosis, whatever they envision and speak will come to pass (Vehayah). Yet, when they gather together, the power of the assembly of the elect lies in the continuum of spiritual practice and spiritual living of each individual member of the mystical body. Only when each member of the body performs his or her sacred duty and function is the body strong and healthy, and capable of performing the divine labor for which it is intended. If one member of the body does not perform his or her sacred duty, the body is drained of strength and weakened, and part of the divine labor will surely remain incomplete. What is the fullness and wholeness of the mystical body formed by the solitary and elect? I tell you, it is the soul of the Messiah.

Wherever one is established in the name of the Holy One, the Spirit of the Messiah is present in that one. Where there are two or more, a greater portion of the Holy Spirit is present and manifest in that sacred space. Where there are ten, the flow of the Divine powers is manifest in full. Where there are twelve, the Divine presence and power of the holy tzaddik is completely embodied in the material world and, thus, something of the soul of the Messiah is brought upon the earth.

Now, there is a secret continuum of the Light-transmission upon the earth: ten tzaddikim of the Old Covenant and twelve apostles of the New Covenant, thus, twenty-two holy ones who maintain the embodiment of the Word of the Lord upon the earth. It is said that, if ever there are fewer than twenty-two holy ones living upon the earth, the world will fall into great darkness and horror. If there are ever fewer than ten righteous ones, then humanity will cease to exist upon the earth. Hence, this secret continuum is the source of blessings and the sustenance of life on earth. Those who tend the holy continuum are the spiritual guardians and guides of humanity.

While we might speak of this inner and secret heart of the holy continuum of the Light-transmission, there are, indeed, many other holy ones laboring in the great work. There are, for example, the secret Lamed-Vau Tzaddikim, the thirty-six holy ones who constantly labor for the sake of divine justice and tikkune. Likewise, there are many adepts and masters who labor in secret in every generation to uplift humanity Godward. The spiritual practices and spiritual living of the faithful empower the holy ones in their mission and keep the precious balance of spiritual forces that allow the holy ones to continue to incarnate in the world and so maintain the continuum of the Light-transmission in humanity.

What is the continuum of the Light-transmission? It is the living presence of God. God has a body and life in the world when you give God your life and body. God has hands through your hands, feet through your feet, eyes through your eyes, ears through your ears, a tangible appearance and voice through your appearance and voice. Inviting the Spirit of the Lord into yourself and giving yourself to the holy Shekinah, walking in holiness, you bring forth the living presence of God into the world. The Lord God enters the material world through those who embody something of the Spirit of God. It is for this that we were created and this is the ultimate mission of every human soul in life.

VERSE 31

Jesus said, "No prophet is accepted in his own village; no physician heals those who know him."

Indeed, it is true. The family and the mundane community who knew the person before the Spirit of the prophets has come into that one will see only the projection they have imprinted upon the person and that projection will blind them to the Spirit of the prophet. It is a simple Truth. Yet there is a more sublime Truth implied here. Just as you might fail to recognize a prophet or apostle of God, so in bondage to your self-identity, to your own name and form and limited ordinary consciousness, you do not recognize and know your own soul and the bornless Spirit within yourself. Recognizing and accepting the prophet or apostle of God, you are recognizing the Divine self within yourself. The inside and outside are intimately connected!

What does it mean to be in the world but not of the world? One who is of the world, in ignorance, believes he or she is this name and form and the outer person birthed and shaped by the world. But the one who is in the world, although not of the world, knows he or she is not this name and form and outer person. Instead, one is aware of the inner self and that self as a child of the Light that has come from the Light and will return to the Light. Thus, truly, one is in the world, but not of the world. Only one who has a sense of this mystery or one in whom this awareness is dawning can recognize a holy tzaddik, for such recognition is a recognition of something within oneself. If it is not within oneself, one cannot perceive it.

You cannot deny the divinity of a master or adept on account of his or her humanness nor can you deny the humanness on account of his or her divinity. To deny either is to deny something of yourself and so make the enlightenment experience impossible for you. It is in your humanity that you will find your divinity, and it is your divinity that will perfect and fulfill your humanity. Righteousness and holiness mean your humanity and divinity are united. The righteous ones will know and follow a prophet or apostle, for that Spirit is awakening in them and is their guiding Light.

VERSE 32

Jesus said, "A city being built on a high mountain and forti-
fied cannot fall, nor can it be hidden."

I s not the center of the holy city the temple of Light and
the fortification the Divine powers? Indeed it is, and the
high mountain is the holy mountain upon which the divine
revelation occurs, the mountain of initiation. Once the divine
revelation transpires, how can that Light be hidden? It reveals
itself and extends itself naturally and spontaneously as surely
as the sun shines at dawn. It cannot be hidden.

Now a city is a place of dwelling and a mountaintop is the
place where the sky and earth meet, where form and form-
lessness touch one another, where the heavens and the earth
embrace. The Master is speaking of a higher form of consciousness and living from that state of Divine consciousness,
a Divine presence and power that will naturally express and
reveal itself whenever your heart and mind and life are manifest in harmony with it.

Now it must be understood that the attainment of higher
awareness must be guarded and strengthened. Enlightenment
is not a fixed state; it is a way of life to be lived. One does not
engage in spiritual practice and spiritual living merely to attain a certain degree of enlightenment, but rather because
spiritual practice and spiritual living are enlightenment and
liberation itself. The Way itself is enlightenment. Remembering and practicing it, so are you blessed!

You establish yourself in a higher state of awareness through study and contemplation of sacred Scripture and the secret wisdom contained in it, through holy discourse, prayer, meditation, sacred ceremony, and living a spiritual life in which the principles of the wisdom teachings are lived. This is the fortification the Lord is speaking about, which includes the cultivation of Christ-like qualities in yourself, so that in every possible way you shape yourself in the image of the Lord. When you shape yourself in the image of the Lord, then surely that holy image is revealed and cannot be hidden. The role of the teachings and initiations is to empower you in spiritual practice and spiritual living so that the Truth and Light might be revealed in your own experience and you might partake of some degree of the enlightenment experience in your own life. Initiations introduce you to higher states of consciousness and the teachings instruct you in how to embody those higher forms of consciousness. It is this personal experience of the Living Christ that is salvation. Living in the Way, Truth, and Light, you cannot fall into ignorance and forgetfulness again, nor do the forces of admixture or the dark and hostile forces have any power over you.

Here, there is an allusion that you must not only sojourn the path to enlightenment yourself, but must labor to bring others to the path and so to uplift humanity. Verse 33 draws out this allusion, directly charging the elect in a ministry and priesthood of the Spirit.

There are many inner and secret levels of teaching within this verse, as with most of them. Here, the Lord is speaking about binding one's soul to the spiritual flow of Divine powers we call Sefirot and, equally, of binding the Sefirot to oneself. He is also speaking of ascending and descending the Ladder of Lights and bringing forth something of the Light into the world each day. If you come to understand how to do this and engage in the practice, the Divine powers will move with you in the world. If you master it, you will find that worlds within worlds, and the whole universe of worlds within worlds move with you, as with the perfect Master. One meaning of the "city" is Malkut and the top of the mountain is Keter, and the fortifications are the remaining Sefirot. The city on top of the mountain also alludes to certain practices of the Melchizedek initiations, one of which, just before sunrise and just after sunset, is a meditation upon a mountaintop where the heavens and earth meet.

VERSE 33

Jesus said, "Preach from your housetops that which you will hear in your ear. For no one lights a lamp and puts it under a bushel, nor does he put it in a hidden place, but rather he sets it on a lampstand so that everyone who enters and leaves can see its light."

Though certainly there are secret teachings of the mysteries only spoken among initiates in the assembly of the elect, the foundation of the teachings are open to anyone willing to receive them. Receiving, we are called to impart; finding, we are called to share with others. It is this that establishes the flow of blessings and Grace.

How could it be that messengers should come and share the Word of the Lord with us, that we should receive it and benefit from it, but not ourselves also bear forth the Holy Word and Wisdom, sharing it with others and bringing others into the path and spiritual fellowship? Indeed, upon hearing the Holy Word and Wisdom, it becomes our duty to speak of and share it. The prophets and apostles of God have not extended the Light to us in order for us to hide it, but rather that we might also engage in the divine labor of bearing that Light in the world. Everyone has a part in the responsibility of the ministry of Light and bringing other souls to the Way. Every student and disciple is a gate to the holy tzaddik. Every initiate of Gnostic Christianity is a minister and priest of the holy covenant. Every aspirant to the Light is also a child of the Light and bearer of the Light in the world. It is a sacred duty.

Here, the Master calls you to preach and minister from your house-top. What does it mean to preach from your housetop? It certainly doesn't suggest the violence of going door to door or any such thing. Neither does it suggest the self-righteousness of believing one knows the only way to heaven and to God. Rather, it is a communication within the natural boundaries of one's own life, with one's family and friends and people one meets under the guidance and inspiration of the Holy Spirit. It means one spreads the Word and extends the Light whenever possible in one's own way, not going out of the way, but imparting to all individuals encountered who are receptive and who naturally cross one's path or enter one's life. In this way, one acts as a laborer in the fields of sentient existence, seeking to find the ripe and mature souls, the chosen ones, and actively participating in the harvest of souls along with the prophets and apostles of God. It is a joyful and wonderful thing to do—being on fire with the Lord!

Becoming an initiate in a mystical order or Wisdom Tradition means we each bear responsibility for the great work, every person according to his or her capacity and talents. Some sacred tasks are specialized by talents and the call of the Spirit, while others are duties everyone equally shares. Just as every member of a mystical fellowship has a sacred duty to materially support the spiritual work, so does every member share the sacred duty of the ministry and priestly function of bringing others to the path and tending to the growth of the fellowship. For this reason, all initiates in the Gnostic Christian Tradition are ordained to impart the first three rites of initiation—baptism, chrism, and the Holy Eucharist—upon having received those initiations themselves, as these are the sacraments of entering the path.

Fundamentally, a mystical fellowship is found by word of mouth. A student or disciple acts as a living link between the apostle and the seeker. The circle of Yeshua functioned in this way, as do virtually all esoteric orders. While such circles may be found, at times, through their open publications in modern times, nevertheless their central way of growth remains word of mouth, something more organic and living. If a fellowship does not bear fruit and grow through the ministry of its members, then it is in danger of withering and passing away.

In this verse, the Master alludes to an esoteric truth. The students and disciples function around a master as the master's connection with the world. They bring down something of the Divine presence and power to levels at which it can be received by new aspirants. The truth is that the students and disciples form links to different levels of consciousness, allowing others to make a connection through them with the holy tzaddik. Very rarely can there be a direct link between a new aspirant and an adept or master. Thus, indirect links become necessary until the aspirant has developed sufficiently enough to establish his or her own direct link. Without the manifestation of the Divine presence and power upon different levels through their spiritual companions, the tzaddikim and maggidim could not maintain a connection with the world. Hence, together, a spiritual fellowship does, in fact, act as a mystical body of the Divine presence, each member of the body playing an important and necessary role.

VERSE 34

Jesus said, "If a blind man leads a blind man, they will both fall into a pit."

In this saying, Lord Yeshua is speaking not only of faith, but of gnosis. Faith is the beginning of the enlightenment experience, but gnosis is the fruit. While faith is the intuitive glimpse of the Truth and Light, gnosis is the actual experience of it, the recognition and realization of the Christ-self within oneself. It is from this experience that an apostle of God teaches and guides the disciple.

While the exoteric and orthodox churches of Christianity have founded themselves upon faith, the original church, the sacred circle of disciples gathered round the perfect Master, was founded upon gnosis. The Lord taught a path of gnosis, an actual enlightenment experience, without which the Christian Tradition proceeds in blindness as an empty shell lacking the kernel of Truth and Light.

You are first awakened through faith, but your faith must become an active invocation of direct spiritual experience. Through spiritual practice and spiritual living, receiving the teachings and initiations of secret wisdom, you are called not only to cultivate an ever-stronger faith, but to seek direct spiritual experience of the Spirit of the Messiah. And more, you are called to embody something of that Holy Spirit. We must seek from the Lord the healing of our spiritual blindness and spiritual deafness, so that we might see and hear the Spirit of God. We are to pray and meditate, seeking the fulfillment of our faith in true Gnosis of the Living Christ.

Now, you must understand that the Way itself is the enlightenment experience. The path itself is the noble ideal and goal. There is no goal but the Way, which is the Truth and the Light, the Divine Life. To remember and practice it is to gain direct spiritual experience of Messianic consciousness and to receive a flow of Divine Grace. Receiving teachings and initiations is receiving the seeds of blessings, but all blessings are brought to fruition through practicing and living the Truth and Light. Not only will we believe with understanding, we will also know it in our own experience. We will not speak what we believe or think to be true. Instead, as Saint John has said, "We declare to you what was from the beginning, what we have heard, what we have seen with our eyes, what we have looked at and touched with our hands, concerning the Word of Life." We will speak what we know and understand, having directly experienced the Truth and Light. This is what Gnostic Christianity means, a Christianity of spiritual knowledge (Gnosis)—hence, a Christianity based upon the direct experience of Messianic consciousness. It is this experience that is the very essence of ordination into the apostolic succession, without which an apostle of God is not yet an apostle. It is this direct experience of Messianic consciousness that distinguishes the succession of prophets from the succession of apostles—hence, two different levels of the holy covenant.

The faith of which the Master is speaking is a faith in the direct experience of the Spirit of God and Messianic consciousness, faith in the indwelling Christ-Spirit and the Divine potential in your humanity. It is a faith in the possibility of direct spiritual experience and knowledge, which is called true Gnosis. It is this that gives spiritual sight and spiritual hearing and the coming into being of the subtle body as the Body of Light.

Such gnosis is acquired through initiation and the metanoia or change in consciousness that follows. Initiation is an introduction to a higher state of consciousness or recognition of something within oneself. One must then integrate this experience through one's own spiritual practice and daily living. It is this process that brings initiation to fruition. Thus, one who has initiation and has brought it to fruition is not blind but seeing, and those who see are fit to guide others. Conversely, one devoid of initiation, and the realization that comes from spiritual practice according to the Spirit of Truth, is blind and unfit to guide others.

The Master is speaking of initiates, those who have direct experience of the Truth, as teachers and guides acting with Divine authority. One must first be a disciple before becoming an apostle, and one must be an apostle before engaging fully in teaching and initiating others. One must act with Divine authority.

In this sense, the Master is also speaking to the truth-seeker regarding identifying a teacher who has sight and is not spiritually blind. The seeker must sense or see that the apostle embodies something of a higher consciousness and that the Divine presence and power moves with the apostle. It is the Divine presence that distinguishes one who sees and has Divine authority. It is not authority of any human being or any human theology or dogma that must teach and guide, but the living presence and the Holy Spirit. Ultimately, it is the Holy Spirit that will teach and initiate the aspirant.

VERSE 35

Jesus said, "It is not possible for anyone to enter the house of
a strong man and take it by force unless he binds his hands;
then he will (be able to) ransack his house."

You must rein in your bestial nature and train the beast according to your inward and godly soul. You must restrain
the evil inclination completely. Only then will your "house,"
your life, be your own, and only then can you offer it up as a
holy temple of the Living Christ. Indeed, you must exercise
self-discipline and develop self-control, so that in heart, soul,
mind, and life you might be obedient to the Spirit of God indwelling you. Only in this way will you truly possess your life
and be counted among the living in the book of Life.

Only in delusion does it seem that self-discipline is a lack
of freedom, for without self-discipline, one is not free at all
but bound to the compulsions of the bestial part of the vital
soul and to a constant impulse to evil. In truth, a lack of self-
discipline is a lack of freedom. Without self-control, you have
little or no choice in what you think, feel, say, or do. Rather,
you live constantly under the compulsion of habits engendered in ignorance and the influence of unwholesome spiritual forces. To exercise your God-given free will, you must be
in control of yourself, in control of your mind and heart and
body, and the inclination to evil must be held in check.

Before going on, it must be said that not only is the "strong
man" one's own bestial nature and evil inclination, it is that

very power of ignorance in the collective human consciousness or mass consciousness, the only real "devil."

If I cannot concentrate my mind, how shall I attain a continuity of consciousness throughout all states of existence? If I have no continuity of consciousness, how shall I master my destiny, as God intends me to do? If my heart, emotions, feelings, and imagination are out of my control, how shall I direct myself Godward or enter the enlightenment experience? If I cannot control my desire, surely I am in slavery! If I live compelled by my fears and insecurity, surely I am in prison! If my mind wanders aimlessly, surely I am lost! Then all I can pray is, "Dear Lord, find me, for I cannot find myself!"

But even if the Lord were to find me, until I bind this strong man who holds my life and me hostage, how can I open the door and invite the Lord in? For the strong man will prevent me. No. It is not the Lord who must bind the strong man in me or restrain the bestial nature and refuse the evil inclination. It is I who must accomplish this part of my salvation, although, indeed, the Lord shall be my comfort and strength. Belief is not enough for salvation. There is a labor to be done! Self-discipline and self-control are called for!

Words like self-discipline, self-control, duty, responsibility, submission, obedience, and so on, have become to us as dirty words, concepts against which we rebel, words we don't want to think or talk about. Yet these very principles, among others, are all crucial to the development and evolution of our soul and our soul's enlightenment and liberation. Perhaps we need to look into these principles, consider the real meaning of such words, and find their rightful place in our lives. Without them, we cannot live as a spiritual or holy people.

Now, all of these words deal with the left side of the Tree of Life, the Pillar of Boaz in the Temple of King Solomon, and righteous judgment. Here, the Master teaches that the aspirant must exercise severity or rigor in a work upon oneself, as much as mercy and loving-kindness. Only in this way can the beauty of the Christ-Spirit illuminate you and shine through you.

There is a secret level of teaching hidden in this verse that speaks of one understanding of the rite of ransom. First, the initiate binds away from him- or herself the forces of admixture and the dark and hostile powers. Then, invoking the Divine powers and uniting him- or herself with the Anointed One, the initiate takes the ransom to be given from the powers that hold the soul hostage, giving the ransom back only when they bless and release the soul. Thereafter, the soul has dominion through the Christ-Spirit over the cosmic forces. So the Master is speaking of the holy covenant of this gnostic rite. Presently, I can say no more than this, although if you know the sacred rituals composing this rite and practice them, from what has been said you will undoubtedly discern a great deal more.

At any moment, there is an interesting question one might ask of oneself: "Who is in control of my life?"

VERSE 36

*Jesus said, "Do not be concerned from morning until evening
and from evening until morning about what you will wear."*

There are two meanings to this verse. The first is this. You
must have faith in God and the Divine potential in you,
and live with faith in order to receive gnosis. The quality of
this faith is such that the aspirant trusts the Lord God to provide everything needed to perform the great work. Hence, in
our faith, we trust that God will provide, as our spiritual father,
Abraham, said to his son Isaac at the time of the sacrifice.

Our faith and trust in God, the Life-power, to provide all
that we need to accomplish our soul's mission in this life naturally extends further. For in such faith, we know that all the
situations, circumstances, and events we encounter are a manifestation of God's Will and God's Spirit speaking to our secret,
undying soul, educating our soul in righteousness and truth.
Whether in auspicious circumstances or in the midst of trials
and tribulations, our faith informs us that God's hand is at work
and Grace is accomplishing the Will of the Lord in our lives.
Thus, we learn to meet all circumstances with equanimity, and
seek to see the working of the Lord in all that transpires.

With life's wisdom, we discover that often the greatest
blessings are bestowed upon us through the natural circumstances of suffering in life and the trials and tribulations we
face. While we might prefer the auspicious times that bring
pleasure and ease, our soul often benefits more through the

hardships we endure than the brighter times. A mature faith perceives in hard times a secret work of the Holy Spirit and seeks to draw out the blessings contained in them, embracing trials and tribulations with confidence and joy in the Lord that is equal to the times of good fortune. With such faith, surely we will discover a center of repose and joy within that transcends the relative conditions of happiness and sadness, good times and bad times, illness and wellness, living and dying. It is to this secret center Lord Yeshua would point so that we might discover it.

Discovering this secret center of repose and joy within, this Christ-center behind the heart, through faith we can learn to live within, letting the Christ-Spirit more and more guide and direct our lives and shape us in the image of itself. This very process is the transformation of faith into gnosis and the emergence of a new faith, and so we advance from faith to gnosis in an unfolding self-realization in Christ. In order to do this, we must learn to gather our consciousness inward, living within and living with faith.

The second meaning to this verse corresponds with the first meaning, and it is this: you must live according to righteousness and truth, according to the Truth and Light revealed in your experience. You must follow in the way of the Holy Spirit and not the way of the world. To do this, you cannot worry about how you appear to others or what other people think of you. Rather, you must concern yourself with the will of the indwelling Christ and what the Holy Spirit directs you to do. One cannot live within and live according to one's faith while remaining preoccupied and self-conscious regarding what people or unenlightened society might think. One who is concerned about what people will think or how one appears to others is not serving God but, instead, is serving the false idols of one's projections of how others want one to appear or what others think. Moreover, such a person lives a lie and is unreal.

Conforming to the world and way of society will not lead to heaven or enlightenment. Living according to what others think or in concern about how you appear will not bring you either health or happiness. You must learn to be who you are and be who you are in Christ.

The Lord is speaking a simple but profound truth, which is also a spiritual practice in daily living.

VERSE 37

His disciples said, "When will you become revealed to us and
when shall we see you?"

Jesus said, "When you disrobe without being ashamed
and take up your garments and place them under your feet
like little children and tread on them, then [will you see] the
son of the living one, and you will not be afraid."

The physical body is a matrix and garment of the soul in
the material plane of existence. In death, the soul sheds
this garment and moves beyond it. Yet here the Master is not
speaking merely about the soul's exodus that we call death,
but of the development of consciousness beyond the body
and generation of the Body of Light in life. Only with such a
development in life will we have the capacity of which he is
speaking in death.

This higher state of consciousness is developed only through
the practice of meditation, in which the mind and emotions
are so concentrated that the consciousness or soul can be
projected out of the physical body, transferred into a subtle
astral body or Body of Light. In this sense, advanced stages of
meditation can be akin to the experience of death, although
in meditation the life connection between the soul and the
body are not severed but a subtle connection is maintained.
Rightly, we might speak of such meditations as a mystical
death and rebirth.

To gain a sense of what such an experience might mean or how it might change your consciousness, your view of life, and who you are, you can imagine what it might be like to have this ability fully developed in your present life. For example, if you actually experienced the separation of your consciousness-soul from your body and its transference into a more subtle and self-luminous form, how would that alter your view of life and the transition we call "death"? If in such a subtle body you could enter into afterlife states or worlds existing in more subtle inner dimensions of consciousness, how would that change your view of the reality you presently experience and your view of yourself? Truly, such a development could radically change your experience of this life and certainly would change your experience of death. At the time of death, you could consciously project your soul from your body, as in so many meditations previously, and then transfer your soul directly into its next mode of existence, whether a heavenly state in the spiritual planes or an auspicious incarnation once again in the material world.

It is this very capacity that we see the Master use in the resurrection of Lazarus and, on another occasion, when he brings the soul of a little girl back to her body. Likewise, if we ever encounter a master imparting an initiation concerning the afterlife states, in which the holy tzaddik sends the soul of a disciple into those states during the ceremony, it is this development in consciousness that is being used. The development of this ability leads directly to the development of the ability to help guide other souls to and from their bodies. Thus, not only does such a development in consciousness lead toward one's own awakening and liberation, but the ability to help liberate others as well.

What the Master is teaching here is quite complex and it is unlikely that we can explore it in full in this present letter. However, the essence of the verse speaks of the necessity of meditation, along with spiritual practice, study and contemplation, mystical prayer and sacred ceremony, and general discourse and worship in Spirit and Truth. Without specific meditation practices it is unlikely that this capacity will be developed. It is possible, on account of previous merit, that study, contemplation, and mystical prayer could establish the conditions necessary for Grace to accomplish this at the time of one's death, or that through one's spiritual link to their holy tzaddik, with the help and blessing of one's master, it could be done through the power of the Holy Spirit. However, full development remains dependent upon meditation directed toward this higher awareness; thus Lord Yeshua is directing his disciples toward the development of certain advanced meditative states.

There are many experiences that may open through such a development, the central experience being a direct knowledge of the soul of the Messiah and embodiment of a holy spark of the soul of souls, namely one's own Yechidah or Divine spark. But before this most advanced attainment, which would represent the most rare state of enlightenment, one would develop the subtle body of Ruach and Neshamah, a Body of Light that would allow direct communion with angelic beings of the Divine powers, entrance into the realms and worlds of the Divine powers themselves, as well as a direct communion with the saints, the sages, prophets, and apostles that have sojourned the path before oneself. Here, we have an indication of what would be meant by the "Communion of the Saints" in terms of the teachings of the inner and secret wisdom.

The intention of initiates entering into such mystical experiences is simple. Such spiritual experiences accelerate development and evolution of the soul and empower the initiate in the great work, empowering him or her to minister to other souls, both on outward and visible levels as well as more subtle levels. With such experiences an initiate would know who and what Christ is in their own experience and be able to perform something of the divine labors the Master himself performed.

Bear in mind that the Master has called us, as his disciples, to perform the divine labors we have seen him perform. Yet more, he has said that, ultimately, we are to perform other divine labors and greater works than we have seen him perform through the Grace of the Holy Spirit.

The state of nakedness and not being ashamed, like a little child, is a state of purity and openness and honesty, but even more than this, a state of self-transcendence. The development of which the Master is speaking comes through self-transcendence, letting go of rigid self-identity and self-consciousness, letting go of who and what we think we are, everything we think we know and all that we think God or reality to be, in order to allow Divine Grace to reveal to us the Spirit and Truth. This requires self-discipline and sacrifice, a total surrender of oneself to the Christ-Spirit.

With self-transcendence and development of consciousness beyond the body, it is quite true that we will no longer live in bondage to the cosmic forces of ignorance, nor will we be afraid before the adversary, the angel of death, or God. Rather, we will know eternal life in conscious unity with God through the indwelling Spirit of the Messiah. How wonderful! There could not be any news so good!

Let us accept this possibility on faith and aspire toward it, and so let our faith move us toward this true Gnosis. May the Lord bless our meditations! Amen.

VERSE 38

Jesus said, "Many times you have desired to hear these words which I am saying to you, and you have no one else to hear them from. There will be days when you will look for me and will not find me."

The prophets, the sons and daughters of the prophets, and all the sages and righteous ones of Israel longed in their inmost being to hear the teachings of the Messiah and to receive initiation from the Holy One who would embody the soul of the Messiah. Lord Yeshua embodied holy sparks of the soul of the Messiah and taught and initiated disciples from a higher level of awareness than any adept or master had previously imparted. In the perfect Master, a new level of the holy covenant was manifest on earth, an inner and secret level never revealed before.

The Master then reminds his disciples that the physical manifestation of his person on earth is limited in duration; hence, time is precious. He is encouraging the disciples to learn all the teachings they possibly can and to seek initiation in the fullest possible sense while he is yet with them, for they do not know how long he will be with them. Indeed! The disciple has the most precious jewel in the holy tzaddik, a priceless treasure sought through many lives. Only knowing this will disciples act accordingly and seek to receive as much as they can while the source of all blessing is present for them.

While the Master is speaking of himself and his relationship with his own disciples, he is also speaking on another level of the spiritual connection between any apostle of God and his or her disciples. The soul passes through many lives before encountering the soul of the holy tzaddik with whom it shares a soul-root and positive karmic connection. Not only must the soul encounter a holy tzaddik in one life or another, the conditions must be present to become a companion and receive teachings and initiations.

Even having met one's tzaddik, the sacred relationship may span a few or several lives. The soul of the holy one is the gate through which the disciple will enter into the enlightenment experience. Thus, once a connection and continuum is established between the soul of the aspirant-disciple and a given adept or master, that tzaddik becomes the only one from whom the disciple will receive the teachings and initiations of the inner and secret wisdom. Although, indeed, our soul may have many teachers along the way, there is no spiritual guide other than our soul's master. Encountering the holy tzaddik that is our soul's true spiritual guide, then, is a great blessing. The wise aspirant, knowing this, will make the best possible use of this precious gift while he or she has it. For one never knows how long the lifespan of the tzaddik will be nor when one will encounter the holy one again. Time is priceless in the presence of one's holy tzaddik, for time is limited upon the earth for the righteous and the wicked alike.

Now the soul of the tzaddik into whose care the Holy Spirit has entrusted us is not the only soul that we share a connection with. In truth, we share connections with a vast number of souls, connections of a positive, negative, and admixed nature. In any given life, most of the significant people in our life are individuals with whom we already have a soul connection of one form or another. We encounter one another to continue, transform, or conclude what we have formerly begun in an exchange of energy-intelligence and experience. With some souls, we might just be forming a connection in this life, while with others we may have had a connection for many lives. We exist in a vast and infinite matrix of interconnectedness and interdependence, including not only "human souls," but all manner of souls and beings-forces, including the cosmic forces of ignorance. It is our teachers and our holy tzaddik who hold the keys to our liberation from this karmic web.

Much could be written on this subject. However, it is only through contemplation and meditation upon the matrix of karmic connections that a true and deeper knowledge comes, and with knowledge, understanding. Hence, the Master says only enough to inspire the disciple to look and see on an inner level for him- or herself.

VERSE 39

Jesus said, "The pharisees and scribes have taken the keys of knowledge (gnosis) and hidden them. They themselves have not entered, nor have they allowed to enter those who wish to. You, however, be as wise as serpents and as innocent as doves."

Today, undoubtedly, the Lord would speak this way of the priests and clergy and seminaries of the exoteric and dogmatic Christian churches, for the keys of the holy mysteries and gnosis have been hidden and lost by the exterior church, and only in the congregations of the interior church can they now be found. Indeed, for hundreds of years, of necessity, the teachings and initiations of the apostolic succession have passed from master to disciple within secret societies. It was not the desire to hide the keys of the mysteries that forced the mystical orders to maintain their teachings and lineages in secret, but to avoid their total destruction at the hands of the dogmatic exterior church. Thus, today, congregations of the interior church are few and difficult to find. Their teachings and initiations are something alien to the majority who would call themselves Christians.

The institutions of dogmatic religion are physical expressions of the dominion of cosmic forces of ignorance. The cosmic forces of ignorance have usurped the divine authority of those chosen by God to bear forth the Light; these forces act to hinder, obstruct, and destroy the streams of the Light-transmission that the prophets and apostles of God bring into the world. Truly, the leaders of dogmatic religion are the blind leading the blind, devoid of the empowerment and higher awareness that direct spiritual and mystical experience naturally brings. This phenomenon has been present throughout the course of human history, and, just as in the time of Lord Yeshua, so it is now.

If you discover that the priests and clergy of the churches have hidden the keys of gnosis and have, ultimately, lost them altogether, what will you do?

If the Holy Spirit descends upon you, and you become on fire with the Lord, what will you do?

I tell you, it is time for a spiritual revolution, a holy revival of the mysteries and true Gnosis!

The Lord tells his disciples to become as "wise as serpents and innocent as doves." What is the meaning of "serpents" and "doves"? The serpent is a symbol of initiation and knowledge that transforms or heals. The dove is the symbol of purity, peace, and the flight of consciousness in ascent beyond the body. They are also allusions to the holy Shekinah below and the holy Shekinah above, thus an ascending and descending power of the Holy Spirit, what in the Eastern orders is called "Kundalini energy." The Master tells the disciples to seek the awakening of this Divine presence and power within themselves and, thus, seek to enter into true Gnosis of God directly.

What are the keys of the mysteries and gnosis? They are practices of mystical prayer and prophetic meditation that create the conditions in consciousness for the aspirant to enter into the direct spiritual experience of the Truth and Light. Hence, they are spiritual disciplines that lead to the awakening of the Divine powers in the soul and the conscious union of the soul with God. Such mystical practices are empowered through initiations, transmissions of energy-intelligence, and shared experiences between an adept or master and his or her disciple. Gnosis is real power.

VERSE 40

Jesus said, "A grapevine has been planted outside of the fa-
ther, but being unsound, it will be pulled up by its roots and
destroyed."

Lord Yeshua speaks of himself as a true vine, one that bears
forth the holy wine of the Beloved. And rightly so, for
one chosen by Divine authority and anointed with the Supernal Light bears a true message and transmission, having the
direct spiritual experience, and therefore gnosis, of the Spirit
and Truth. Such a prophet or apostle of God initiates a
stream of the Light-transmission in the world, which in turn
is passed from one generation to another, from an apostle to
his or her disciples, forming a living lineage or "vine of transmission" The holy root of this vine is in God and is the first
prophet or apostle that embodied and initiated the current. A
living lineage that continues to bear the fruit of the Divine
presence and power is a grapevine rooted within the heavenly Father-Mother.

Frequently, there are offshoots of the authentic lineages.
With the passage of time and generations, various aspects of
the teachings and initiations are lost and corruption enters.
Doctrines are formed and crystalized around fragments of the
true Gnosis. Often, many doctrines are conjured up, not based
upon any ground of the original teachings and transmission; in
the process, what truth that might remain is typically gravely
distorted. This is a natural function of ignorance. It gives way

to the birth of exoteric and dogmatic forms of religion that present themselves as the only right interpreters and bearers of the original teachings and practices of the Master. In fact, they are far from any real knowledge of the Spirit and Truth. Such are grapevines planted outside of the heavenly Father-Mother that will not bear fruit and that will be pulled up by their roots and destroyed.

It must be understood that dogmatic religion itself tends to bring about its own demise. It tends to be self-destructive. It destroys its own members, and anyone doing injury to their own body undermines their own life. More so, by nature, dogmatic religion prevents and cuts off a direct Spirit-connectedness, without which it cannot endure.

Typically, exoteric religions speak of God outside of oneself and separate from oneself, and thus sorely limit the range of experience and growth of the soul. Anytime religion and state are combined, the result is an oppressive environment that places a stranglehold upon the activity of the Spirit and Truth, which will eventually come to a head in its own shattering. What can be said is that there are always spiritual revolutions and revivals when necessary, and God continues to send his messengers. The Holy Spirit will not allow herself to be silenced!

Here, the Lord is speaking of religious institutions of his own day, although we certainly have our own version in modern times. By such sayings, he not only warns us away from exoteric and dogmatic religion, he clearly states that he is a teacher of a spiritual path and not a religious teacher. Indeed, the authentic mystic and spiritual individual has no need for dogmatic doctrines or hollow practices that accomplish nothing in the way of actual spiritual growth and evolution. Rather, mystics are worshippers of God in Spirit and Truth, guided by the Holy Spirit of God, and seek teachings and practices that lead toward direct spiritual experience and union with God.

Perhaps there is a place for exoteric religion in that it may serve souls in their early states of development and evolution, yet those in whom a mystical inclination is emerging are called within themselves to seek out the esoteric and mystical path and to depart from exoteric religion and its dogmas. The dawn of the mystical inclination calls for a living spirituality that needs a far more spacious view and consciousness than dogmatic religion can allow. This is certainly the case with Yeshua and his disciples, including his disciples today.

VERSE 41

Jesus said, "Whoever has something in his hand will receive more, and whoever has nothing will be deprived of even the little he has."

Listen and hear! For you are called to enter into the holy sanctuary of the mystery, to be counted among the chosen ones to receive the baptism of water and fire and Spirit, and to take up your place in the mystical body of the Messiah. You are called, but you must listen and hear the call of the Holy Spirit in you and answer the call, so that you might also be chosen. I tell you, those who choose the Lord are chosen by the Lord, that they should be unto the Lord a holy people and living temples of the holy Shekinah of the Lord.

Look and see! There is a great wealth that has come to dwell in this poverty. The soul within you is a priceless pearl formed in the womb of the Creator and destined to shine with the Light and Glory of the Living God, becoming like unto God. So like unto God is the soul destined to be and become, that, in union with God through the Spirit of the Messiah, there shall be no distance, nor any difference between the godly soul and God Itself. The godly soul shall be the holy name of the Lord God, the Spirit of God and the Divine powers of the Godhead indwelling it. So it is written, "On that holy day, he and his holy name shall be One."

How shall I come to the Lord? If I am a son or daughter of the heavenly Father-Mother and heir to the throne of celestial Jerusalem and all the treasuries of the kingdom of heaven, as the perfect Master has said, should I come unto the Lord in my delusion of poverty as though a beggar? Or should I come before the Lord in Spirit and Truth as a noble son or daughter, entering with the noble bearing and confidence of a child of Light? Indeed! To enter in poverty as a beggar is false and untrue, a seeking of Divine Gnosis through ignorance! But such ignorance shall never attain true Gnosis. Only the gnostic being of the Godly soul, the Neshamah, shall attain true Gnosis, for only the child and heir inherits what belongs to the Divine parent, for the child is of that holy kingdom and the Spirit of the Divine parent is in that child. He or she has been born in the image of the Holy One of Being who is the heir's Creator.

Yes, you are a child of Light and you are blessed and ordained as a holy priest-king of the Supernal Light in the world, an heir, with the Soul of the Messiah, to the kingdom of God. It is in this way that you must come to the Lord, with the wealth of your noble being and royalty, not according to the delusion of lack and poverty, as though you were a beggar. It is unseemly and inappropriate that a holy prince or princess should enter into the presence of the Lord like a beggar. The heir must enter into the court of the Holy One as a child of the Living God, one who is chosen and anointed as a holy priest-king. Be not an outsider to the heavenly court, nor to the assembly of the elect on earth. Be an insider. Know the wealth that is within you and bring it forth so that you might have an offering for the Lord our God and so draw near unto the Holy One.

I tell you, the guardians of the Palace of Lights will not let a beggar in to see the Holy Queen, nor will they bring a beggar into the feast of the priest-king, let alone allow a beggar to enter into the bridal chamber! Only the sons and daughters of the Holy One can know the beloved bride of the Holy One as their constant companion and partake of the wedding feast and have a place in the bridal chamber. A stranger has no place in the inmost chambers of the Palace of Lights!

You are richly blessed. There is a wealth in you. The Lord has showered blessings upon you. Your faculties, your talents and gifts, the resources you possess, and the life that is in you, all of these are the blessings of the Lord upon you. All that you have and all that you are comes from the Lord so that you might have an offering through which to draw near unto the Lord. You are created in the image of the Lord so that you might unite with the Holy One and dwell in the Holy One and the Spirit of the Holy One might dwell in you.

Your faculties, your talents and gifts, the resources of your life, and your very life itself, are the holy offering you are to bring with you when you come to be received by your holy tzaddik and seek to receive teachings and initiations into the mysteries of God. They are the offering you are to place upon the altar of the Lord. Only in giving of yourself are you received and so receive in full the spiritual flow of the Divine powers and Grace upon Grace. You must come with something in your hand in order to receive more.

Surely, a beggar shall not pass the holy guardians of the Palace of Lights. Only one bearing the holy seal shall enter. If a beggar cannot enter but is prevented, what would happen to the thief who enters? Indeed! Whatever the thief had when entering would certainly be taken—his freedom, or perhaps even his life!

Although at the outset you might seek to enter into the holy covenant and continuum of the Light-transmission seeking to receive for yourself alone, ignorant of the wealth you bring with you, you cannot allow yourself to remain in this ignorance. You must cultivate the holy desire to receive so that you might impart. We are not called into the assembly of the elect only to receive for ourselves alone, but to act as a conscious agent of the great work. We are not chosen as a member of the mystical body of the Messiah only to labor for the enlightenment and liberation of our own soul, but to participate in the divine labor of the redemption of all living souls. You are given a wealth to bring into the great work, and you are that wealth.

Now there is a secret spoken here, for in cultivating your God-given faculties, talent, and gifts, using your resources and life in the way of the righteousness of one's godly soul, remembering and practicing the righteousness of your godly soul, your spirit, Ruach, and your heavenly soul, Neshamah, are naturally and spontaneously added unto you. New spiritual faculties, talents, and gifts are given to you, the Divine powers awaken in you, and so you are reborn of the Holy Spirit, fashioned through Grace in the image of the Lord. Cultivating what you have and what you are, you will naturally grow and evolve. Yet not cultivating yourself in this way, you cannot grow, the Divine potential remaining only potential, the holy tree only a spark as yet trapped in the shells.

There is another level of this secret spoken here, for it is said that the rider of the Merkavah can only speak of the mysteries of the holy Merkavah and chambers of the Palace of Lights to one who knows already. Indeed, only to one who has attained a glimpse or taste or something of the actual spiritual experience, can the inmost mysteries be spoken. Only an insider of the experience will understand what is said and have a share in the mystical experience. Without spiritual study and contemplation, mystical prayer and meditation, coupled with spiritual living, the conditions necessary to receive the inmost teachings are not present.

Remember, you are a child of Light! Practicing the Way, Truth, and Light, so shall you be greatly blessed, for, in truth, your very soul is the blessing you shall receive when you give yourself to the Lord in this way. The Way is the experience of the Light-transmission itself. Practicing it, you bring forth the Holy Light from within yourself and so receive and share the Light.

VERSE 42

Jesus said, "Become passers-by."

One who knows him- or herself a traveler, passing through the world and the experience of this life, cannot be bound by the dominion of cosmic forces that rules over this world when the time comes to pass out of the world. Knowing oneself as a traveler, a soul of Light coming from the source of Light and Life, one is free to ascend and pass beyond. Yet anyone attached to this world, and the name and form assumed in this life, is not free to pass beyond. Attached to things under the dominion of the cosmic forces of ignorance, one is bound to that dominion by attachment. This reflects a central teaching of the secret wisdom among the Gnostic Christian circles. Knowledge of your true being, the soul of Light and Christ-self, is what brings about liberation from the dominion of cosmic ignorance.

Here, the Master is speaking once again of a divine pride in which the initiate lives with the awareness of oneself as a child of Light, identified not with name and form and the world, but rather identifying with his or her soul and the indwelling Christ-Spirit. The gnosis of the soul of Light reveals that oneself is, indeed, a traveler passing through this world, that this life is merely part of a far longer sojourn of the soul that spans countless lives and passes through many worlds. This knowledge naturally tends to dispel attachments to the world and things of the world, producing a detached attitude.

This detached attitude allows one to live more fully within and to be guided by the Holy Spirit and Christ-Self.

This verse may be taken another way. Not only does it hold the meaning of a spiritual detachment from the outer person of the world and the world itself, so that, with the awareness of oneself as a traveler, one might follow the guidance of the Spirit and enjoy life in the Spirit of God, it also holds the meaning of becoming a traveler in inner space, the journey of Merkavah or the throne-chariot. Ascending and descending through the chambers of the Palace of Lights in meditation, the initiate of the discipline of Merkavah is rightly called a sojourner or traveler in Spirit. There is a secret in the teachings of Ma'aseh Merkavah that is implied in this verse, for the chambers of the Palace of Lights are the heavens, spiritual realms or worlds contacted in higher states of consciousness. At one and the same time, the Palace of Lights is also the soul in which the Christ-self dwells.

These two principal meanings of the verse go hand in hand. Without the awareness of oneself as a traveler in this world and the spiritual attitude of detachment that comes with it, you cannot be a rider of the Merkavah. Spiritual detachment is essential in order to free the soul for the interior journey and unfolding self-realization. It is as simple as what you desire most and so bind yourself to—the world of name and form, or the world of Supernal Light.

Here, it must be said that one who knows the world of Supernal Light within and all around oneself is truly alive in this world. Knowing oneself as a child of Light is not a removal from life and daily living. Rather it is a bringing down of the Holy Light from above and a drawing out of the Holy Light that is below. The aim of the initiate in the Kabbalah and Gnostic Christianity is the union of heaven and earth, not a choice of one over the other. Ultimately, the intention of the great work is manifestation of the kingdom of heaven on earth— the advent of Messianic consciousness in humanity and on earth.

VERSE 43

His disciples said to him, "Who are you, that you should say these things to us?"

Jesus said to them, "You do not realize who I am from what I say to you, but have become like the Jews, for they (either) love the tree and hate its fruit (or) love the fruit and hate the tree."

In this verse, we discover the struggle of discipleship. To receive the teachings, initiations, and blessings the Christ-Spirit poured out upon us through an apostle of God, as a disciple of the Anointed One, we must be able to recognize and remember the Christ-Spirit, both in the apostle and in ourselves. This requires a progressive development of higher awareness within ourselves and a capacity to maintain that higher state of awareness.

It is like a person who has to wake up early in the morning, but upon awakening, feels very tired and has a strong desire to go back to sleep. The person must struggle to remain awake. If one does not have a strong enough desire to accomplish the purpose for which one is arising, it is only through the force of will that one will overcome sleepiness and get up. What if one is going to do something strongly desired? Then instead of the force of will, it will be the force of desire energy that awakens the person.

Developing and maintaining a higher state of awareness is like this. If our love of the Spirit and Truth, our desire for the

Lord, is absent, it will take a force of will on principle to develop and maintain a higher state of awareness, but if we have a love of Spirit and Truth, a true desire for the Lord, then the force of our holy desire will bring us to the presence of awareness. Naturally, the struggle is easier through love than through the force of will on principle. With love, the struggle is not a struggle, it is effortless, like a little child awakening on Christmas morning to receive and open gifts.

Yeshua Messiah is speaking from a far higher level of Divine consciousness than any prophet or apostle before him. His disciples have to struggle to maintain a high enough state of awareness to remain consciously connected to the Christ-Spirit flowing through him and to receive the teachings and initiations of the Anointed One. At times, they are able to do so very well, while at other times, it proves very difficult as they fall back into a lower state of consciousness and a more humanistic and materialistic view. Anyone who has ever become a student of an authentic spiritual teacher and guide will have had something of this experience, and those who have actually entered into discipleship with an adept or master will know this struggle most intimately. It is a natural part of becoming a companion of a holy tzaddik and part of the natural ordeal of initiation.

Knowing this is important. It prevents our falling into self-negativity when we find ourselves in this struggle. Such self-negativity, if allowed to go too far, could cause us to stray from the path and to break our connection with our spiritual master, bringing us to spiritual and psychic harm. However, if we know this struggle is natural and, indeed, noble, extreme self-negativity will not be engendered, and we may even find ourselves encouraged to greater strength or resolve. Not only does the knowledge help in this regard, it also encourages us to bear in mind that our teacher speaks from a different view and different level of awareness than our own. Thus, we come to realize why we will naturally struggle at times to understand his or her teachings. Moreover, we will listen and hear differently, realizing that frequently there are layers of meanings in what our teacher says beyond what we may presently understand, and we will remain open and sensitive. Perhaps even more important than this, we will realize our need for spiritual practice, for the only way to develop and maintain higher awareness so that we might understand the wisdom teachings more deeply is through spiritual practice.

What does it mean to "either love the tree and hate the fruit or love the fruit and hate the tree?" One meaning is that I might love the spiritual teachings but hate spiritual practice, or love spiritual practice but not live according to the teachings. Likewise, I might love spiritual practice but find I have an aversion or fear when spiritual experiences arise, or having had some spiritual and mystical experiences, I prevent them from penetrating and changing me. There are really many meanings to these words of the Master along these lines, the core of which are contradictions that hinder or obstruct our receptivity. Here the Master indicates that the aspirant must learn to watch for such contradictions and seek to resolve them.

VERSE 44

Jesus said, "Whoever blasphemes against the father will be forgiven, and whoever blasphemes against the son will be forgiven, but whoever blasphemes against the holy spirit will not be forgiven either on earth or in heaven."

If you strike the Mother, you endanger the Holy Child and distance yourself from the heavenly Father, and so it is said that blasphemy of the Holy Spirit is an unforgivable sin. She is your connection to the Father-Mother and Spiritual Sun. To cut yourself off from her is to cut yourself off from your very own soul and the Living God. It is best not to hit the mother of your soul!

There are many forms of the blasphemy of the Holy Spirit. Perhaps the most commonly understood blasphemy is the act of suicide, for the Life-power in you is an operation of the Holy Spirit and your life is a gift from God. To take your own life, then, is to stop the operation of the Holy Spirit in you and to totally disrespect and discard the most precious gift of life the Lord has given you. Our masters are able to help the dying through their transition, reaching beyond the threshold of death into the afterlife states to render invisible assistance to the soul in its transmigration into the next life. It is the custom of initiations in the Gnostic Christian Tradition to minister to the spirits of the living and the spirits of the dead, spirits both visible and invisible, but our masters tell us that, though they have tried, they have never been able to successfully help any soul who has crossed into the afterlife by an act of suicide. In so doing, by the very action itself, one has cut oneself off from every source of Divine intervention.

Thus, one will have to pass through the experience of the consequences of such an action and the karma engendered will have to play itself out. Typically, the karma of suicide is not exhausted for many lives, and the nature of the experience in the afterlife states is naturally hellish, as the state of mind at the instant of dying is the largest determining factor in what the soul experiences in the afterlife. The state of mind and heart in which one actually takes one's own life is surely a hell, and that hell goes with the soul and manifests in the afterlife. That it stays on earth and in heaven means that one's next incarnation will be plagued with the fruit of such negative karma and one will have to face the negativity one refused to face before, until at last one is able to endure and overcome it.

Suicide is one form of blasphemy of the Holy Spirit, but there are other forms also. To speak against the Spirit of God that indwells you or to disbelieve in the indwelling Spirit is another form. In this way, one cuts oneself off from the soul and God, effectively severing one's connection to the source of all blessings. If heaven is connectedness and nearness to God, then hell is disconnectedness and distance from God, and the natural result of such disbelief and ignorance is the experience of hell.

Yet another form is the betrayal of the Truth and Light revealed in one's own experience. This particular form of blasphemy can only be performed by an initiate, or one who has directly experienced the Divine power of the Holy Spirit. It is one thing if I live as the ordinary person in the world and have had no other conscious experience than the world. Then I act in complete ignorance, not making a conscious choice. It is another thing if I have received initiation and had some experience of the Truth and Light directly or if I have been present and witnessed the power of the Holy Spirit and then consciously choose to follow in the way of the world and live in the way of an ordinary person. Once I have knowledge through experience, I cannot forget or deny completely what I know. If I betray that gnosis, it will naturally haunt me, both in this life and the next.

There is also the situation of an initiate or one spontaneously touched by God in whom the power of the Holy Spirit manifests, yet the person claims the power as one's own and does not give glory to God. In this case, the Holy Spirit will depart and another spirit will enter and, under the spell of self-intoxication, lead the soul where it does not want to go.

One may also speak of the circumstance in which one consciously seeks to hinder, obstruct, harm, or kill a holy one that bears the Divine presence and power. Such an action cuts one off from one's very own source of being.

Now other examples could be given, although these should suffice for an understanding of the blasphemy of the Holy Spirit. What is important to understand is that "unforgivable" means that the action cannot be instantly dispelled or the injury to oneself swiftly healed, but rather that it has lasting and long-term affects/effects and that there is no mitigation of the karma other than it playing itself out. It certainly does not suggest that any soul would be cut off from God forever or that any soul would spend eternity in hell. Although, without a doubt, one day in hell could well seem like forever. According to the masters, there is no such thing as eternal damnation. God is a merciful God!

VERSE 45

Jesus said, "Grapes are not harvested from thorns, nor are
figs gathered from thistles, for they do not produce fruit. A
good man brings forth good from his storehouse; an evil man
brings forth evil things from his evil storehouse, which is in
their heart, and says evil things. For out of the abundance of
the heart he brings forth evil things."

If your heart is true and good, your words and actions will
accord with one another and be true and good; if your
heart is false and bad, your words and actions will not accord
with one another and will bear the taint of the evil inclination. It is a simple Truth no one can really deny in experience
and it is a measuring rod, as it were, of one's spiritual development and evolution.

It has been said that what you most love, your soul (*nefesh*)
shall become, whether godly or ungodly, whether an entrance
into heaven, hell, or a world of admixture. Your desire brings
you into the experiences you have in your soul's journey.
Only when you master your desire energy can you consciously direct your soul toward your inmost heart's desire,
the holy desire to unite with the Beloved.

What is this love that the soul follows? It is your thoughts,
emotions, and feelings that shape this *love* or desire energy.
What you allow your mind and heart to dwell on most is
what you most love or desire, whether that be a negative or
positive manifestation. If you wonder what you most love,

merely observe your thoughts, emotions, and feelings, where your mind and heart naturally tend to wander, and there you will see where your soul travels. When you look and see, listen and hear your thoughts and emotions, do they reflect the indwelling Christ or something else? If the image they form were placed before a mirror, would that image be self-luminous and beautiful or something shadowy and unbecoming? Are you who you want to be and going where you want to go?

In this way, you will discover what is in your storehouse, which is your heart, and take an inventory of the stock that fills it, whether foods good for the soul or poisons that bring the soul to sorrow, suffering, and death. When you look and see in this way, you must understand that you are not what appears. Look and see with detachment and without judgment, accepting what you discover as the present condition of your consciousness, although not the truth of your inmost being. Every state of consciousness is transitory, the radiant display of being ever-becoming. If you find thoughts and emotions that are not good or that do not reflect the image of the Lord, then you must root them out, either banishing and dispelling them or subjugating and transforming them. In any case, negative thoughts and emotions cannot be constantly entertained, for allowing negativity to dominate oneself is inherently self-destructive and undermines your health and happiness.

Let it be clearly said that it is possible to attain self-control and to direct thought and emotion as you wish. You can master your mind and heart through consistent self-discipline, and in so doing, Divine Grace will enter in and accomplish that part of the transformation of consciousness you cannot, but you must do your part of the divine labor. Then the Holy Spirit can accomplish her part, and you experience a victory for Christ.

Indeed! Anyone who claims that he or she cannot change thought and emotion is mistaken. One who believes oneself a victim of circumstance will remain a slave and victim, until at last one is willing to discipline oneself and work out one's own salvation. The Savior cannot save one who is unwilling to save oneself. You must be ready and willing to work with the Lord, your inner self, for your enlightenment and liberation.

In the Torah, Jacob wrestled with the angel of Esau and attained dominion. Who is this angel of the Lord with whom Jacob wrestled? It is none other than his twin, Nefesh Behamit, his bestial soul. He wrestled with his own insecurity, desires, and fears, the impurity of negative thoughts and emotions that hindered and obstructed his Nefesh Elokit, his godly soul. He wrestled the angel of the Lord through the night and was wounded in his thigh. Yet with dawn's light, the Divine power of the Spiritual Sun within, he attained victory, and the angel of Esau blessed him and gave him the name Israel, which means "One who wrestled with the God and attained victory." What was the nature of the blessing such an angel placed upon Jacob? It was the blessing of harmony and peace, Nefesh Behamit becoming subject and obedient to Nefesh Elokit. In that instant, Ruach and Neshamah were added unto Jacob and he was, in truth, a new man. He had become Israel, the holy man of God.

Every soul that would pass through the gate of initiation must also wrestle this angel of the Lord and attain dominion over the mind, heart, and bestial soul. It is not by oneself alone that victory is attained, but through the Divine power of the Spiritual Sun within oneself and the Grace of the Holy Spirit. One who says he or she cannot transform negative thoughts and emotions but rather are helpless before them is, in part, correct. You must rely upon the Lord and the saving Grace of the Holy Spirit. Like Jacob, although in bondage, you must wrestle with faith in the One-Who-Delivers.

Now you may ask, "How can I change negative thoughts and emotions?" For such change or transformation in consciousness, you must pray and meditate and discipline yourself daily, until at last there truly is a metanoia and the Divine illumination enters into you and flows out from you. You must uplift all negativity to the Lord in prayer, and through holy meditation, you must cultivate your intelligence and the powers of your godly soul. This alone will liberate you from bondage and bring you to the other shore—a dynamic aspiration with faith in the Anointed One of God. Remember, the Truth of the Anointed One is the Light that is in you, which only you can choose to let shine from within you!

VERSE 46

Jesus said, "Among those born of women, from Adam until John the Baptist, there is no one superior to John the Baptist that his eyes should not be lowered (before him). Yet I have said, whichever one of you comes to be a child will be acquainted with the kingdom and will become superior to John."

The holy sparks of the soul of Elijah incarnated as John the Baptist. The Spirit of the prophets was manifest in complete fullness in John, so that, through him, the way might be opened for the incarnation of the soul of the Messiah and there might be a holy tzaddik to teach and initiate the perfect Master. To accomplish this sacred mission, the soul of John the Baptist had to ascend higher than the soul of Moshenu and had to bring down in full the Spirit of the prophets. Only in this way, through Divine Grace, could John be the spiritual teacher and guide of the great teacher, Yeshua Messiah. Therefore, among all of the prophets, it is rightly said that John is superior.

Not only did Yeshua take upon himself the burden of the world's sin, John also took upon himself the weight of the sin of Israel. When the holy soul that incarnated as John was previously incarnate as the prophet Elijah, he established the karmic connection for his own sacrifice at the hands of King Herod when he beheaded and slew the priests of Baal. Then, in his death, he took upon himself the burden of Israel's sin and, with his own life, marked the conclusion of the succession of prophets under the old covenant, sealing it with his own blood. This holy act opened the way for the dawn of the new covenant and the succession of apostles. Lord Yeshua is alluding to this in this verse.

Elisha, the disciple of Elijah, asked his holy tzaddik for the great blessing of twice the power of the master of the assembly of prophets, namely Elijah himself. The disciple was granted his request and received twice the power of the holy Shekinah that was with his tzaddik. Thus, this precious soul ascended beyond his holy master, becoming the soul that would first bring down to earth the holy sparks of the soul of the Messiah. The soul incarnate as Yeshua was this precious, holy soul. Thus, in John the Baptist and Yeshua, something that was begun between Elijah and Elisha was fulfilled and made complete.

What does it mean that the disciple of the Anointed One who becomes a child will be greater than John? First, that the soul of the Messiah imparts a far greater blessing, revealing keys to the mysteries that were formerly hidden and opening the way to the world of Supernal Light. It also means that the new covenant and apostolic succession is a superior Light-transmission to that of the patriarchs and that of the prophets. The teachings and initiations of the Messiah come from above all those previously manifest.

Here, too, there is a holy promise of spiritual development and evolution beyond that state of the prophets, the prophecy of an evolution to Christhood. For one who fully becomes a son or daughter of the Living God, a holy child of the Light, embodies exactly the same Son of God. Any soul that embodies the Spirit of the Messiah is both son of man and Son of God, the very same Word and Wisdom coming into being through his or her soul and spirit.

Along with divine pride, which we have spoken about in much detail, Yeshua indicates the necessary balance of spiritual humility, for one cannot have divine pride without spiritual humility, lest one become extremely unbalanced. He demonstrates humility by giving praise to his own holy tzaddik, as do all true and faithful disciples. In so doing, he becomes like a window through which the Light-transmission flows to his disciples. We also wish to have such humility coupled with divine pride.

VERSE 47

Jesus said, "It is impossible for a man to mount two horses or to stretch two bows. And it is impossible for a servant to serve two masters; otherwise, he will honor the one and treat the other contemptuously. No man drinks old wine and immediately desires to drink new wine. And new wine is not put into old wineskins, lest they burst; nor is old wine put into a new wineskin, lest it spoil it. An old patch is not sewn into a new garment, because a tear would result."

When God is your God and you seek no other, then you shall know God and the Lord shall be your God. In that very instant that you give yourself so fully to God, God will give itself fully to you—and in a natural and spontaneous way, you will find yourself in union with God. There is no struggle or conflict in this, any more than when you enter the embrace of your lover, carried into your lover's arms upon the swift currents of desire. It is completely effortless, beginning and ending in repose and joy. When the Lord is your God and there is no other, the path is all-joy!

You enter into the Way of Christ through the holy rite of baptism. Being received into the baptism of the Lord, you receive also the holy chrism. Going down into the waters, you are crucified with Yeshua Messiah; rising up, you are resurrected with him to the Divine Life. You also have become a holy sacrifice for redemption of the world and humanity, that is to say, drawn near unto the Lord so as to embody something of the Christ-Spirit and so extend the Light. And this is your salvation, that you are dead in Christ, having descended with him, and so you are arisen, made alive in him, and shall ascend with him to perfect repose and joy in the Lord God. Baptism is a passage through the tomb, a mystical death in which the old, ignorant self passes away and is no more. Thus, you are free of the sin and karma of that old ignorant self. Baptism is also the womb, the womb of Mother Wisdom, from which you are reborn in the Spirit of the Messiah, putting on a new and enlightened self, destined to enter the great ascension. Indeed! The child of Darkness dies and the child of Light is born in the holy rite of baptism. Having died and been reborn in the Christ-Spirit, you receive the chrism of Light, becoming one anointed with the Light as the Lord himself.

Now having received baptism and chrism and partaking of the Holy Eucharist, you are set upon the path of enlightenment. You have been ransomed from the dominion of the cosmic forces of ignorance so that your soul might enter into the bridal chamber, to know and be known by the Lord God and so enter into a conscious union. You have been ransomed. Yet you must seek your Beloved and live as one united with the Holy One, serving the Lord, as your very own soul and self, with faith, hope, and love. In this way, you ransom yourself and others along with you and enter into the bridal chamber. If, having been ransomed, you return again to the dominion of the cosmic forces of ignorance, binding yourself to them and serving one among them as your god, then surely any ransom paid for the freedom of your soul is nullified. Likewise, if there is another whom you desire more than the Beloved, you will not enter into the bridal chamber to unite with the Holy One. Your desire will carry your soul away from the Beloved to a lesser god or goddess, or perhaps even a demon lover. In any case, there will be a division in you, the upper world and lower world will be separated from you, and so your soul must continue its aimless wandering, neither ready nor willing for the great ascension.

Entering into the holy gate of initiation, you must not look back, lest you suffer the fate of Lot's wife, whose reward is the fruit of the unenlightened past, not the promise of the enlightened present and future self. You can no longer live as one born of the world and the dark powers of the world; you must live as a child of the Light, one reborn in the Holy Spirit and anointed with Light. You can no longer serve the world or anything of the world; you must serve the Spirit and Light and Truth. Freedom is before you and bondage is behind you. There, on the threshold, you must choose whom you shall serve. Until you choose, letting go of the way of the world and taking up the Way of the Spirit, you cannot pass through the holy gate of the kingdom.

The Master is speaking to the disciple. The disciple is more than a religious person who, like any other ordinary person, serves the world and things of the world, although having some inclination toward enlightenment or God. It is fine that religious persons remain of the world, for they are on the wheel of life, death, and rebirth, as on a vine. They shall remain on the vine to ripen and mature. For one called to discipleship, such conflicts of interest are unacceptable and present an obstruction. One cannot be a true and faithful lover of the Beloved unless there is only the Beloved in one's life. It is this that distinguishes the disciple from the religious person and seeker. For the disciple has found the Beloved and seeks only the embrace of the Beloved. Indeed! One may enjoy life abundantly as a disciple of the Messiah, but in everything it is the Spirit of the Messiah that is sought and found. The disciple has found life in God. For the disciple of Lord Yeshua, the Lord is always first and everything else is second. This is the natural order of the Divine Life.

VERSE 48

Jesus said, "If two make peace with each other in this one house, they will say to the mountain, 'Move away,' and it will move away."

The house is your body and life. The two between whom there must come peace are, on the one hand, your heart and mind; on the other hand, they are your Nefesh Behamit and Nefesh Elokit. Why would we speak of four when the verse speaks only of two? As long as you are double-minded and the heart is veiled and disobedient to Spirit and Truth, there can be no peace between the mind and heart. The duality in mind and heart and the division between them are caused by the inner conflict within the vital soul. When there is peace between Nefesh Behamit and Nefesh Elokit, only then does peace and harmony come between the mind, heart, body, and soul.

So long as you are double-minded, doubting, and the heart is disobedient and easily lead astray, Divine Grace is obstructed and the power of your faith can only remain weak, at best. As St. James says, such a person in whom disbelief remains, who is double-minded, is like a wave of the sea, driven and tossed by the wind, and thus unstable in every way, able to receive very little, if anything, from the Lord. Until there is unification between the various levels of consciousness and all are brought in the harmony of an authentic individuality, the Holy

Spirit cannot freely work within you and through you in order to transform you and to transform the world.

Faith is essential. By faith, you are set upon the path to enlightenment, and by faith you are empowered to walk the path in holiness. Likewise, it is faith that brings forth gnosis. Receiving knowledge of the lesser mysteries, through your growing faith, you might also receive knowledge of the greater mysteries. Established in the perfect faith of Yeshua Messiah, you might also receive knowledge of the supreme mystery and enter completely into the bridal chamber. Faith, then, is the gate to salvation, just as gnosis is the fruition of salvation in the Spirit of the Messiah. Faith is not idle, but labors always in the Spirit of Christ for self-transformation and the transformation of humanity and the world. Faith actively aspires and hopes for all good things. Faith is an unconditional love that holds compassion in its heart for everyone and every thing in Creation. But faith is yet more. It is a very real and potent spiritual power, the power through which all gnosis and spiritual gifts come, and through which great miracles occur. It is the holy gate of all good things and the foundation of the healing power of God, whether on a spiritual, psychic, or material level.

Faith is the intuitive sense of experience not yet had, and thus your faith is a power of your inner teacher and guide. While you can labor to establish the conditions within yourself to receive the blessing of faith and an ever-increasing and stronger faith, all your efforts will not result in the dawn of faith, for faith is a gift given by the Lord through the agency of the Holy Spirit. Therefore, it is your duty to labor to establish the conditions necessary for you to receive this gift. Along with the divine labor, you must also pray for the gift of faith. As the Lord has said, "Ask and you shall receive!"

Now I will tell you an open secret. When you are solitary so that you become elect—that is to say, when you are an authentic individual in the Christ-Spirit—you will find within a secret center of perfect peace and joy that is beyond the passing waves of happiness and sadness, pleasure and pain, wellness and illness, living and dying. Gathering your consciousness inward and living from that Holy Being, there will be a great power manifest in you and working through you.

The holy Shekinah will come to manifest as you and you will not experience death. You will abide in a continuity of conscious existence throughout all states of existence, and you will have dominion over all hidden and spiritual forces. Like the Lord himself, through Divine Grace, you will have the power to transform others around you and the worlds through which your soul passes in the Way. Faith shall bring you all blessings. Have faith, therefore, so that the promise of the Lord might be fulfilled in you.

VERSE 49

Jesus said, "Blessed are the solitary and elect, for you will find the kingdom. For you are from it, and to it you will return."

We have spoken of becoming solitary and chosen. But what does it mean that the chosen ones have come from the kingdom of God and will return to it? Do not all souls come into being from the kingdom of God and are therefore destined to return to it? Are there living souls not from the kingdom of God, but born from another domain? The answer to both questions is yes! All souls come from the kingdom of God and are destined to return to it. Yet there are living souls that do not come from God's kingdom, but are born from another dominion. How can this be?

First, you must understand, there is the earthly part of the soul and the heavenly part of the soul, Nefesh and Neshamah, respectively. Nefesh comes into being from the dominion of the cosmic forces of ignorance. Until Nefesh is unified and redeemed, ransomed from the cosmic forces of ignorance and reborn of the Holy Spirit, it is not of heaven. It lacks its mediating intelligence and the influence of the heavenly part of the soul. Before redemption, Nefesh is of the world, not of God. It dwells in ignorance and forgetfulness until enlightened by the Holy Spirit, receiving both the Ruach and the influence of Neshamah. Every living being in the world has something of the Nefesh, but only the human being who has become solitary and elect has received his or her Neshamah, or heavenly soul. The Neshamah comes from the kingdom of God, and therefore shall return to God's kingdom. Nefesh returns again and again to worlds of admixture and darkness until it is reborn of the Holy Spirit and is joined with Neshamah and thereby redeemed.

Receiving Ruach, your human spirit, and the influence of your Neshamah, your heavenly soul, you are empowered in the Holy Spirit to discover the kingdom of God. When you receive your Neshamah fully, you will know yourself as a child of Light, come into being from the world of Supernal Light and destined to return to it. So, indeed, you are destined to have a place in the world to come, as is every living soul when redeemed in the Spirit of the Messiah.

Here, we must make a distinction between actual and potential. All are destined to be children of Light, having this potential within themselves—but until something of that potential is awakened and actualized, an individual is in bondage to ignorance and is a child of Darkness. Thus, in Gnostic Christianity, the Masters speak of the children of Darkness and children of Light upon the earth, making this distinction, yet speak of all souls being ultimately redeemed at the end of time. No living soul shall be lost from the Lord God forever. The Lord our God is merciful and compassionate and shall bring the Spirit of redemption even to the heart of evil itself. We have cause for our spiritual hope in the presence and essence of the soul of Messiah! Praise the Lord! Blessed be the Holy Name of the Lord! Amen.

VERSE 50

Jesus said, "If they say to you, 'Where did you come from?'
say to them, 'We came from the light, the place where the
light came into being on its own accord and established [it-
self] and became manifest through their image.' If they say to
you, 'Is it you?' say, 'We are its children, we are the elect of
the living father.' If they ask you, 'What is the sign of the fa-
ther in you?' say to them, 'It is movement and repose.' "

I tell you, with the blood of Christ you have been ransomed
from the dominion of the powers of the world. With the
blood of the perfect Holy Lamb of God, you have been redeemed so that your soul might ascend to repose and delight
in the bosom of the Lord our God. Baptized into the mystical
death and resurrection of the Lord and having received the
anointing of the Supernal Light and awakened the indwelling
Christ-Spirit, there is upon your brow the holy sign of initiation. It is the holy sign of the new covenant in the Anointed
One of God. Having that holy sign upon you, in faith and
knowledge of Christ, you are empowered to pass by the
guardians of the gates in ascent, to pass through the domains
of the cosmic forces of ignorance, and to ascend beyond into
the world of Supernal Light. Indeed! You have undergone a
rite of passage and so are empowered to pass by the cosmic
forces that would hold your soul in bondage to their dominion. Through the Spirit of the Messiah, you have repose in

the Lord our God and the angels of the Lord and the authorities and dominions and spiritual powers are made subject unto you. Through the grace of Yeshua Messiah, your soul is free to ascend into the kingdom of heaven. Praise the Lord!

Already, we have spoken of the play of cosmic forces, divine forces, admixed forces, and demonic forces that form the matrix of God's Creation. You must understand that there are realms and worlds corresponding to these beings-forces existing within the inner space of consciousness and as real in their dimension as the present world of our experience. These are heavens and hells and worlds of admixture, such as our own, that are neither a heaven nor hell, but have the influence of both the heavens and hells in them. In its journey to the world of Supernal Light, the soul, in its ascent, must pass through these lower realms and worlds, and the realms and worlds within and above them, whether in dream and sleep, in holy meditation, or the transmigration of the soul in death. In its passage through these domains, the soul is naturally challenged by the beings-forces that dwell in them. If the soul is ignorant of its true nature and of its origin in the Light, it can be led astray from the path of the ascension, prevented from passing through, and bound to the dominion of cosmic forces in that realm or world. Only through faith in the Spirit of the Messiah and knowledge of itself as a child of Light is the soul empowered to pass by the guardians of the gates in ascent.

The cords that bind the soul to the realms and worlds below come from a false self-identification and the self-cherishing that naturally follows, which give rise to the desire and fear (attachment and aversion) that binds the soul. Hence, the soul's connection to these various realms and worlds is formed by misdirected desire energy and fear, habitual patterns of thought, feeling or emotion, word and deed that are in affinity with and correspond to these realms and worlds below. The soul is drawn into these realms or worlds and bound to them in ignorance. As we have previously said, desire and fear lead the soul-being where it will go, and the soul-being becomes what it has most loved, whether of heaven, hell, or a realm or world of admixture.

Now, it must be said that all of these realms and worlds occupy the same space at the same time, existing within one another in the inner dimensions of space-time consciousness. Thus, all of these realms and worlds, as with the world of Supernal Light, exist within and all around you. The ordinary person does not merely have eyes to see these realms or ears to hear the spirits of these realms. One perceives only what one has a karmic affinity to perceive, according to the vibratory level of one's consciousness and one's openness and sensitivity. The initiate, however, seeks to cultivate his or her capacity to shift levels of consciousness, to become progressively more and more open, sensitive and conscious of the influence of the cosmic forces, and to master them in the Christ-Spirit while yet in this life. Thus, in the transmigration of the soul, the initiate might consciously direct the soul into the next existence or, if it is time, to ascend with the Spirit of the Messiah into perfect repose in the heavenly Father/ Mother—hence to enter into the "eighth heaven," the world of the Supernal Light.

Here, the Master is giving instruction in Merkavah, essential teachings and initiation on how to ascend, riding the Merkavah, and to pass by the guardians of the gates and the dominion of cosmic forces along the way. Rather than complex teachings of the names of the spirits and angelic guardians one will meet and many words of power and signs given to corresponding guardians, the Master reveals a universal key of faith and gnosis that unlocks every celestial gate and everlasting door, the simple Truth of the soul as a soul of Supernal Light and of the indwelling Christ-Spirit. These are not words spoken to visible and mortal beings. They are spoken to spiritual beings-forces that would seek to hinder, obstruct, and prevent the soul's passage in the great ascension.

There is a secret here, for the Master is teaching from the holy books of Enoch, and he is instructing the disciples in understanding of such Holy Scriptures. If one would seek a deeper insight and understanding of this saying, one must seek to understand the prophets, and especially the initiate, Enoch. For therein is the holy mystery made known of what we are to become in Christ and the path of the great ascension.

VERSE 51

His disciples said to him, "When will the repose of the dead
come about, and when will the new world come?"
    He said to them, "What you look forward to has already
come, but you do not recognize it."

The dead wander aimlessly through one reality to another, from one existence to another, and do not see where
they are going or reality as it is. The dead do not see as the
living see, hear as the living hear, nor feel and sense as the living feel and sense. They can neither speak and be heard nor
act for themselves in the world. They are no longer in their
body and cannot enter it, although they might attempt to do
so, and may linger about their corpse with this vain hope.
What is the state, then, of the children of Darkness who are
dead to the Spirit? Indeed, they wander aimlessly through life
and do not see or know where they are going, nor can they
perceive reality as it is. They live in ignorance of the Sacred
Unity that God is and ignorant of their Spirit-connectedness.
Born of the world under the dominion of the cosmic forces of
ignorance, they are blind, deaf, and dumb in Spirit. They do
not know the Spirit and Truth that they might speak it, and
they are compelled by cosmic forces, not able to act freely
for themselves in the world. Likewise, their Neshamah, their
spiritual nature, cannot enter into their body and life. Ever
seeking to enter and illuminate them, their Neshamah is al-

ways near, yet, in truth, far from them. They are, as it were, without their soul and dead.

Look and see the plight of the ignorant and ordinary person. Not reborn of the Holy Spirit and awake in the Anointed One, they are as though dead and aimlessly wandering as earth-bound spirits. They live and die and are reborn of the world, only to live and die again, entering empty and leaving empty, for all that they value and seek is as dust and ashes, empty and impermanent by nature. They grope about in the darkness of ignorance, seeking to fulfill their inmost heart's desire. Ignorant of that holy desire for the Beloved, they seek after strange gods and sell themselves into bondage.

When will these living dead enter into repose and the world to come? When they die to the world and are reborn of the Holy Spirit, recognizing the indwelling Christ and receiving their soul of Light. Then they shall be alive, awake to the eternal Light and Light of the Lord's promise.

If I do not know that I am dead, how shall I seek the resurrection and find it? If I do not see the sorrow and suffering of this world and the wickedness of the way of the world, how will I seek to practice righteousness and attain salvation? Will I know the necessity of faith and gnosis of the Anointed One if I cannot see the nature of this reality or the spiritual forces within and behind it?

First you must realize that you are a slave and recognize what freedom is, in order to seek and find it. You cannot be free unless you first realize that you are in bondage and recognize the path to enlightenment and liberation. In truth, it is that which binds you that will set you free. You must look and see this, and seeing, you must practice the Truth and Light revealed in your experience.

From the above, we understand that rebirth in the Holy Spirit and awakening the indwelling Christ is the resurrection. Until we are reborn in the Christ-Spirit, we are dead to the Lord, our God, and surely, unless we experience something of the resurrection in this life, we will not experience the resurrection on the Day of Reckoning—the day of our death. Having lived unconsciously, we shall surely die unconscious; having lived in sin we shall surely die in sin, and our soul shall find no peace or rest.

Praise be to the Lord our God in our Lord and Savior, Yeshua Messiah; for through Lord Yeshua, Divine Grace has come into the world and we have resurrection to eternal life through the power of the Holy Spirit which he imparted and the keys of the mysteries he revealed. In the blood of Christ, we are alive this day and we shall continue in Life and Light in the Day of Reckoning, ascending with him to repose in our heavenly Father-Mother! The resurrection is now, always! The world to come, the world of Supernal Light, has come upon the earth and is within and all around you. You must only become open and sensitive, reborn in the Holy Spirit, to receive it. What the Lord is speaking about is not distant but is the nearest thing, as near as your very breath and the beat of your heart. Ever near is your Neshamah and the kingdom of heaven. When you recognize the Light in you, then you shall enter into the kingdom of Light on that very day. Is this not what happened to Enoch, when walking with the Lord, he arose and was united with the Lord God above as he was below? Yes, indeed, what you manifest below shall be manifest above; what you bring into this life you shall also have in the afterlife. Or have you not heard of how St. Thomas built heavenly palaces for kings of India, so that they might have an abode in the kingdom of heaven? Where shall you dwell longer—in this passing world or in the world to come? For this reason, the wise and righteous ones labor for the world to come and remain undistracted by the world of delusions.

Now there is a secret given here, for not only is the apostle of the Anointed One sent to minister to the living but also to the dead. Indeed, the spirits of the dead, seeking the Word of the Lord and healing and liberation from spiritual forces of wickedness, come to the apostles and prophets of God, just as the living do, and the wise among the dead seek teachings and initiation also. The assembly of the elect gathered about a holy tzaddik is composed of both visible and invisible spirits and the tzaddik ministers to invisible and spiritual beings as well as to incarnate souls. Truly, wherever there is worship of God in Spirit and Truth, the spirits of the saints and sages are present, and the angels of the Lord and all manner of spirits come and go, seeking the blessing of the Lord in holy worship. Likewise, when you study and contemplate holy and secret things, or whenever you pray, meditate, or perform sacred ritual, spirits come to receive from you in the Lord. Or have you not heard that the fallen sought Enoch to pray to the Lord for them, that the Lord might hear the prayers of Enoch and have mercy upon them?

But let it be clearly said that it is ungodly to bind to yourself the spirits of the dead or to seek their service for your own interests. To do so is to make links with unwholesome spiritual forces and do great harm to your vital soul, and likewise, you bring harm to the dead, further agitating them and drawing them deeper into bondage. You are not to seek the ministry of the spirits of the unenlightened dead. You are to minister unto them, bearing forth the Word and Wisdom of the Lord for their redemption. The Lord, himself, ministered to the spirits of the dead bound in Sheol, and so also shall those anointed in his Holy Name.

VERSE 52

His disciples said to him, "Twenty-four prophets spoke in Israel, and all of them spoke in you."

He said to them, "You have omitted the one living in your presence and have spoken (only) of the dead."

The Lord is speaking, first, of John the Baptist, the Baal Shem or master of the great name, living in his generation, who was the twenty-fifth of the great prophets known. The Lord, himself, was the twenty-sixth, fulfilling the prophets and embodying the Divine presence and power of the holy name whose number is twenty-six, the Tetragrammaton. This fulfillment is the initiation of the new covenant and the apostolic succession, which fulfills and takes the place of the old covenant and the succession of the prophets. Yeshua was the last of the holy prophets in Israel and the first of the apostles of God anointed in the Supernal Light.

More than any personality display of any given prophet, even himself, the Master is directing the attention of the disciples beyond personalities and the idolatry of personality cults to the Holy Spirit that has spoken in all of the prophets and shall speak in all of the apostles of God. It is not the personality-display of the prophets and apostles that the aspirant to the mysteries is to focus upon, but rather the Spirit of God that speaks in the prophets and apostles so that, ultimately, that very same Spirit of holiness might come to speak within the disciple as within the Master himself. The divine labor of the prophets or apostles of God is not about the prophet or apostle, but about the Holy Spirit that works within and through them and the Word of God revealed. It is not the personality of the adept or master that is to be worshipped, but rather it is the Spirit of God within and beyond them and within and beyond oneself. Our worship is of the Living God, a worship in Spirit and Truth.

The disciples speak correctly. All of the prophets had spoken in the same Holy Spirit, and it was the soul of the Messiah, the Logos and Sophia of God, that inspired and guided them all. But the disciples speak in past tense, of history, not of the present living reality of the Holy Spirit among them. For the Light-transmission to occur, the disciple must know and focus upon the living presence here and now, in the moment, and enter into that Divine presence and live from that Spirit. Only then will the inmost initiations happen and they will also become bearers of the Light and Spirit in the fullest sense.

Many would make the same mistake today, looking back to Lord Yeshua and the first apostles, ignorant of the apostles of Christ and the living presence moving with them today. Most who count themselves as "Christians" would turn to times past and to letters in a book rather than the Spirit of the living Messiah dwelling among them today. Yet, here in their midst are adepts and masters of the mysteries who embody something of the Supernal Light, a living myth transpiring in every generation, although very few are they who realize the divine revelation continuing in their own times. This tendency to look into the romantic past or fanciful futures prevents the would-be aspirant from entering into the living presence and being reborn of the Holy Spirit as an actual experience. The Master rightly calls the attention of his disciples back into the living presence where their own enlightenment and liberation is to be found.

Listen and hear! This very day the Holy Spirit, the Spirit of the prophets, the Spirit of the initiates, the Spirit of the Messiah, lives and moves among us. The apostolic succession continues in the assembly of the elect. Pray that you should meet a living apostle of God, and encountering one that you should receive teachings and initiations from him or her, entering into the stream of the Light-transmission, that the Spirit of Christ should come to dwell in you. Seek the living presence and embody it! Amen.

VERSE 53

His disciples said to him, "Is circumcision beneficial or not?"
He said to them, "If it were beneficial, their father would beget
them already circumcised from their mother. Rather, the true
circumcision in spirit has become completely profitable."

What is the meaning of any outward sign or gesture if
the truth of that sign or gesture is not inwardly manifest? If one bears the sign of the holy covenant outwardly, but
their heart, mind, and life are not purified and consecrated to
the Lord our God, then surely they cannot be counted
among the chosen ones, for one is not living as a holy person
unto God. Likewise, if one refrains from eating pig but acts
like a pig, like an insatiable consumer, surely consuming like a
pig, one is a pig-man or pig-woman, and not eating the meat
of pigs means nothing. If one is intoxicated with self-cherishing and the desires of the world, does it mean anything if one
does not partake of alcoholic drinks? Yet consecrated wine
may well bring the holy Shekinah to rest upon the one who is
faithful and righteous, and who drinks of it!

Here, the Master addresses the question of holiness and
righteousness. Holiness is an inward state and righteousness
the activity that proceeds from holiness. Holiness is dependent upon no outward sign or thing. It is a state of higher
awareness in one who is reborn of the Spirit of holiness. It
naturally follows that the holy person will live according
to the Truth and Light revealed in his or her experience of

rebirth in the Spirit, and will worship God in Spirit and Truth. The holy person will live according to faith, hope, and love—most especially by love and compassion.

What is to be cut off so that the Christ-Spirit might indwell us and the Light shine from within us? I tell you, it is self-cherishing and selfishness, attachment and aversion, and all negative thoughts, emotions, and perverse imaginations that must be cut off, the poisons of pride, jealousy, arrogance, greed, lust, ignorance, fear, anger, envy, falsehood, gossip, slander, gluttony, intolerance, mean-spiritedness, and the like. We are to circumcise our heart, mind, and life of all these and, ultimately, the roots of these evils, which are self-cherishing, attachment, and aversion. Indeed, how can we continue to entertain such darkness and walk in holiness, to walk in the Light? We cannot walk in the Light with the Lord and continue to practice the ways of darkness. Rather we must actively purify ourselves of all darkness in the Lord and practice the way of Light.

When you contemplate the holy sign of the covenant, you will realize that it represents an openness and sensitivity, and that it is specifically related to the purification and consecration of desire-energy and the creative spirit—that is to say, the power of the imagination. This creative power is crucial for conscious evolution. It is a power that creates and destroys for good or for ill. The aspirant must master it so that he or she might subject this great power to God's Will. So long as this power is directed to things of the world and negativity, the soul cannot seek God and unite with God. Rather, the soul suffers a seeking of fullness in emptiness and a union with that which dies; therefore suffering death again and again. When this creative power is turned away from the world, turned inward and Godward, it is this very power that moves the holy Merkavah in ascent and that accomplishes all manner of good works.

Under the old covenant, the holy sign of circumcision related only to men. In the new covenant it includes women also; for man and woman alike can circumcise their heart and mind in the Spirit and so bear forth the holy sign of the covenant equally. This reflects the priestly function to which both men and women are called in Christ. This also reflects the truth of the Neshamah, which is neither male nor female but contains the potential of both the male and the female. Thus, under the new covenant, there is an aspiration to become "like unto the angels of the Lord," one meaning of which is transcendence of gender.

The Master speaks secretly of a mystery of Yesod, the foundation, for the sign of the covenant corresponds to Yesod and the flow of the astral tides. The subtle body at the level nearest to the physical is etheric and astral in nature and is mostly shaped by the emotions and passions. Therefore, the appearance of this body, as with the aura of a person, is determined by the vibratory frequency of the emotions. If the vital feelings and emotions are positive, bearing a resemblance to the human spirit, and are Christ-like, then the astral body shines with light and is beautiful to behold, appearing angelic—but if the vital feelings and emotions are impure and negative, then the astral body is darkened and distorted, taking on a demonic appearance. The state of the astral body, in turn, invokes spiritual forces in affinity with its condition, and links are formed with the spiritual forces attracted, whether angelic, admixed or demonic. This is true at the level of the mental and causal bodies as well, the mental body shaped by thought-forms and concepts held in the mind and the causal body by previous evolution or karmas.

The subtle body, composed of these various levels, corresponding to Asiyah, Yetzirah, and Beriyah, must be purified and consecrated and shaped in likeness to Christ, so that, receiving the spiritual body, corresponding to Atzilut, the subtle body might be transformed into the Body of Light or Solar Body of the resurrection. This transformation begins with the purification and dedication of each level of consciousness to the Lord, the active cutting off or transformation of all thoughts, feelings, emotions, speech, or activities not in harmony with the Spirit and Truth. This very activity makes the subtle body more and more self-luminous, forms links with Divine and angelic forces, and opens the way for the greater metanoia, when the Holy Spirit enters to transform every level of consciousness into a vehicle of the Christ-self. With any thought or emotion, one might contemplate whether one is linking with the Divine powers and heaven or with some other spiritual forces and domain. This very question represents a knowledge of what true circumcision means.

VERSE 54

Jesus said, "Blessed are the poor, for yours is the kingdom of heaven."

First we might speak of the natural faith and devotion of those who live in poverty. Not having resources in the world, they tend to value the Spirit and heaven more. Go and attend a service of worship in a poor community of the Third World or, better yet, attend a religious festival, and you will learn something about faith and the power of the Spirit not so easily found in our land of personal kingdoms and queendoms and, certainly, almost never among the wealthy. Hence, you will see that the surface meaning here speaks a fundamental truth.

Now whatever our circumstance in life, we must find the blessing and Grace of God in it and make the best use of the life we are experiencing. This is as true of seemingly unfortunate circumstances as it is of those appearing fortunate. Here, the Lord is making a point of teaching this principle, but he is not necessarily teaching a retreat from the world or life, so that, having resources, one should abandon one's responsibility or disregard the sacred trust. The wealthy ought to use their wealth for the sake of heaven, as much as the poor should use their poverty for heaven's sake.

Such a saying tends to turn our own societal values on their ear. Without any doubt, the Master teaches that our values are largely upside down and out of right order. Material wealth is certainly not the greatest aspiration, but the whole purpose of the money-power is a service to something greater and not something in itself. If one of the spiritual-material powers given to you is the money-power, like any other spiritual gift, talent, or power, it is to be sublimated and mastered and so restored to God's Will, rather than merely the service of egoistic vanity. The real value of money lays in what it can accomplish in charity, the betterment of humanity, and the great work. It is a resource of divine energy given for the sake of the development and evolution of the human spirit toward divinity. In ignorance, it is rarely used in this way, or if used, only in a tokenistic way. Here, we may remember the Master's comment regarding the businessperson who does not know the real purpose and meaning of his or her gift in life. The businessperson cannot enter into the kingdom of heaven. The ardent and self-centered materialist will not evolve very swiftly spiritually.

Much more than this is being said here, for the meaning of poverty is not so much about our physical or material condition. Rather it is about our psychic and spiritual condition. Hence, it is about an awareness of our nothingness or emptiness that allows a true perception of the nature of the self and realization of that Divine self. We might say it this way; "Blessed are those who become empty of themselves, for they shall be Spirit-filled." Indeed, as long as we remain full of ourselves, full of all our preconceptions, preconditions, and expectations, obstructed by what we think we know, who we think we are, and who or what we think reality or God to be, it is unlikely we will truly know ourselves or God. We certainly will not know reality as it is in this way. To be filled with God's Spirit, we must become empty of all of this, open and receptive to the Spirit and Truth. What a wonderful blessing such receptivity is, for through it, we enter into the kingdom of heaven, not only in the afterlife but here and now. Blessed are those who are poor in this way!

There is more to be said of this emptiness. If I know I am nothing and that nothing I am or that I possess is my own, but, rather, that it all belongs to the Lord, in that moment I am free of all bondage to my self-identity and possessions and can finally really enjoy all that the Life-power of God has given me. Therefore, I naturally restore all these things to their proper function in Creation, the service of God's own Will. I dare say that whatever I have and whatever I am is given to me that I might have a fit offering to the Lord.

This awareness of nothingness or emptiness is the key to the sublimation of all spiritual-material powers. When self-grasping and attachment are gone, I have no need to withdraw myself from such powers or the world, but I may more deeply involve myself and consciously cultivate those powers for heaven's sake, and I may thus live fully in the world, although not being of the world. Hence the nothingness or emptiness of which the Master speaks is something truly powerful and dynamic insomuch as it is a complete transparency to the Spirit of God.

Now some might argue, saying, "I clearly am something, somebody, and my possessions are my own." I would have to answer, "Well yes, for a little while you are something or somebody and there certainly are things at your disposal, but both your life and possessions really are disposable. For who were you before you were born and who or what shall you be when you die? Moreover, whose possessions will your possessions be when you die? If you cannot possess these things in death, are they actually your possessions now?"

I will tell you a secret. Whoever you are and whatever it is you have in the way of resources at your disposal—if you give all you are and all you have to the Lord and use it fully for heaven's sake—all of it will be with you when you die and you will have even more in the world to come than you can possibly imagine now. Yes, there is a way to keep it all and to generate more, but you must give it away and use it as a sacred trust in order to do this—although wealthy, you must be poor in Spirit.

Let me share another secret connected to this one. When you become nothing, in that instant, you will be everything. When you give everything away, you will receive everything as your very own. When you are empty, you will be completely filled with the Spirit of the Light of God. Consider what the Master said, "I do nothing of myself, but only what I see my heavenly Father do." On account of this, he could also say, "He who has seen me has seen the Father." So our Lord and Savior is completely poor and totally wealthy. This is the state of perfect delight.

VERSE 55

Jesus said, "Whoever does not hate his father and his mother cannot become a disciple to me. And whoever does not hate his brothers and sisters and take up his cross in my way will not be worthy of me."

Surely, the Lord of Love does not invoke us to hatred. Anger and hatred are the dominion of the creatures of pain and the darkest demons. Hate is the poison of the deepest pit of hell, the greatest distance from the Lord, our God. Hatred is born of fear, for fear leads to anger, and anger transforms into hatred, a downward spiral into the bottomless pit from which the greatest horror and evil emerge. No! The Lord is not encouraging hatred but rather is the champion of love, a love so powerful that he gave his life as a holy sacrifice for his friends, obedient to God even unto death, and on account of the obedience of love, the Lord is victorious over death and Hades. Having passed through the gate of death and descended into the realms of hell to minister to the spirits in bondage, he has arisen in resurrection and ascended to repose at the right hand of the heavenly Father-Mother.

The Lord commands not hatred, but that you put aside all attachments and aversions and follow him. The word is wrongly translated as "hatred." It ought to read, "put aside." If you seek anything in Creation more than the Lord our God, or love any creature more than you love the Holy One, then the Lord cannot give himself to you in full, nor can the Holy Spirit possess you completely. If you seek God for any other reason than God itself, it is as though, to you, God is a lamp to be lit so that you might find whatever else it is that you want other than God. Surely, if you seek in this way, the Holy Light will remain outside of you, for seeking to be fulfilled in something else, you do not desire the Holy Light to enter and fill you.

The Lord has said, "Let your eye be single and your whole body shall be filled with Light." Yes, it is true. On the one hand, this eye is desire, and the Lord is saying let your desire be only for the Lord our God, the Beloved of the inmost part of your soul. Yet, on the other hand, the Lord is speaking of something more esoteric—an interior star in your brow, the center of Divine energy in your head. If you are attached to things below, you cannot cleave to things above. If your desire moves through your body, heart, or mind seeking the objects of your desire in the world, your soul is thus held in bondage to those things and cannot ascend into the kingdom of heaven. "Let the dead bury the dead!"

To shift your consciousness to this Divine center in the head, you must let go and let be, and you must go inward and upward, cleaving to our Lord and Savior. Indeed, you must cleave unto the Lord with a passion as powerful as though the Lord were pulling you from a burning building! Truly, that is exactly what the Savior is doing, for the world is on fire with unholy desire and is being consumed and burning away. The earth shall pass away, and heaven shall pass away, and the heaven above it shall pass away. It is all a house on fire, and the Lord is pulling you out of it and into himself. Cleaving unto the Lord, our Lord and Savior will draw your soul upward in ascent. Uniting you in himself and himself in you, he will bring you into union with the Lord God above, but you must put aside everything and everyone else and follow in the way of the Lord, so that you also might take everyone and everything up with you, even as the Messiah himself. If you do not put the world aside, you cannot uplift it. Only by letting go and letting be can you ascend with the Lord and, having ascended, bring down something of the Supernal Light to transform yourself and the world.

Here is spoken the mystery of the holy cross. For descending and ascending, running and returning, the vertical axis of the cross is established, the various levels of consciousness brought into harmony and linked together, the earth and the heavens united. Like the Holy One himself, you are the Ladder of Lights upon which angels of the Lord and the Grace of God ascend and descend. Therefore, the Holy Light is in you and this Light illuminates the whole world. This extension of Light is the horizontal axis of the cross. In this, you will understand the meaning of taking up your cross in the way of the Lord.

The Master has said, "And now, therefore, as I have come, I have opened the gates of Light. And I have opened the ways which lead into the Light. And now, therefore, the person who will do what is worthy of the mysteries, let that person receive the mysteries and enter into the Light." (Pistis Sophia 135). Yes, the Way is opened before you and the Lord has poured out the Light upon you, anointing you in the Light as he himself is One Anointed in the Supernal Light. Giving yourself to the Lord in love as he has given himself to you, entering into him and receiving him within yourself, through faith you are made worthy of true Gnosis and Divine Grace will accomplish everything good in you and through you.

You are made worthy through faith, hope, and love. You are made worthy through faith because, in belief with understanding, you link and unite yourself with the Anointed One within and beyond yourself and so are redeemed in the presence and essence of the Messiah— that is to say, in the mystical body and blood of Christ. You are made worthy through hope because, believing in the Holy One, you follow in the way of the Holy One, actively aspiring and shaping yourself in the image of the Lord, becoming like unto Christ himself, and seeking the fulfillment of the Lord's Will in you. You are made worthy through love because, in love, you make yourself obedient unto the Lord, surrendering and opening yourself to the power of the Holy Spirit, and perfect your conscious union with God, both above and below.

You are not who or what you think you are. Your mother is not your mother, your father is not your father, your sisters and brothers are not your sisters and brothers. No, indeed! You are a child of God, a child of the Light, born not of the world of darkness below but the world of Supernal Light above. The Lord God is your Father-Mother and all who follow in the Way of Light and are children of Light are your sisters and brothers. You are a soul of Light, a bornless Spirit. Do not be deceived by the world of darkness and death, nor taken hostage by the power of ignorance and forgetfulness. If you are taken hostage, know that a ransom has been paid and you are free to go whenever you like. As one sage has said, "If not now, when?"

VERSE 56

Jesus said, "Whoever has come to understand the world has found (only) a corpse, and whoever has found a corpse is su-perior to the world."

The world and universe are as a body animated by the Spirit of God; the soul of the world is the Word and Wisdom of God. A body without a soul indwelling it is a corpse—stardust blown by cosmic winds! To grasp at the body rather than cleave to the soul is an ignorant thing, for everyone knows that every form eventually dissolves and everybody ultimately dies. Consider this, who would keep a corpse in one's house or sleep with a corpse or attach oneself to a corpse or place a greater value on a corpse than on the Life-power that was once in it? Would it not be insanity for anyone to do such a thing?

Look and see! The flesh does not endure forever; neither shall the world of flesh and blood endure forever. This body is an animated corpse and so is the world! If you know the body will eventually pass away and the world will eventually pass away, why cling to the body or chase after anything of the world? Why not seek your immortal soul and the soul of the world? Why cleave to the world instead of the Spirit of God, the Life-power? Surely only ignorance would have you attach yourself to a corpse!

In this passage, the Lord asks you this question, "If you gain everything you desire in the world and the whole world itself, but you lose your immortal soul, what good is that to you?" The answer is obvious. Everyone knows the answer perfectly well and would swiftly respond, "It would be no good to me, for when I die, I will not have the world, and losing my soul for the sake of the world, neither will I have my soul in death!" Everyone knows the answer, but who lives and conducts him- or herself according to this common knowledge? If I do not live according to a simple and earthly truth that everyone knows, then how shall I live according to the greater Truth and Light of the kingdom of heaven? If I do not honor that which I can see in plain view, how shall I honor that which is hidden within and above?

Many are called by the Holy Spirit and seek the gate of initiation, but few are they who pass through the gate to enter the path of the great ascension. Only those who discover both in mind and heart that the world is as empty as a corpse are actually set upon the path and established in the Way, for only they are willing to put the world aside and follow the Lord our Savior in the worship of God in Spirit. You must know the world is a corpse so that you might develop your consciousness beyond it. You must see that it is empty in order to seek Divine fullness. Unless you let go of the illusion of the world, you cannot look and see reality as it is! I tell you, you must pray and meditate deeply until the delusion of lack and the power of ignorance is dispelled once and for all time!

When you cleave to the soul of the world, instead of the body of the world, you will be superior to the world. That is to say, when you bind yourself to the Spirit of God, to God's Holy Word and Wisdom, and so bind God's Spirit to you, then you shall be free of the ruler of the world, the power of ignorance, and abide in true Gnosis.

Now if I speak of what you already know, there is no need for many words. With few words you are reminded, so that, remembering, you might pray and meditate and be blessed never to forget again. Yes, I pray you remember and seek your soul and the soul of the world in the Lord our God. Amen.

VERSE 57

Jesus said, " The kingdom of the father is like a man who had [good] seed. His enemy came by night and sowed weeds among the good seed. The man did not allow them to pull up the weeds; he said to them, 'I am afraid that you will go intending to pull up the weeds and pull up the wheat along with them.' For on the day of the harvest the weeds will be plainly visible, and they will be pulled up and burned."

Shall we call the prophets and the Lord liars and say, "There will be no day of reckoning"? God forbid that we should contradict the Lord as though children of rebellion. May it never be so, or the Lord has said in the prophets that there shall come a day of reckoning, when, in the presence of God, we shall behold all we have done, whether for good or for ill, and according to the balance, the soul shall find its place, whether nearer or farther from the Lord our God.

Suppose your life story is a book you write up until the moment of your death, and in the afterlife, you must read this book again and again, reliving the story. Is the story of your life one you would desire to live again? Would it be a blessing or a curse to you? Would it become as a gate to heaven or some other place?

For every soul there comes a day of reckoning, when the soul undresses of the body and passes out of this world. Before passing in ascent, it enters a life review and passes through the judgment in the presence of the Lord. It is not the presence of the Lord, but the soul itself, that stands in judgment, and the balance of that judgment determines the nature of the next existence the soul shall enter.

There is also another Day of Reckoning, not merely for the individual but for the whole of humanity and the world. There shall come a time when the presence of the Lord shall enter the world as never before. The Lord shall come as a raging fire and brilliant light, as though the fire and light of countless stars gathered together. For the children of Light, it shall be a day of great peace and joy. Yet unto the children of Darkness, it shall be a day of great horror and wrath. You must understand that the presence of the Lord is the same. There is not a wrathful and a merciful presence of God. The presence of God is always the same and transcends the appearance of peace and wrath. It is like this, one who has made him or herself like unto the Lord, who has become the holy fire and Light, will experience joy upon joy and Light upon Light. Conversely, one who has not made oneself like unto the Lord, who remains ignorant and cleaves to Darkness, will experience this same Divine presence as a consuming fire of apocalyptic horror. To the child of the Light who has become the Light, it seems a blessing, but to the child of Darkness who remains separate from the Holy Light, it seems a dread curse. Such is the nature of the Day of Reckoning.

Why should the Lord allow the unrighteous and wicked to remain upon the earth and thrive in the world, when clearly we see that the children of God suffer on account of the evil they bring into the world? The Lord is the same with all of his children. The Holy Mother looks after every one of her children as though her one and only child. The Lord is compassionate, merciful, and loving. The Lord seeks the repentance and redemption of all of his creatures. The Lord seeks to bless and embrace saint and sinner alike. God waits upon all to turn unto her and to seek her most intimate embrace. Yet if the hour of God comes and there remain souls living as children of Darkness, then in that day they shall be shattered and driven out from before the presence of the Lord, given over to another world until at last they are ripe and mature in the Spirit and Truth.

Why does the Lord allow the demonic forces to play amid humanity and to reign over the earth until that Day of Reckoning? Could
there be a righteous warrior without a worthy enemy with which to
do battle? Can a true and strong evolution occur without a force of resistance and opposition? No, indeed! There can be no righteous warriors without a worthy enemy to do battle with. The evolution of
God's Creation could not happen without forces of resistance and opposition. Likewise, it is the knowledge of good and evil that gives
human beings free will to choose between good and evil. What lover
would seek a beloved whose love was given by demand and not according to free will? Where is the joy in love unless it is freely given
and received? Truly, love is delightful and powerful when it comes on
account of love and for no other reason, and such is the desire of the
Lord—that we should freely choose to love him and so turn to God
of our own free will. If the evil one and the dark hosts did not exist,
there could not be this freedom to love or to hate!

Many things can be said of the Day of Reckoning, for much has
been revealed in the prophets concerning the hour of God, and the
Messiah has also revealed deep mysteries concerning that holy day.
One thing is for certain. It is a day of holy fire, Light, and Divine revelation, and it is wise to live in such a way so as to be ready at any
moment for the coming of that holy day. Only the Lord our God
knows when that day will come, and it shall not go well with those
who are unprepared to meet their Lord.

It must be said that no soul shall be damned to hell forever, nor shall
any soul be separated and lost to the Lord God for all eternity. Nothing in all of Creation shall be lost. Everything shall return into the
bosom of the Lord, having come forth from it, but let it not be said
there is no such thing as hell or the dread experience of damnation. Indeed, there are many hells—realms and worlds of shadow play and admixture. Many are they who will experience such realms and worlds
before, at last, they repent and are redeemed. Ultimately, even the
demons and the evil one shall repent and be redeemed.

What is the Day of Reckoning? It is a radical transformation and
transition in consciousness, a crossing over, as it were, from one state
of consciousness to another, whether manifesting in an individual or

on a collective level. Of this holy day, the Master has said, "Then two will be in the field; one will be taken and one will be left. Two women will be grinding meal together; one will be taken and one will be left." Such is the nature of the advent of supernal consciousness. Those who are open and ready to receive it will be taken up by it and embody it, and it will transform every level of consciousness, even the physical body. Those who are not open and ready to receive it will not be taken up and transformed by it, but will, in effect, be passed over by the Divine presence and left behind in the former state of being. Thus, we understand, by the "Day of Reckoning," the day of our death and transition from this life, a crucial time of transition in the collective human consciousness, and the advent of supernal or Messianic consciousness on earth.

VERSE 58

Jesus said, "Blessed is the man who has suffered and found Life."

This life is naturally fraught with sorrow and suffering and great challenges. Trials and tribulations come and go and they are unavoidable. If you must endure sorrow and suffering, then let it not be without purpose and meaning. Seek to draw from it the blessings that may be found in it, so that, when the period of sorrow or suffering has passed, you will have the good from it. When you meet the challenges of life in this way, you will naturally be blessed and your faith will grow stronger and your soul more refined. You will find Life!

St. James has written, "Whenever you face trials of any kind, consider it joy, because you know that the testing of your faith produces endurance; and let your endurance have its full effect, so that you may be mature and complete, lacking in nothing." Yes, indeed! Be joyful in the face of trials and tribulations and sorrow and suffering will be transformed! When met in this way, every challenge of life is an opportunity for growth and development of the soul and spiritual evolution toward Christ-consciousness.

You might say to me, "This is impossible!" but I would say that nothing is impossible with God, and if you ask the Lord with faith to bless you to endure every trial and tribulation with joy, the Lord will be with you, will empower you, and will give you what you ask. So it is with anything you might feel lacking—wisdom, understanding, patience, compassion, forgiveness, hope, love, and so on. Anything you need, if you become open and receptive, the Holy Spirit will deliver to you as a gift from the Lord God above. You must only have faith and seek to walk in holiness.

There is nothing gained by falling into oneself in times of sorrow or suffering. Rather, the trials that come are the call to let go and let be and to get out of oneself, a call to self-transcendence and compassion. You can use the suffering that comes to open your heart with love and compassion for all who are experiencing such suffering and to lift you up out of yourself into the Christ-self. This is what it means to find life.

When trials come and you fall into yourself and close your heart, suffering is increased and intensified. When you open your heart, making room for everyone and everything and for the Lord, suffering is decreased and passes more swiftly. This is simple wisdom of life experience. There is also profound spiritual wisdom involved here, for if you endure suffering for the sake of dispelling the negative karma and sins of the world, you enter into a covenant-continuum with the Lord himself, uplifting the holy sparks of the klippot, which are bound in the Darkness, and restoring them to the Body of Light of Adam Kadmon. In this way, you draw yourself nearer unto the Lord, putting on the image of the Lord and uniting yourself with the Christ-Spirit. One who passes through times of suffering in this way has, in the face of trial, the joy of the resurrection and eternal life.

It must be said that there will naturally be a testing of the faith of an initiate and that part of the process of initiation are the ordeals that precede fruition. They are as labor pains in the birth of the Holy Child, and you need to understand that such suffering is an integral part of the joy of rebirth in the Holy Spirit. One who is unwilling to undergo the pains of labor is unwilling to experience the joy of the birth of the Christ-self, and surely there shall be no birth without also the pains of the labor. You must bear in mind, in the midst of the ordeals that come, that, when the Holy Child is born in you, all suffering shall swiftly be forgotten and there will come a perfect peace and delight. You must not turn back from the ordeal; instead, you must look forward and pass through it. May you endure with joy the pains of labor consciously and so receive the blessing the Lord would have for you—eternal life!

VERSE 59

Jesus said, "Take heed of the living one while you are alive,
lest you die and seek to see him and be unable to do so."

How wonderful that the Word and Wisdom of God has become flesh, the Christ-Spirit incarnate, living and moving among us, that we might see, hear, touch, be touched, and therefore know the Spirit of the Messiah and receive that Holy Spirit within ourselves! What a great blessing it is that the prophets and apostles of God live among us and come to us, imparting the Holy Light. If it were not through the agency of physical bodies, the life and personality displays of the holy ones, how would we behold the Christ-Spirit that is invisible and hidden within or behold the Divine presence before we had eyes to see in the Spirit vision? It is the mercy and grace of God that it is so! Praise the Lord!

If you do not know the Living Yeshua in life, how will you know him in death? If you have not given birth to the Christ-Spirit in your life, how shall that Holy Spirit live in you in the afterlife? Indeed, the purpose of this life is your awakening and liberation in the Lord. Awakening to the Spirit of the Messiah in this life, you will also be awake and free in the Anointed One in the afterlife. Yet one who does not turn to the Lord in life will not meet the Lord and ascend with him when they pass out of this world. Rather, when the Holy Light of God dawns for them, they will not recognize it and will turn away from it. Now is the time for self-realization. There is no other time for it but now!

Fundamentally, we die as we have lived. The afterlife experience directly reflects the life we have lived, and the next existence experienced by the soul is largely determined by the present life. In this life, right here and now, you are generating the next life. If you seek an entrance into the kingdom of heaven, then reflect the kingdom of heaven in this life and you shall enter into it now and at the time of your passage out of this world. Whatever good you would seek, bring it into this life and you will surely have it in the next. It is a basic principle of Truth.

What a great blessing it was for the disciples of Lord Yeshua! How very rare and precious to have met the incarnation of the soul of the Messiah in this world and to have been a disciple of the Holy One. Yeshua Messiah is the rarest of all spiritual masters, a perfect Master and incarnation of the great World Teacher. There are many different levels of spiritual masters and adepts. In every generation, these various levels of prophets and apostles live among us, but the perfect Masters come only in very few generations when it is time for a radical shift in human consciousness and a new level of the divine revelation. It is completely justified that the Master would encourage his disciples to make the most of this very special blessing.

Now I tell you, if you seek to see Yeshua Messiah in dream or vision, the Lord will come and appear to you and confirm your faith, establishing you in gnosis. Already we have spoken of the Way of this holy seeking, of prayer and meditation, holding the holy image of the risen Messiah in your mind. What begins as an activity of imagination will come to fruition with the presence of the Lord entering into it and imparting teachings and initiations to you. Yes, indeed, everyone can receive the blessings of Yeshua Messiah directly. As the Lord has said, "Wherever two or more are gathered in my name, I am there. Whenever you pray with faith in me, I am there with you."

So initiates understand that, through the person of their spiritual teacher, the Lord comes to them, teaching and initiating them into the holy mysteries. Receiving their teacher in this way, they receive the Anointed One himself and they receive the very same blessing as the beloved disciples of our Lord and Savior. Surely, they will meet their spiritual master again in the kingdom of heaven and enjoy the communion of the saints with their holy tzaddik in the presence of the Lord. Praise the Lord for such a wonderful blessing!

At the level of the inmost teaching in this saying, the "Living One" is your holy Neshamah, your spiritual nature. So the Master is saying that you are to seek your heavenly soul in this life, that, bringing it into incarnation, you should have your Neshamah always. Only when the Neshamah is incarnate fully in a life will you be fully awakened and liberated once and for all. It is here and now that Neshamah must be realized. This is the true purpose and meaning of life. If you do nothing else in life but only this one thing, you will have accomplished everything and will know eternal life in this very life and beyond it. I pray to the Lord that you should receive the blessing of the influence of your Neshamah, and yet more, that you might receive your heavenly soul within you! Amen.

VERSE 60

They saw a Samaritan carrying a lamb on his way to Judea.

He said to his disciples, "That man is round about the lamb."

They said to him, "So that he may kill it and eat it."

He said to them, "While it is alive he will not eat it, but only when he has killed it and it has become a corpse."

They said, "He cannot do so otherwise."

He said to them, "You, too, look for a place for yourselves within repose, lest you become a corpse and be eaten."

Nature herself is pure and selfless. The Word of the Lord is her spirit and the Wisdom of God her soul; she, herself, the grace and glory of the Lord of Creation. If you look into Nature and see her, you will see the Truth of God; if you listen to hear and hear her, you will hear the voice of the Almighty speaking within her and through her. She is, indeed, the delight and revelation of the Lord our God, the outpouring of the Holy Spirit of God in the act of Creation ongoing. Although evil appears in Creation in the separation of the Light and the Darkness, Nature herself is not evil. Rather evil is the product of ignorance and unconsciousness through which disbalance and disharmony manifest in Nature and the forces of chaos play out their mindless impulses.

While we can speak of the necessity of the redemption of Nature from the bondage of ignorance and forgetfulness, in her created essence, we cannot speak of her in any way as evil or opposed to the Lord God. For of every aspect of Nature in Creation, the Lord God has said, "It is good," and Nature herself is the manifestation of the grace and glory of God.

Indeed, the garden of Eden represents the purity of Nature in union and harmony with God, paradise being the state of Nature before the involution and the operation of cosmic ignorance. Through involution, cosmic ignorance came into being and Nature became unconscious of herself for the sake of evolution and awakening. Truly, the sorrow and suffering of division is as nothing in the face of the perfect delight of union. Only a little while is there the illusion of division and separation, all for the sake of the joy of mystical union in lucidity and freedom. Understanding this, we know even cosmic ignorance as a secret operation of the Holy Spirit.

Now why should I speak of Nature here? Because Nature must be distinguished from the "world" and the "way of the world" as spoken of in the wisdom teachings, lest, as so many of dogmatic faith, we make the mistake of considering Nature herself evil or against the Lord. Nothing could be further from the truth, but with the dawn of mental being and humanity, the cosmic forces of ignorance come into play. They create the world through the agency of humanity and move through the human being, just as Nature is becoming conscious of herself through humanity. By "world" is not meant the heavens and the earth, the land and sea and creatures of nature. Rather, what is meant are unenlightened conceptions of mental being, the worldview and activities of human beings ignorant of the Truth and Light; hence ignorant of the Lord God. By "world" is meant the human or mental world created under the power of cosmic ignorance in which the powers of ignorance reign supreme and the Truth and Light, the Lord our God, is completely forgotten and forsaken. It is a world of injustice and selfishness, lacking love and compassion, a world ruled by self-cherishing and selfish interests, desire, fear, and hatred. The way of the world is the way of selfishness, self-seeking, and violence, and, in truth, a path of wickedness—that is, a path of self-destruction.

Only by understanding this will you understand the present verse or the saying of St. James when he writes: "You want something and you do not have it; so you commit murder. And you covet something and cannot obtain it; so you engage in disputes and conflicts. You do not have it because you do not ask. You ask and you do not receive, because you ask wrongly, in order to spend what you get on your pleasures. Adulterers! Do you not know that friendship with the world is enmity with God? Therefore whoever wishes to be a friend of the world becomes the enemy of God" (James 4:2–4). What is meant by the "world" and the "way of the world" is the evil that comes from self-cherishing and selfishness, which is to say that self-cherishing and selfishness is the enemy of enlightenment or God, and those who practice it make themselves opposed to the Lord.

So powerful is selfishness that we bring it to the path—so that we seek our spirituality and religion to serve our own selfish interests rather than actually entering the path for the sake of heaven and seeking God for the sake of God. Indeed, many would-be seekers or spiritual persons merely seek, in their spirituality and religion, the fulfillment of their own selfish ambitions and worldly interests, justifying their self-cherishing with terms like "spiritual person" or "God." Yet the truth is, the Lord is not their god. Their god is other than God; their god is a lesser god or goddess of selfish desire. So we see false preachers addressing messages and teachings toward greed they call "abundance" and false prophets giving false teachings that do not challenge egotism but instead encourage selfishness under the guise of "spirituality." One need only look into teachings of new theology and so-called modern spirituality to discover what the Lord is speaking about. Where is the power of the Holy Spirit in most churches today? Where are the teachings of righteousness in modern spirituality? Have we, then, tamed God so that God should submit to our own self-will and agree with us? When we sojourn on the path with a worldly mind serving only our own worldly interests, will it result in anything less than the killing and devouring of our spiritual nature? Will it not kill the Lamb of God, the Christ-Spirit in us? Yes!

Dare to consider exactly what put our Lord and Savior to death! Was it not worldly interests and egotism that brought so great a prophet and apostle of God to the cross? Have not all martyrs died on account of the selfishness, which is the way of the world? So we understand how St. James can speak in such strong terms of what becoming the friend of the world means. It means we then crucify Christ, as surely as if we, ourselves, drove the nails through the Holy One's body into the wood! If you kill your own Savior, how shall you be redeemed and saved?

There is a grave danger, and I shall dare say a "mortal sin," in suggesting that Lord Yeshua is the Son of God and you are only human and cannot live as the son or daughter of God. To say Yeshua was the Son of God, but I am only human and therefore am justified in continuing to live in selfishness according to the ways of an unenlightened society—the way of the world—is a missing of the mark of Truth that leads straight to hell! That is to say, that leads to a great separation and distance from the Lord our God. The reason for the coming of the Messiah was to close the gap and link us once again most intimately with God's Spirit. The perfect Master has called us out of the world and our worldly interests into the kingdom of heaven and the interests of heaven, and exactly this is what it means to be Christ-like or "Christian."

Now here the Master says to the disciple, "Seek a place for yourself within peace," the perfect peace of the kingdom of heaven, not merely in the afterlife but right here in this present life. Seek the Christ center within, behind your heart and above your head, and live in the way of that Holy Spirit within and beyond you—the way of selflessness that gives rise to cosmic consciousness, and the Messianic consciousness that is within and beyond it, hence supernal consciousness. Serve that noble ideal rather than the way of the world; serve the real idea of the indwelling Christ. It is this that brings the realization of eternal life.

VERSE 61

Jesus said, "Two will rest on a bed; the one will die, and the other will live."

What is death but a loss of consciousness and forgetfulness? Life, then, is a continuity of consciousness and remembrance of the bornless Spirit. One will lose consciousness and the other will maintain consciousness. If we say this is the deathbed, what is the difference between these two, the one who will die and the one who will live? The difference is this. The one who will die is identified with name and form and therefore with a corpse that dies and is eaten. How horrible an end of life! But the one who will live has let go of name and form and is identified with the Neshamah, or heavenly soul, and the Christ-self that indwells it. Therefore, he or she will depart the material body as though worn out clothing to continue life in the Body of Light. How wonderful a beginning of life!

Initiating the rite of the Holy Eucharist, the Lord has said, "Do this in remembrance of me," the Word and Wisdom of God within you—the Spirit of Messiah indwelling you. Do this in remembrance of your secret and undying soul and bornless Spirit, so that always you know yourselves alive and have eternal life in the Spirit of God. It is as the manna of heaven and waters of life that we partake of in the Holy Eucharist, the bread of heaven and wine of the Beloved, and partaking, we know ourselves united with the Anointed One in the presence of the living God.

What does it mean to have faith in Yeshua Messiah, in his death and resurrection? It means that I receive the Grace that the Lord has imparted and that, receiving the Holy Spirit, I am united with the Lord, both in his death and his resurrection, and will ascend with him into repose when I depart this material existence. Knowing consciousness beyond the body in this life, I shall know life in the world to come. The Holy Eucharist is a rite of divine theurgy through which you not only affirm your faith, you partake of the presence and essence of the Lord, feeding your soul and Body of Light, as it were, and so, even in death, you shall know Life and Light.

The one who shall die has not received the Divine Grace of the Lord nor performed the divine labors of faith, through which the Body of Light comes into being and his or her heavenly mansion is built. That one has focused upon making a place in this world, but neglected making a place in the world to come, and so has no place in repose but will continue in aimless and unconscious wandering, passing through the gate of death again and again. It would seem the one who dies has spiritually starved to death!

Now on another level, the Master is speaking of the Second Coming and the Day of Reckoning, as we have discussed previously. To carry our exploration a bit further, let us ask a question. When Uzzah saw the ark of covenant unsteady and about to fall, and reached out his hand and touched the ark of God to prevent it from falling, why was the wrath of the Lord kindled against Uzzah so that he was struck dead? Surely, one who would protect the holy ark of God should receive mercy! First, it must be said that the whole tale is told from a mortal perspective, so that, when the name and form that appears in the world falls dead, death is the consequence and life is gone. This being the case, from the mortal perspective, it would appear as though the wrath of the Lord was upon Uzzah. Yet, what if, in this action, God called Uzzah to itself, taking Uzzah into the kingdom of heaven on account of his faithfulness, a faith even willing to face death to defend the holy ark of God. There was no prophet there to say what transpired, only David, who was afraid to lose his life at the hands of the Lord. Indeed, who in the world that remains in worldly mindedness can say how the Lord works?

Let us assume that the wrath of the Lord did come upon Uzzah. How can this be? Quite simply, Uzzah was in a state of impurity in consciousness and not wholly consecrated unto the Lord God, and so receiving an influx of Divine Grace directly—it was as wrath to him, a flashing fire taking his life. Uzzah was not near unto the Lord nor like unto the Divine presence; therefore, as one drawing near unto the sun without first becoming like unto the sun, he died in the presence. You must become like unto God to draw near unto the Lord God. In this way, you preserve your life.

There shall come a day when the presence of the Lord is everywhere on earth, as it was upon the ark of the covenant. To some, it shall be as mercy and a great blessing; to others, it shall be as wrath and a horrible curse. As we have said, the presence of the Lord is the same; it is we who are different, whether righteous or unrighteous, like unto the Lord our God or dissimilar to the Lord. Whether meeting the Lord in death or in the Second Coming, it is all a question of how like or unlike we are to the presence of the Lord. The selfish die in their selfishness while yet in life. The unselfish live in the Christ-self, both in life and in death, so there is no death for them. Was Uzzah taken up or not? Who but the Lord can say? As for you, are you on the path of the ascension, that is to say, day by day becoming more and more Christ-like? If you are, then you will be taken up and know eternal life in the presence of the Lord, for already you are drawing near and ascending in life and so it shall be in the afterlife. This is the promise our Lord and Savior has given to us. If we are willing and surrender ourselves, the Holy Spirit will fulfill it. Let us invite and welcome the Christ-Spirit within ourselves and our lives and so live in Christ!

VERSE 61
(Continued)

Salome said, *"Who are you, man, that you, a mortal being,*
have come upon my couch and eaten from my table?"

Jesus said to her, *"I am he who exists from the undivided.*
I was given some of the things of my Father."

... *"I am your disciple."*

... *"Therefore I say, if he is destroyed he will be filled with*
Light, but if he is divided, he will be filled with Darkness."

Look and see! The ministry of the Lord is to both visible
and invisible spirits. Among his disciples are noble cosmic
forces, spirits, and even the holy angels. Here, an angel of
peace inquires of the Lord as to his inmost nature and his
teaching. He reveals something of himself to her and she becomes his disciple, receiving teaching and initiation from
him. So also, before the Lord ascends, we hear that he ministered to spirits and souls bound in Hades and the domains of
the rulers, bearing forth the Light of God even into the darkest of realms to redeem all who would receive the Word of
the Lord. The mercy and compassion of the Lord abounds!
Praise the Lord for the Grace he freely imparts to those who
will to receive it!

Now, it is this way with all the tzaddikim, the apostles of
God. Their circle of companions extends beyond visible souls
and spirits; it includes invisible souls and spirits. Our ministry

is to both visible and invisible spirits. In the Christ-Spirit, we are given authority over the rulers and spiritual forces of cosmic ignorance established in celestial places. We are even set over the angels of the Lord, so that we minister to the angels even as the angels minister to us. You also are to minister to both visible and invisible spirits. Spirits of the living and the dead, noble elemental and cosmic spirits, the angels of the Lord, and whatever spirit might come to you, you are to put to the test, to see if it is from the Lord or not, and to minister accordingly. It is through the Spirit of the Messiah within humanity that all beings, visible and invisible, and Nature herself are redeemed. This is one of the central teachings of this saying.

The Master is also teaching of the ascension and passage through domains of cosmic and heavenly forces. He is speaking of both faith and gnosis of your inmost essence, the Christ-Spirit, through which you receive the right of passage through all realms and worlds, as we have spoken of previously. In this saying, he teaches that even the angels of the Lord shall challenge the soul in its ascent and that one must be prepared in faith to meet their challenge, just as with any other spiritual force or being.

The Lord makes the nature of our gnostic faith clear. We must meet the challenge of all spiritual forces, whether in this life or the afterlife, with complete faith and trust in the indwelling Christ, knowing that if we are destroyed, we shall be uplifted in the Lord and grow even stronger in the Christ-Spirit. We must have faith in the Spirit of God that dwells in us, even in the face of certain death and destruction. Unified with Christ in this way, we shall be filled with Light, but if we are divided by self-cherishing, desire, and fear, our faith being weak, the powers of ignorance shall overcome us and we shall be subject to their dominion.

This saying has deep mystical and magical teachings contained in it. It is part of the most esoteric level of the Master's teachings that only his inmost disciples can receive. For this reason, the saying that follows speaks of the Lord imparting teachings on the inmost mysteries only to those "worthy" of receiving them. We gain a glimpse of what he means in this present saying, for how many individuals today are able to hear and understand the teachings contained in it? If there is a reaction to this most superficial level I have given, who can hear the inner levels of teaching that are also present in it, such as how to put the spirits to the test or to minister to invisible spirits? In an age of arrogant reason, it is hard for us to receive the crazy wisdom of the Lord. Only one who has become a disciple can receive the transmission of the secret wisdom. I pray you find an apostle of the Lord and become a true and faithful disciple, that you might receive the hidden wisdom that can only be given through oral transmission and shared spiritual experience.

VERSE 62

Jesus said, "It is to those [who are worthy of my] mysteries that I tell my mysteries. Do not let your left hand know what your right hand is doing."

Seek the keys of the mysteries and the Lord shall give them to you. Be ready and willing to receive the teachings and initiations of the secret wisdom and the Holy Spirit shall impart them. Let your faith become openness, sensitivity, and a complete surrender to the Holy Spirit, aspiring with your heart, soul, mind, and life to true Gnosis, and she will manifest the Christ-mind in you. To do this, you must let go and let be; you must abide in holy awe and wonder of the mysteries of God and Creation. Put away all preconceptions, preconditions, and expectations, everything you think you know, all that you think you are, and all concepts of reality or God you hold dear. You must become empty of yourself so that you might be filled with the Holy Spirit of the Lord. Then you shall receive all the spiritual knowledge and gifts you desire, all things given to you according to your faith, aspiration, and surrender.

What is the promise of the Lord our God in the prophet Isaiah? The Lord proclaims, "I will give you the treasures of darkness and the riches hidden in secret places, so that you may know that it is I, the Lord, the God of Israel, who calls you by your name" (Isaiah 45:3). This is the promise the Lord has made to the faithful and elect who seek knowledge of the Lord and who worship the Lord in Spirit and Truth.

I tell you, if I think I know anything in the presence of the Lord, then I abide in ignorance and prevent any reception. Although a prophet or apostle of the Lord should bring the Word of the Lord to me, I will set myself up as the judge of what to accept or not accept, and the Holy Spirit will not be with me in my receiving. For I am not open and sensitive to the Spirit of the Lord but remain in the darkness with my heart and mind closed. No wonder I can receive very little or nothing at all of the mysteries, for I am unwilling and not ready to receive. Equally, if I believe, in my ignorance, more than the promise of the Lord, so that I do not trust in the Lord and the power of the Holy Spirit to enlighten me, I also prevent my receiving on account of a weakness in my faith. Whether through pride and arrogance or insecurity and lack of faith in the Spirit of the Lord, the Light-transmission is hindered and obstructed.

Now, let it be said that prophecy or divine revelation is only as clear as the mind and heart of the prophet or apostle of God or the one to whom the Lord chooses to speak and reveal his mysteries. To the degree the mind, heart, and life are pure, free of self-cherishing, selfish motivations and ambitions, desires and fears, the Light of the Lord will shine within and through the one who receives. Wherever there is darkness and negativity, however, the presence of the Lord cannot abide, and the Word of the Lord is surely tainted and distorted. Thus, seeking knowledge of the mysteries, I must purify myself of all that would taint, hinder, or obstruct the Word of the Lord. Becoming empty of myself, I must let the Word of the Lord possess me and fill me with the Holy Spirit.

Jesus said, "I have brought the keys of the mysteries of the kingdom of heaven, otherwise no flesh in the world would be saved. For without the mysteries no one enters into the kingdom of Light, be that person righteous or a sinner. For this cause, therefore, have I brought the keys of the mysteries into the world, so that I may release the sinners who will believe in me and harken unto me" (Pistis Sophia 133).

You cannot rely upon ordinary and superficial consciousness to gain knowledge and understanding of the holy mysteries. Linear and finite reason cannot grasp or comprehend the mysteries nor receive the keys that open the gates of gnosis. In order to gain insight and knowledge, you must shift from the reasoning mind to the intuitive and creative mind. You must learn to enter into higher states of consciousness that are able to receive the divine revelation.

We may consider this shift in consciousness in terms of sound and vibration. There are various frequencies of vibration that produce the sounds we hear. We hear only those frequencies we are attuned to and our physical ears allow us to hear. Although we may hear a great deal, there are many dimensions of sound we are not able to hear because the frequencies are either above or below our range of hearing. In essence, we are not physically attuned to those frequencies of vibration and so do not receive them. To us, it is as though they do not exist at all, yet they are present in the atmosphere nevertheless. If we had different ears that were able to attune themselves to these frequencies, we would be able to hear these other dimensions of sound. The same is true with our other physical senses: taste, smell, touch, and sight. Just as we hear only a certain range of vibratory frequencies of sound, so we only perceive a certain range in the spectrum of light and so on. There are whole levels or dimensions of the physical universe we cannot perceive with our physical senses.

Just as our physical bodies have senses, so also do our subtle bodies. While most ordinary individuals have the potential of psychic and spiritual senses but have not actualized them, the potential is present within every human being. The actual range of the physical senses cannot be extended, save through the agency of our machines. However, not only can psychic and spiritual senses be activated, they can also be extended through shifts into higher states of consciousness. Machines have allowed us to perceive and experience levels or dimensions of physical reality that formerly were hidden and unknown to us. Likewise, if the inner senses of our subtle bodies are awakened and we are able to shift to higher states of consciousness, we will perceive and experience levels or dimensions of reality that were, in effect, formerly nonexistent to us.

Here, it must be made clear that material, psychic, and spiritual dimensions of reality are not separate from one another; rather, they are different levels of one reality-truth-continuum and we are speaking of one meta-dimensional matrix of reality.

Unless the prophets and apostles reveal the keys of the mysteries to us, how would we receive knowledge of the mysteries? As the Master says, as souls involved so deeply in the material plane of existence, unless there were tzaddikim and maggidim to give us the keys, we could not receive them. This is especially true of the inmost and highest mysteries of the kingdom of heaven and soul of the Messiah. Were it not for the incarnation of the Spirit of the Messiah and the mystery drama played out by the perfect Master, we would not have the keys of the mysteries that are in our possession today.

What are the keys of the mysteries? They are teachings on the metaphysical order and inner dimensions of the reality-truth-continuum. They are methods of mystical prayer and prophetic meditation that allow an initiate to awaken the psychic and spiritual senses of his or her soul, and to shift into higher states of consciousness. Having these keys, an initiate is able to enter into direct experience of inner psychic and spiritual dimensions. Along with these teachings and instruction, there is also transmission of substantial spiritual energy-intelligence, a Light-transmission, that empowers the spiritual practices and helps awaken the inner and higher senses and powers of the soul and spirit. The substantial energy-intelligence and teachings of the secret wisdom transmitted are the keys to the mysteries, and through them, an initiate can open the gates of the mysteries and experience the divine revelation directly.

What does it mean to be worthy? Fundamentally, it means that you have faith in the reality and possibility of Messianic consciousness and actively seek to consciously evolve toward that self-realization. It means that you are ready and willing to receive teachings, instruction, and initiations, and to actively follow and practice the Way opened to you, entering into the great work as a conscious agent for the enlightenment and liberation of yourself, humanity, and the world.

VERSE 63

*Jesus said, "There was a rich man who had much money. He
said, 'I shall put my money to use so that I may sow, reap,
plant and fill my storehouse with produce, with the result that
I shall lack nothing.' Such were his intentions, but that same
night he died. Let one who has ears hear."*

Now it is an obvious truth that, when death comes, regardless of our intentions and however noble they
might have been, all is said and done. What has not been
done and not been said remains unsaid and undone, and we
take with us only what we have sown and therefore reaped
from this life. Life is short and it is best to make the most of
it, especially in terms of refinement and evolution of the soul.
Life is precious.

It must be understood that, while incarnation again and
again into the material plane of existence is, in a certain
sense, bondage and exile, at the same time it is a great blessing, for it is in the material or physical plane of existence that
the soul has the greatest possibility for swift refinement and
evolution. Although, according to the masters of all Wisdom
Traditions, these times in which we live are extremely dark
and degenerate, at the same time they tell us that incarnation
in these times holds more potential for conscious evolution
than times past. Although some degree of advancement in
the development and evolution of the soul can occur in more

subtle realms and worlds—such as those in astral, mental, causal, and spiritual planes experienced during the transition through afterlife states—what progress might be made is very slow and happens only over the course of vast spans of existence. Typically, whatever is accomplished in more subtle dimensions must ultimately be embodied in the physical or material plane to be brought to fruition. In truth, the actual advancement of the soul happens through incarnation in the material plane, whatever is attained here in the physical plane being a true and lasting attainment. When we understand this, we become aware of why this life in the material plane is considered so precious by initiates of the mysteries, for they know life not only in the ordinary and mundane context but in terms of its vast potential for conscious spiritual evolution. If one truly realizes this greater purpose and meaning of life to the soul-being, one certainly is not so inclined to squander such a priceless opportunity upon vain and worldly things, but will naturally direct more time and energy toward one's psychic and spiritual evolution and the attainment of the kingdom of heaven.

Frankly, just as one does not know the hour of one's death, one also does not know when one will again have the opportunity for swift and radical advancement of the soul. The truth is that, if one incarnates rapidly into the material plane following this life, there is no certainty of what the conditions of the next life will be, whether they will afford auspicious circumstances for spiritual practice and spiritual living that lead to advancement, or instead they will be very inau-spicious circumstances. Likewise, rather than a swift return into incarnation in the material plane, the soul could get caught up into incarnation within the domains of the cosmic forces on another plane, the duration of which could last a very long time. While some incarnations of this nature may prove relatively pleasurable, they could also prove dread and terrible, as in the case of the entrance of the soul-being into one of the realms of hell. Even in the case of a pleasurable incarnation in a more subtle realm or world, the possibility of the advancement of the soul would most likely be very slight, if at all. Departing such an incarnation might prove to be a deeply sorrowful and painful thing—so much so that it could lead to a vital recoil, producing a far less favorable incarnation because of the violence of the vital nature at the time of death or transition. Thus, the opportunity of this present incarnation is something you cannot be certain will come again so soon in the future, and it is most special in the case of a noble soul who has encountered their holy tzaddik and has consciously entered into the path of the ascension.

The wealthy individual that the Master is speaking of is the disciple. Teachings and initiation, the opportunity to invest that precious good fortune in actual practice and life, is a great wealth and treasury—an enlightenment treasury. Since one does not know when they will be so spiritually wealthy again, it is best if they make the most of the opportunity while they have it, lest in not making use of it, they lose it and do not find it again for a very long time.

Now is the time to generate and manifest the Body of Light, to realize the resurrection and eternal life. Now is the time to seek to receive your Ruach and Neshamah, to embody your heavenly soul and unite yourself completely with the indwelling Christ. Now is the time to make for yourself a place in the kingdom of heaven and to build your heavenly mansion, the reward of good and noble works. Now is the time—there is no other—for if you do not accomplish these things in life, then you will not attain them in the afterlife. You will receive in the afterlife the fruit of your labors.

If that labor was only for vain and empty things, then vanity and emptiness—poverty—will be yours. If, on the other hand, that labor was for things good and noble and Spirit-filled, then good and noble things will be yours, and you will receive the Divine fullness and be wealthy in the Holy Spirit. What is spoken here is a simple truth that, if you search your heart, somewhere deep inside yourself, you already know. Thus, let your holy intention bear the good fruits of righteousness and holiness and good works, investing what the Lord has given you wisely, so that you might receive yet more and have more to share and to give. Fill your storehouse with good produce and treasures now, so that you may have them when you seek and need them.

Bear this in mind: Whatever you attain now, you will have always. Whatever you do not attain will not be with you when you depart this world. Let those who have ears, listen and hear!

VERSE 64

*Jesus said, "A man had received visitors. And when he had
prepared the dinner, he sent his servant to invite the guests. He
went first to one and said to him, 'My master invites you.' He
said, 'I have claims against some merchants. They are coming
to me this evening. I must go and give them my orders. I ask to
be excused from the dinner.' He went to another and said to
him, 'My master has invited you.' He said to him, 'I have
bought a house and am required for the day. I shall not have
any spare time.' He went to another and said to him, 'My
master invites you.' He said to him, 'My friend is going to get
married, and I am to prepare the banquet. I shall not be able to
come. I ask to be excused from the dinner.' He went to another
and said to him, 'My master invites you.' He said to him, 'I
have just bought a farm, and I am on my way to collect the
rent. I shall not be able to come. I ask to be excused.' The servant returned and said to his master, 'Those whom you had
invited to the dinner have asked to be excused.' The master said
to his servant, 'Go outside to the streets and bring back those
whom you happen to meet, so that they may dine.' Business-
men and merchants [will] not enter the places of my father."*

B lessed are you, O Lord our God, who sends forth the prophets and apostles, your holy servants, bearing the Spirit
and Truth, your Word and Wisdom, to your people! Through
your prophets, you give voice to the divine vision and make

yourself and your mysteries known. Through your apostles, you come among us, to live and walk with us and open the way before us, so that not only might we receive your ongoing divine revelation, but we might aspire and ascend in union with you and be called your sons and daughters.

Praise be to your Holy Name, O Lord our God. We listen and hear your heavenly voice. We receive your Holy Word and the instruction of your ageless Wisdom, and we thirst and hunger no more. You have given to us the living water and bread of heaven, nourishing and restoring our soul and spirit with your Divine presence and power, and you have established us in the Spirit of holiness. The blessings and Grace you have imparted through your prophets and apostles you have poured out upon us, saint and sinner alike, so that all who are willing to receive shall receive and shall be fulfilled in receiving and giving to others.

Blessed are you, O Lord our God, the life of the prophets and apostles and all your people is in your hand, for you are the holy root and sustenance of one and all.

You spoke to the man of God. You showed yourself to the prophet. You sent the ravens to feed your prophet meat and bread. Morning and evening you sent your holy angels ministering, and from your own mouth, you gave your chosen living waters.

With the righteous crone and the lad, you gave your messenger shelter. Under the wings of the holy Shekinah you gave refuge and life. In the hour of trial and tribulation you gave witness with your fire and lights. And you, yourself, come to the Holy One, anointing with your Holy Spirit and Light.

In due season, through the prophet, you blessed and ordained the apostle, giving to your holy apostle a double portion of the Spirit of the prophet, and bound to the apostle the soul of the Messiah above.

You sent your prophet to initiate and open the way before you came into the world. You have become in him the Holy Lamb of Passover for one and all. You spread out a holy feast upon the banquet table.

You enter your house to dine and commune with those who also enter. You give your peace and joy and all good things to those who would know you. From the wedding feast, you bring the soul of the elect into your bridal chamber. You fulfill the promise of your holy covenant and uplift your servants above the angels.

Praise be to your Holy Name, O Lord of the prophets.

Holy, holy, holy are you, O God of the apostles.

Blessed are you, O Lord our God.

You are our heavenly Father-Mother, and we are your children in the Spirit of the Messiah, your sons and daughters of gnosis in the Holy Spirit.

Bless us to become as your holy image.

Let the Spirit of the prophets remain with us.

Let the Spirit of the initiates move among us.

Let the Spirit of the Messiah indwell us.

O Lord, let us enter your house and dine with you. Pour forth your Holy Spirit upon us and let the living waters flow from within us.

May the Light be in extension and your kingdom manifest upon the earth. Amen and amen.

What does this prayer have to do with the parable the Master is speaking? The Lord our God is the Master of the house, and the prophets and apostles of God, the men and women of God, are the servants of the Lord who bear forth his Holy Word and Wisdom, giving an invitation to the elect and receiving the elect into the feast of Divine ideas, the real ideal of the Will of God for the secret and undying soul. Whoever is willing to answer the call of the Holy Spirit, the servants of the Lord will receive and share the blessings and Grace of the Lord, giving to the righteous and unrighteous alike, according to the Word of the Lord. The true prayer here is not that the Light should be in extension, but that there should be among humanity those who are ready and willing to receive it and to let the Supernal Light shine within them and through them to illuminate the world. As the Master has said, the harvest is plentiful. Pray the Lord sends out laborers into the fields, so that the harvest might be gathered in. Thus the prayer for extension of Light is a prayer for souls to receive it, and receiving it, to give and share that Divine illumination.

It is true that there are certain souls for whom a holy tzaddik is sent into the world. However, if those souls will not be received, then the tzaddik is free to receive any soul who might cross his or her path, and to set his or her blessing upon anyone who is ready and willing to receive it. While the holy tzaddik is sent into the world for the sake of righteous souls, the healer also comes for the sake of those who are ill and dis-eased. The holy tzaddikim come for the righteous and unrighteous alike, and it is often among the unrighteous that a repentance and righteousness is to be found, for in the midst of sorrow and suffering, the soul is more likely to turn unto the Lord and cry out from deep within. Here, you might contemplate the harlot Rahab, who became as a shining star lifted from within the pit of darkness, a sinner become a saint. Likewise, you might consider the conversion of St. Paul, a rebellious son who became a great messenger of Divine Grace.

Along this line, we may well say that the Lord works in strange and mysterious ways, for hardening the heart of some, the Lord brings Light to others, and in the end all are to be redeemed. But who can comprehend how the Spirit of the Lord works or know and understand the ultimate fruition the Lord seeks? If the heart of Pharaoh was not hardened, would the glory of the Lord have been so fully revealed to the chosen ones? If the children of Israel did not reject the Anointed One, would the gentiles have received the Light and been brought into the assembly of the elect? Without the secret operation of the Holy Spirit through the powers of cosmic ignorance, could Creation evolve as the Lord intends and the joy of reunion be known? Indeed! The Way of the Lord our God is a great mystery! No one can explain it, but everyone is invited to experience it.

Now, let it be said that the Lord seeks you out so that you might find the Lord and receive within yourself the Spirit of the Lord. You are the house of the Lord, the living temple of God, and going within, you will dine with the Holy One and unite yourself with the Holy One. Shaping the outer person and your life according to the way of the inner self or Christ-self, you will become as the image of the Lord upon the earth, even as the perfect Master. The Spirit of the prophets, the Spirit of the initiates, and the Spirit of the Messiah is not something separate and apart from you. You are invited to partake of the Holy Spirit, to be fulfilled in the Holy Spirit, and to enter into the mystery drama yourself. You are called as sons and daughters of the living God to become men and women of God, apostles of the Lord laboring for the Second Coming. God seeks you out so that you might return to a conscious unity and harmony with him. The Lord lays out a feast of divine ideas before your intuition, so that you and anyone who is willing might partake and so consciously evolve toward the real idea of your secret and undying soul—the image of Christ.

Many are the holy mysteries indicated in this way of interpreting the present saying, and we have drawn some of them out for contemplation and meditation. Yet there is another way of interpreting this saying quite differently. That is to consider yourself this host who is disappointed. Life naturally tends to shatter our preconceptions, preconditions, and expectations. Life challenges our false beliefs and immature stages of faith, until, at last, we look and see reality as it is and accept life on life's terms and so let go and let be. Perhaps our greatest suffering comes from our striving against life to maintain our delusions, trying to keep them from suddenly collapsing. Yet eventually, all our illusions will be revealed for what they are. Only when we can accept the downfall of our false beliefs can we be free to embrace a real and noble faith—a belief with understanding.

VERSE 65

He said, "There was a good man who owned a vineyard. He leased it to tenant farmers so that they might work it and he might collect the produce from them. He sent his servant so that the tenants might give him the produce of the vineyard. They seized his servant and beat him, all but killing him. The servant went back and told his master. The master said, 'Perhaps they did not recognize him.' He sent another servant. The tenants beat this one as well. Then the owner sent his son and said, 'Perhaps they will show respect for my son.' Because the tenants knew that it was he who was the heir to the vineyard, they seized him and killed him. Let him who has ears hear."

This saying focuses upon the plight of the prophets in Israel, and not only Israel but the world at large, and is a prophecy of the complete rejection of the Great Prophet of God who embodied the soul of Messiah. At the same time, the Master gives a teaching on the purpose of humanity in the material world and the fields of sentient existence and why you and I are incarnate in this life. The purpose of humanity is Nature awakening and becoming conscious of herself and uniting herself to the Beloved, the Lord our God. The Lord has made us caretakers of his Creation, of the world and all that lives in it, and of each other, and he has made us co-creators with himself, destined to evolve into a Divine human being, one anointed with the Supernal Light as Yeshua Messiah and Lady Mary. We do not come into the world for ourselves. We come for a divine labor for the sake of the evolution of our soul and God's Creation; for the sake of heaven and the Lord. The children of Light know they are from the Light and of the Light and serve the Light and Spirit, but the children of Darkness live in ignorance and forgetfulness, and do not know they are from the Light and so rebel against it. To this very day, we see the conflict and struggle between the Light and the Darkness in the dualistic state as we watch the great evils humanity commits and the perpetual destruction of life on earth because of selfishness, greed, and hatred. Believing we are here for ourselves alone, we act in such a way as to destroy the blessings and good that God has given to us and we lose our human spirit and the Spirit of God to gross materialism. We do not serve the Lord our God; only our own deluded interest, and, quite naturally, we suffer on account of it.

It is certainly not that the advancement of humanity on any given level is inherently wrong or evil. Neither is it evil or wrong that we should advance ourselves in life or seek to live life more abundantly. It is the intention of God that we evolve and advance as a species of his creatures, and that we access and actualize all possible material, psychic, and spiritual powers, the powers of nature and our soul. It is the Will of God that we live life abundantly, but the fruit of our labor is not our own—rather, it belongs to the Lord. Our role is that of a co-creator with God, to evolve and awaken Creation and bring it into fruition in God itself. As we activate the powers of Nature and powers of our soul, we are to put them into the service of the Lord's plan for Creation and to restore all powers to God. We are to use all resources and powers wisely, not as though they are our own, but use them for the sake of heaven. In so doing, we become more and more like unto God and unite ourselves with God.

How wonderful! The Lord reveals to us the purpose and meaning of our lives, so that knowing the purpose and meaning of our lives, we might live life abundantly. The Lord does not call us out of life, but out of materialism, worldly mindedness, and the selfishness that leads us to destruction and death. The Lord calls us to the Divine Life, the development and evolution of our soul, to become more than human—to become like unto the angels and to ascend in our evolution even beyond the heavenly hosts. Likewise, the Lord calls us to develop and evolve the world into the image of the heavens and to unite heaven and earth within and through ourselves. How awesome and marvelous the calling of the human spirit! Let us praise the Lord who has fashioned us in the Divine image!

So the Master is speaking of the purpose and meaning of our life on earth. Yet he is also addressing the ignorance and forgetfulness in humanity of its purpose on earth and the dominion of the cosmic forces that holds the majority of humanity in bondage. So great is the power of cosmic ignorance and the intoxication of materialism in the world that, when the Lord sends prophets and apostles to the people, the people turn against the holy ones and seek to destroy them. Worldly people, under the influence of cosmic ignorance, would seek to destroy even an incarnation of the soul of the Messiah, the great World Teacher, so that they can continue to gather in power for themselves and serve their own self-interests. Perhaps today we may not physically beat and kill the prophets, but we continue to persecute them, to ignore them, and to shun them. We may not act to kill their body, but we do seek to kill their spirit and to crush their zeal. The result is the same. Business, politics, academics, dogmatic religion, and mass humanity is the same today as in the day of Yeshua; unenlightened society remains fundamentally the same, and the response to the holy and enlightened ones whom the Lord sends is the same.

Now it must be said that even the cosmic forces of ignorance serve the Lord, although not intending to do so. In fact, they are a secret operation of the Holy Spirit of God working toward the fulfillment of God's plan for Creation. The cosmic forces of ignorance provide the friction, resistance, strife, and opposition necessary for evolution to occur. They put to the test every new development in the progress of evolution to see if it is true and good and strong. We see this in the Holy Scriptures when we read that the Lord hardens the heart of a person. For example, in Exodus, we read that the Lord hardens the heart of Pharaoh. On account of this, the glory and power of the Lord is revealed to a far greater degree, both to the children of Israel and the Egyptians. In the same way, the Lord hardens the hearts of the children of Israel so that they reject and kill the Great Prophet who embodies the soul of the Messiah. Yet on account of the rejection of the Messiah, the Light of the Anointed One is extended not only to the Jews but also to the gentiles. This is not to say that anyone should willfully seek to harden their heart against the Lord, or seek to facilitate the dark and hostile forces, or in any way act in opposition to the Will of the Lord, justifying their evil by a claim of serving God. It is not meant to condone or put a blessing on wickedness. Rather, it is meant to demonstrate how the Lord uses and works through all spiritual forces, even through the cosmic forces of ignorance and the enemy, in order to evolve and perfect his Creation, and to say that these spiritual forces are also in the hands of the Lord, however strange and mysterious that might seem to us.

We learn from the Holy Scriptures that God has a plan on earth for humanity and that the Lord sends messengers to reveal that plan and to establish continuums to link humanity with himself and to carry out that plan. We also learn that humanity has free will and can accept or reject the Will of God, keeping or breaking covenant with the Lord. God changes the plan according to the choices human beings make, ever seeking to bring about the greatest possible blessing and good, and continuing to influence and guide humanity toward its Divine destiny. We come to understand that humanity is part of God's plan and holds within it the potential of the ultimate fruit of Creation and that God needs the human co-creator to bring about the intended fruition. Without humanity, where would be God's ultimate joy in Creation? To whom and through whom would God then reveal and give itself?

You may ask of the threat of punishment when we rebel against the Will of God, but the consequences exist in the act of rebellion and activity of the evil inclination itself. Of all the horror and terrible things that have come or will come, is not the sorrow and suffering of them all a natural result of our creating a distance between ourselves and God, or the ignorance that makes us believe and live as though we are in an isolated self-existence, separate and apart from everyone and everything else in Creation and God itself? In truth, the Lord gives no promise of reward or threat of punishment, but rather informs the soul of consequences of its own actions according to the law upon which Creation has been formed and the human being fashioned. Bear in mind that evil is inherently self-isolating and self-destructive. Indeed! What would the murder of the heir of the vineyard accomplish but the loss of exactly what they were trying to take as their own possession and their own suffering or death? Evil always acts in this way and brings about its own destruction.

Perhaps what is central to the teaching the Master is giving here is the cultivation of our discernment and ability to distinguish between good and evil, and a spiritual practice and spiritual living that empowers us to cut off the evil inclination and to choose the good and godly. The anonymous author of the Letter to the Hebrews writes, "But solid food is for the mature, for those whose faculties have been trained by practice to distinguish good from evil" (Hebrews 5:14). Thus, we see that the ability to discern between good and evil is crucial to our spiritual advancement and the enlightenment and liberation that the Spirit of the Lord would bring to us.

In our immaturity, we do not have this discerning power. How could any individual persecute, shun, ignore, harm, or kill a man or woman of God, save that they could not recognize the holy one and could not distinguish between good and evil? Indeed, without some degree of this faculty, how could I recognize a prophet or apostle of God? Surely, I would write them off as some cult leader or crazy fanatic so as to not have to deal with the challenge and trouble they bring, and so I would persecute them, whether on a gross or subtle level, believing myself righteous in so doing! As Yeshua says to his disciples, "They will persecute you and seek to kill you, believing it righteousness."

I pray to the Lord for you, that the Holy Spirit will manifest the power to discern between good and evil and strengthen you in righteousness, to choose and enact always the greater good. In this way, I pray for the Holy Spirit to guide and protect you and for your success. Amen.

VERSE 66

Jesus said, "Show me the stone which the builders have rejected. That one is the cornerstone."

The measurements of the cornerstone must be precise because it determines every other line and angle in the building. Therefore, only the best-cut stone could serve as the cornerstone. In this parable, it would seem that the quality of the stone is something inward rather than outward and that it corresponds with a different logic than finite and mortal reason, for if the stone is rejected by the builders through ordinary linear reasoning and external appearance, then its true qualities are inward and hidden from plain view.

When the people expect a warrior-king to come as the Anointed One and God sends a priest-king, the karmic vision of the people prevents them from recognizing and accepting the Messiah, for the appearance of the Messiah contradicts their expectations. Likewise, the preconceptions of dogmatic doctrine form another layer of karmic vision, preventing the realization of a greater Divine Truth. Then, of course, there are all the preconditions of the individual that are in opposition to the message of the Anointed One, and this, too, generates karmic vision, obstructing the reception of the Spirit of the Messiah. Fundamentally, individuals see only what they want to see, and how they view what they see and judge it is based upon predetermination, upon previously formed beliefs, opinions, and expectations. What does not conform to their preconceptions or contradicts their world view, they ignore or reject and may even react violently toward, while what agrees with their own ideas and world view, they readily accept and like. Unfortunately, one cannot search for the Truth and find the Truth in this way. At best, one can only find partial truths always mixed with falsehood. The Anointed One of God did not conform to Jewish expectations, and certainly confounded all linear and finite reason. For this reason, very few could recognize and receive the Messiah, and fewer still could listen and hear his teachings and follow him.

Now, it would be expected that Christianity has done better, having accepted and preached the Anointed One of God. Yet, in truth, everything Yeshua had to say of the pharisees and the scribes can be said of the clergy and theologians of our own times. Whether the dogma of Judaism or of orthodox Christianity, neither can understand, let alone experience, the Spirit of the Messiah and the message that the Holy Spirit brings. Like the Jews, the majority of Christians have also rejected the message of the Messiah, making a human being the deity in an improper sense and denying both the indwelling Christ and the Word of the Lord that teaches our destiny to become Christ ourselves.

It is the indwelling Christ-self that has been rejected—the teaching of the Lord that every man and woman is to become a son or daughter of God. The Lord has said that we will do greater things than we have seen him do, and likewise that every person is a child of God destined to become like the angels, hence a Christ-like being. Without a faith and knowledge of the indwelling Christ-self, one cannot receive the teachings of the Messiah in their true context, which certainly prevents the initiation into the Spirit of the Messiah or Messianic consciousness the Lord intends for us. The stone that has been rejected by orthodox and dogmatic religion must be the cornerstone of our orientation and preaching, the indwelling Christ and an evolution of the soul to Christhood.

It is faith and gnosis of the indwelling Spirit of the Messiah that gives a correct basis for our thoughts, feelings, emotions, and likewise for our spiritual practice and spiritual living. This Spirit and Truth alone gives us the proper foundation to build ourselves as temples of the Divine presence and to labor for the Second Coming. The Second Coming is the dawn of Christ-consciousness in the individual. Only through a sufficient number of individuals realizing the Christ-Spirit within themselves, and forming collectives to work together for the advent of Christ-consciousness on earth, will the Second Coming happen in the larger segments of humanity and become a global event. If clergy and theologians do not teach the people the spiritual practices that form the divine labor toward the Second Coming, how will the advent of Messianic consciousness fully come upon the earth? Likewise, if only the doctrine of Logos is taught and not the true doctrine of Sophia, how will the fullness of the soul of the Messiah be known and understood? Yet all of this is dependent on the knowledge of the indwelling Spirit of Christ as the inmost secret essence of the soul—hence, Christ as our own inner and Divine self.

Now, you must understand that the Light-transmission of the apostolic succession is founded upon faith and gnosis of the indwelling Christ-Spirit and that, in rejecting the true teaching of Christ regarding the Christ-self and the evolution of the soul to Christhood, the dogmas of orthodox Christianity prevent the teachings and initiations through which Divine Grace flows forth. The way of the original church of the Anointed One was founded upon actual initiations imparted by ordained apostles to their disciples; hence the cornerstone of transmission was a living relationship between a spiritual master and his or her disciples—discipleship. In the rejection of the indwelling Christ-Spirit within the elect, the succession of apostles and the way of discipleship in Christ was also rejected. The effects of this in Western culture are so extreme that few, if any, believe in or are able to recognize living adepts and masters of the apostolic succession, and almost none have any understanding or inclination to be true and faithful disciples. Save among initiates of small mystical circles, the keys of the mysteries are virtually lost in Christianity today. The mystical lineages themselves are rapidly passing out of the world in our dark and degenerate times. The holy fire the Lord kindled is almost completely extinguished! May we pray the Lord initiate a Spirit-filled revival to stoke the holy fire and rekindle it once again to blazing!

VERSE 67

Jesus said, "If one who knows the all still feels a personal deficiency, that person, he is completely deficient."

I f you know yourself connected to the Sacred Unity that God is, no longer do you suffer from the delusion of lack and separation, and therefore the sorrows of personal deficiency have vanished. Indeed, faith in the death and resurrection of Yeshua Messiah and knowledge of the indwelling Christ-Spirit enlightens the soul and liberates you from the cosmic forces of ignorance and death. Remember the promise of the Master at the very outset of this Gnostic Gospel of Christ, "Whoever discovers the meaning of these sayings will not experience death." Do you believe with understanding— that is to say, have genuine faith? Through faith and the good works of faith do you labor for true Gnosis? Then of a certainty, gnosis will be granted unto you and you are already redeemed! Do you have faith that Christ indwells you and you are delivered from the bondage of ignorance and death? Then for you, the resurrection is now and the advent of Messianic consciousness is near! Praise the Lord!

Now, let it be said that having mystical experiences in and of itself is not enough. You must integrate into yourself the Truth and Light revealed in your experience, letting the spiritual experiences transform you, and so live according to the Truth and Light revealed in your experience. In order to have direct spiritual experience, you must create the conditions in which a shift into a higher state of awareness can occur and through which Divine Grace can move.

If I do not actively engage in prayer and meditation, and worship the Lord my God in Spirit and Truth, I cannot very well expect to enter into higher states of awareness or prophetic levels of consciousness—let alone, were I to enter them by some chance, that such experience would transform me. The Master is once again addressing the possibility and necessity of direct spiritual experience and of the practice and spiritual living that bring it about.

Yet, the Master is also speaking of something even more subtle and sublime. He is saying that it is Divine Grace that accomplishes everything—but only when the disciple suspends the egoistic self, silencing the mental being and calming the vital-emotional, thus allowing Divine Grace to act without obstruction. Entering into the Sacred Unity in this way, there is no one to be deficient. Rather, the Christ-self, in union with the heavenly Father and the Holy Spirit, is the doer of everything. In the egoistic condition, everything is personal, but in this state of self-transcendence nothing is personal at all. Having entered directly into the experience of such self-transcendence and embodying something of that higher consciousness, one can no longer conceive of oneself separate and apart from the Sacred Unity and therefore can in no way be personally deficient. The spiritual experience of which the Master is speaking is deeply healing and liberating!

Let me share with you the ideal that the initiates of our lineage hold in their spiritual practice and spiritual living. The view they hold is that it is the Christ-Spirit in them that prays, meditates, and worships God in Spirit and Truth and that it is the Christ-self who lives their life and labors to accomplish God's plan through it. In everything that is done, it is the Holy Spirit that is the doer and the initiate is the conscious witness and vehicle of this action of Divine Grace. In this sense, the masters of our tradition would ardently agree with St. Paul, who argues salvation through faith by Divine Grace.

If you enter into a practice with this enlightened view, how could you believe a good session of practice is the result of your own doing or a poor session of practice the result of some personal fault? Likewise, if you practice this view in daily living, where shall there be any personal deficiency? All there will be is a divine labor to be done and you will let the Holy Spirit do what she must do, cooperating with her completely. Everything changes with this view, and the nature of the change is profound. When you know you walk with the Lord and that the Spirit of the Lord is with you, the negative self-consciousness that once plagued you is no longer present, or at least is no longer so strong as it once was.

Let it be said clearly that the path is about self-transcendence, service to others and service to the Lord our God. In the midst of service to others, and to the Lord, who has time to become self-conscious? If at any time I find myself too self-conscious, then perhaps I am too self-centered in that moment and serving myself rather than serving the Lord in that situation. I have always found this to be true.

VERSE 68

Jesus said, "Blessed are you when you are hated and perse-
cuted. Wherever you have been persecuted they will find no
place."

There are two paths for the soul to travel, but one consciousness-force. There is the path of unenlightened society, and there is the path of the holy ones, which is the
complete opposite of that of society and conventional wisdom. Both paths are a manifestation of the same mind or consciousness-force; the consciousness that is enlightened and
the consciousness that is unenlightened is the same consciousness-being. It is simply a question of Divine illumination or the lack of it.

So we understand that the Way of Spirit is not the way of
the world. It stands to reason that anyone who walks in the
Way of the Spirit and seeks a conscious unity with God will
find that they naturally meet with gross and subtle opposition
from their society and worldly minded people around them;
in one form or another, they will find themselves persecuted.
Now in the past, such persecution very often led to physical
abuse and even murder at the hands of the powers that be or
the ignorant multitude. Today physical abuse or death is far
less likely, but rather such things as slander and verbal abuse,
being ignored or shunned, considered a "cult leader" or "cult
follower," or some crazy fanatic, are all common forms of

persecution that the disciples and apostles of the Light-transmission may well encounter. This can come from strangers or friends or family, all the same. Likewise, nothing around oneself in society will in any way encourage you to follow in the Way of the Spirit or to engage in spiritual practice and spiritual living, but rather everything will encourage you into a state of worldly mindedness and distraction from the path to enlightenment. Persecution may even come from those claiming to be religious persons or religious authorities who serve the static state of conventional wisdom over and above the Wisdom of God. Nevertheless, persecution, whether obvious or not so obvious, will at some point be met with, even by the most discrete among the faithful and elect. If one walks fully in the way of the Holy Spirit, it will be very obvious. It has been so with the prophets and apostles of God who sojourned the path and served the Lord before you, and it will be so with you, if indeed you take up the mantle of the messengers and apostles of God.

Not only will opposition come from ignorant and worldly minded individuals, but also from the cosmic forces of ignorance. If a prisoner or hostage attempts to escape their capture, will not the captors stop at nothing to prevent escape, and if they cannot prevent escape, even seek the hostage's life? So it is with the cosmic forces of ignorance, or as St. Paul calls them, "the spiritual forces of wickedness established in heavenly places." They will also persecute and attempt to discourage and hinder the mystical aspirant for the enlightenment experience so that the soul might remain in bondage to the ruler of the world, the enemy.

The fact is that, meeting with such opposition, you can be assured you are on the right path. Walking in the way of the world, nothing will oppose or contradict you, but the world will agree with you, yet the world will not agree with you if you follow in the Way of Spirit. As a matter of fact, under certain conditions, the opposition might prove quite violent, even in these modern, "civilized times."

Now this is not spoken to discourage you from the path, nor does it suggest that anyone among the faithful and elect should go out looking for trouble or invoking trouble upon themselves. Rather, it is spoken for the sake of understanding the persecution or opposition one will quite naturally encounter, and to empower us to endure and overcome it. It is actually a teaching on how to face persecution or opposition one may come across and to realize, within it, a blessing of the Lord.

Yes, indeed, whatever persecution or opposition you might encounter is a blessing upon your soul if you maintain your faith and endure it, for your faith will naturally grow stronger and your soul gain refinement in the process. On a psychic and spiritual level, you will grow and be stronger in the long run. You might ask how this is so? Bear in mind that resistance and opposition is necessary for the process of development and evolution. Without it, evolution cannot occur, or occurring, whatever might emerge would be inherently weak and imperfect in nature, unable to thrive on its own. Opposition ensures and cultivates the strength and quality of everything that emerges in evolution. This is truth, whether we are speaking of biological or spiritual evolution. Thus, whatever persecution or opposition one might encounter, the disciple is to realize as a blessing and meet it in this way, receiving the hidden blessing that it brings.

Persecution may come for many reasons, not only on account of our faith and spiritual practice. Nevertheless, we are to respond to it the same and seek to draw out the hidden blessing in whatever situation of oppression we might encounter. Always, we are to seek our refuge and strength in the Lord and let the Holy Spirit guide our response. Some situations may call for an active and dynamic response, while others may call for a passive response. It is the Spirit of Christ that indwells us that will know what is best for all who are involved. Hence, we must put our trust in the Lord and turn to the Lord in the face of any trial or tribulation we might meet. I pray that always you might rejoice in the Lord, in good times and bad times, knowing the whole of life as the blessing of the Lord and receiving every blessing that the Lord sends you. Amen.

VERSE 69

Jesus said, "Blessed are they who have been persecuted within themselves. It is they who have truly come to know the Father. Blessed are the hungry, for the belly of him who desires will be filled."

To sojourn the path, one must have a sense of the mystery and an impulse to seek Truth within. While a man or woman of God may serve to kindle inspiration and motivation through their ministry and teachings, motivations and inspiration that come from outside of oneself are not enough for the actual journey of the path to enlightenment and liberation. Without the inner impulse, one will not have the drive to sojourn very far upon the path and will soon be distracted by the world and things of the world.

Likewise, every aspirant must cultivate and heed his or her conscience and seek to live in such a way as to have a good and clear conscience. One who is ripe and mature for the mystical path must be able to live by way of inner guidance, both of one's conscience and the voice of the Holy Spirit speaking in oneself. Obedience to good conscience and righteousness imposed by any source of external demand will accomplish very little in the way of development, refinement, and evolution of one's soul-being. Although a law given for the sake of the lawless and imposed from the outside may serve to guard against a deeper fall into negativity and karma, it does not actually serve to advance the soul in its development. Actual evolution only occurs from an inner impulse, a holy law of righteousness discovered within one's heart and inmost being. It is this inner impulse toward righteousness and truth that distinguishes one ready for the mystical path, and following it, that reflects one's genuine willingness. The holy tzaddik looks for this tendency in those who seek to enter into discipleship and to receive teachings and initiations in the esoteric wisdom.

When the Master speaks of an internal persecution, he is speaking of an inward conscious struggle for growth and refinement of oneself on moral and spiritual levels—an evolution of the psychic and spiritual dimensions of oneself according to the Truth and Light revealed in one's own experience. During periods of our early development on the path, our conscience is very likely to persecute us, convicting us of our ignorance and missing the mark, so that we are not satisfied to remain in Darkness, but are compelled to seek the Light. The persecution of which the Master is speaking is akin to the dark nights of the soul, of which St. John of the Cross wrote. Only those willing to pass through ordeals of spiritual growth and advancement will come to a full and conscious unity with the Lord and know the most intimate communion in the Spirit of the Lord.

In speaking about one who is hungry or thirsty, in order to understand the implications of the analogy, consider a time when you were extremely hungry or thirsty and had a very strong and deep drive to satisfy your hunger or thirst. If your desire for Spirit and Truth is as strong as this, without a doubt you will ultimately be Spirit-connected and filled with the Divine illumination.

In order to receive the Christ-Spirit, you must desire to receive it. In order to receive the Lord in your life and all good things and all spiritual gifts, you must desire to receive them and actively aspire to them, desiring not only for yourself alone, but that you might give and share all that you receive with others. This holy desire is either in you or it is not, and no one but yourself can give this holy desire to you. You, yourself, must kindle the flame of divine passion within you, and you, yourself, must actively seek and aspire to the Spirit and Truth. One who has this holy desire to receive for the sake of giving and sharing will experience abundance in this life and will come to know a communion in the Living God.

VERSE 70

*Jesus said, "That which you have will save you if you bring
it forth from yourselves. That which you do not have within
you will [kill] you if you do not have it within you."*

L isten and hear what the Master is saying. It is not something outside of yourself that will save you, but it is what
is within you that will deliver you. Although, indeed, the
Lord our God is above and beyond you, at the same time the
Holy One of Being is within you. The Spirit of the Lord indwells you. The presence of God dwells in the inmost part of
your soul and is your very own true self. Look and see your
soul within you; look yet deeper into the inmost part of your
soul, and there you will find the Holy One, the Spirit of the
Messiah, our Lord and Savior.

What is the holy blood of the Lamb that redeems us? It is
the essence of the Spirit of the Messiah that the perfect Master has poured out upon us. Whoever drinks of these living
waters shall thirst no more, for these waters shall spring forth
from within the deepest part of the soul, quenching the
thirst, not only of oneself, but other souls also.

What is the holy body of Christ of which we partake and
eat? It is the presence of the soul of the Messiah that Lord
Yeshua has imparted to us. This holy presence comes from
above and, descending upon us from above, shall also ascend
and return to its place at the right hand of the Father and take
us up into repose in the abode of Supernal Light.

When you partake of the Holy Eucharist, have you received something from outside of yourself? Not really. The Holy Eucharist is an invocation and remembrance of who and what you are in your inmost being and a drawing out of the Divine presence and power of that Holy One. It is a matter of the education of the soul, a drawing out of what is already within you. The activity of the holy rite of Eucharist itself is the manifestation of the Christ-self coming forward, as is every mode of spiritual practice and spiritual living we entertain, so that the holy activity is the blessing itself. The practice of the Way, Truth, and Light is the enlightenment experience, and those who live the Divine Life of Christ, with faith and trust in the Word of the Lord, are already liberated. It is all about drawing out what is within you and letting your light shine to illuminate yourself and the world around you.

Now you must understand that there are three distinct levels or aspects of the soul. They are Neshamah (the heavenly or inmost soul), Ruach (the human spirit and intelligence), and the Nefesh (the vital or earthly soul). When a person actively lives according to the righteousness of his or her inner self, following in the way of Christ and living according to good conscience and what is right in the sight of the Lord, his or her Nefesh and Ruach naturally and spontaneously receives the influence of their Neshamah—the spiritual nature of the heavenly soul. Of the person who sanctifies him or herself in this way, it can be said that it is what is within them, namely the living soul or spiritual nature, that will save the person. Conversely, when a person lives in ways of ignorance and wickedness, not heeding good conscience nor following in the Way of the Lord, in effect, he or she is cut off from the Neshamah and another spirit takes possession of that person, an unclean spirit of destruction and death. Of such a child of Darkness, it is rightly said that it is what one does not have within oneself that will lead to one's destruction and death.

Neshamah literally means "living soul" or "living breath." You will recall the first initiation the risen Messiah imparted to the disciples in their ordination as apostles of Christ. In that initiation, the Lord breathed upon them and they received the Holy Spirit and they received their Neshamah in full. Only when they received, integrated, and embodied their living soul could they then receive the baptism of the holy fire. This baptism of Pentecost is an influx of supernal holiness, the descent of the Shekinah from above, which is the true dawn of Christ-consciousness. Reception of Neshamah and descent of the holy Shekinah from the upper world form the holy rite of the bridal chamber, or the Light-transmission of the apostolic succession.

Now all of this is within you, waiting to be drawn out and lived, and living the Spirit and Truth, you shall possess your life in the Lord and therefore have life eternal in the Spirit of the Lord. Blessed are they who live the Divine Life and cleave unto the Lord, for they are alive this day and shall never die! Praise the Lord!

VERSE 71

Jesus said, "I shall [destroy this] house, and no one will be able to build it [...]"

The earthly temple in Jerusalem has been destroyed and is not to be rebuilt. Here, the Master is speaking a prophecy of the shattering of the old covenant. Yet in so doing, he is speaking of holy mysteries of the new covenant and esoteric wisdom concerning the soul of the Messiah. In the coming of the Messiah into the world, no longer is worship of God based in an earthly temple nor upon the holy mountain; it is a worship in Spirit and Truth everywhere, a worship founded within the heart, soul, mind, and life of the elect. The temple to be built is a Body of Light—hence the solar body or body of the resurrection.

For this reason, the Lord also said, "I will destroy this temple and rebuild it in three days." The temple that will be destroyed, not to be rebuilt again, is the external earthly temple, but the temple the Lord speaks of rebuilding is the body transformed by the supernal consciousness-force. Not only are we to generate and build a Body of Light, ultimately even the matter composing the physical body shall be transfigured to shine with the Supernal Light.

The earthly temple, especially the first tabernacle in the wilderness, was constructed based upon the pattern and image of the heavenly sanctuary. All that the Lord instructed it to contain, and the whole structure itself, directly reflected the holy mysteries of the celestial temple above. Yet this temple below was but a shadow and dim reflection of that holy sanctuary above, a sign of things hidden and stored up for the righteous and elect souls. It was not the holy sanctuary itself, but a physical interpretation and image of the temple of light in heaven. Now such an earthly temple was necessary until the advent of the Messiah, preparing and opening the way for the coming into being of the Anointed One of God upon the earth. Once the Anointed One, the holy priest-king of the celestial temple, brought forth the Supernal Light upon the earth, no longer was the earthly temple needed as before. Consequently, it was destined to be destroyed and never to be rebuilt again. As an affirmation of this prophecy, the Lord inspired the faithful of the Prophet Mohammed to erect a holy place of worship upon the site of the old temple as a guardianship against attempts by the ignorant to return to old ways.

We behold the new holy sanctuary in the resurrected body of our Lord and Savior—a body transformed and radically different in nature from the gross material bodies of our current condition. It is a Body of Light that can appear in any form according to the silent will of the soul and Christ-Spirit. Likewise, it can appear and disappear at will, within any plane of existence, and it can travel incredible distances as swiftly as thinking of them, and it can pass through solid objects. By nature, this body is indestructible and incorruptible, bornless and therefore deathless. It is a self-radiant and subtle body that shines like the sun—hence the term solar body or Body of Light.

In Christ, our body and life, our mind, heart, and soul, is the living temple of the Lord, the holy house in which the Spirit of Christ dwells. To the degree that we bring our Body of Light into substantial being within our physical form, we are the holy sanctuary of the Lord, and wherever we go, that place is holy unto the Lord our God. This is a present truth. Yet at the same time, our faith and hope instruct us of a spiritual evolution and the future in Christ—that this Body of Light shall become a far brighter and greater body than it is at present, one day to become so strongly manifest as to actually transform the matter of the physical body, translating the material body into the image of the glory of the Lord. At present, we know some things of what we are to become; yet much remains a mystery to us and thus we speak of our hope in Christ, our hope for the resurrection and the great transformation. In New Jerusalem, there will be no external temple. The elect shall be the holy sanctuary of God, formed in the image of the Lord—the risen Messiah. Hence, we will be like unto the angels of the Lord, although set above even the highest of the holy angels.

Now when we speak of this Body of Light as the holy temple of the Lord, you must understand that this is the temple of which the Lord speaks in his prophets, saying of it that it is a temple not made with human hands but by the Word and Wisdom of the Lord. It is a holy sanctuary fashioned by the Holy Spirit. Indeed! It is Divine Grace that generates and builds the Body of Light, not we ourselves. Our part is merely the good works that establish the conditions in which Divine Grace can accomplish the Lord's Will. On our part, we need only abide in faith, hope, and love, actively aspiring and surrendering to the Spirit of the Lord and letting the Holy Spirit guide and direct us in the Way, Truth, and Light. How delightful our spiritual hope in the Messiah! How awesome and wonderful are the ways of the Holy Spirit! How amazing and marvelous the good news the messenger of God has come proclaiming! We are truly blessed in the Spirit of the Lord! Praise the Lord! So great is our joy! Amen.

VERSE 72

[A man said] to him, "Tell my brothers to divide my father's possessions with me."

He said to him, "O man, who has made me a divider?"

He turned to his disciples and said to them, "I am not a divider, am I?"

It is an interesting request that this person brings to the Master. Considering that the Master had no legal authority to pass judgment and have that judgment executed, one cannot help but ponder exactly what this person was asking the Master to do. If his brothers were disciples of the Master, then perhaps the Master could act to ensure that the father's possessions were fairly distributed. But if this man's brothers were not disciples, then the only way the Master could intervene would be by the use of the magic-power. Assuming the brothers of this person are not disciples, we have to assume he is asking the Master for a divine intervention through the use of the magic-power, as not only was Master Yeshua known as a mystic and spiritual teacher, but also as a powerful magician and miracle worker. Taking this assumption as our foundation, this saying teaches the role of divine theurgy or magical practice in our tradition, a spiritual art used not for matters of personal gain but rather to render invisible spiritual assistance and to facilitate the great work.

What is divine theurgy or magic? It is a conscious manipulation and directing of invisible or hidden spiritual forces according to the volition of the magical practitioner. While many traditions that teach knowledge of magical arts do so for the sake of serving the personal will of the magical practitioner, that is not the intention of divine theurgy in the Wisdom Traditions. Rather, the aim of divine theurgy is to facilitate the Divine Will. We see this with the Divine power in the prophets and the stories about their use of that Divine conscious-ness-force. They use the Divine power under the intuitive guidance and direction of the Holy Spirit, using the magic-power according to the word of the Lord.

Why do initiates study the magical arts? The reason is twofold. First, in Christ we are to have dominion over all cosmic and spiritual forces, whether divine, admixed, or demonic in nature. Through study and practice of the magical side of the teachings, the initiate awakens and exercises the full range of the soul's powers, both psychic and spiritual. In the process of the development of the soul, he or she attains a certain degree of mastery over the hidden forces. So the first reason is the de-velopment and evolution of the soul as a conscious agent of the great work. Second, in Christ we are to serve the Will of God on earth, la-boring for the Second Coming and the upliftment of humanity. The magical arts are a way of rendering substantial invisible assistance, both openly and in secret. Having knowledge of and communion with the indwelling Christ, the initiate uses his or her knowledge of the magical arts to facilitate the will of the inner or Christ-self.

The human soul is a God-like creature, fashioned in the likeness of God. It is the intention of God that we are endowed with a whole range of spiritual gifts and powers, so that we might be conscious co-creators with the Lord and serve as conscious agents of his Divine plan, as do the holy angels. While the Master taught his disciples to pray for all spiritual gifts, he also taught them methods of practice to develop these gifts and instructed them in the keys to the mysteries of hidden spiritual forces. Yeshua had a profound knowledge and under-standing of not only the mystical Kabbalah but also of the magical or practical Kabbalah. These teachings continue to be imparted from master to disciple in the apostolic succession to this very day. They are part of the oral transmission, not written or communicated in open discourse, but spoken in secret mouth to hear.

You will recall that the Master charges his disciples with the ministry of bearing forth his message, as well as a ministry of healing and exorcism. This ministry is to both the living and the dead, and to visible and invisible spirits alike. The ministry to the dead and to invisible spirits, and the ministry of healing and driving out dark and hostile forces, require a degree of magical knowledge coupled with mystical knowledge of the teachings. Thus we find in the rite of ransom, initiations into the magical knowledge along with the inner mystical dimension of the teachings. Fundamentally, the initiate in the Gnostic Christian Tradition is to be a healer and spiritual warrior, a conscious agent of the great work.

The Master is also speaking of the mystical knowledge that is the core of his teachings. While the magical dimension of the teachings deals with a mastery and conscious direction of hidden spiritual forces, the mystical dimension deals with mystical prayer and prophetic meditation, and the development of a conscious unity with God. It is this mystical development that is considered most important in the teachings and initiations of the apostolic succession, and that shapes the nature of the magical practices of Christian initiates. Unification with God, a conscious awareness of the Sacred Unity that God is, is the heart and core of the message of the Messiah. It is from the awareness of this Sacred Unity, and from the Will of the Lord discerned through the Holy Spirit, that initiates practice their divine science of magic. Hence, initiates will only use the secret wisdom in a way that unites and brings them to the Lord, not in a way that divides and carries one further away from the Light and Truth.

Clearly, Lord Yeshua did not come into this world in order to concern himself with mundane and worldly matters. Rather, he came to bring teachings of heaven and the kingdom of God. His divine labor was not of this world, but for the sake of heaven and upliftment of humanity into unity with God. Likewise, as disciples of the Messiah, we have not come for the sake of the world but for the sake of heaven and the kingdom of God on earth. As the Lord reminds us again and again, like himself, we are from above, not of this world. Thus, he encourages us to practice and live in such a way that, although in this world, we are not of the world. Our aim in the Messiah is to cleave to the supernal holiness that comes from above and to remember ourselves as children of Light.

This is the present Truth of your inmost being—you are a child of Light, ever in union with all that lives and with God itself. Division and separation is an illusion; Sacred Unity is the Divine Truth. I pray you may have a strong faith in the Lord and live with this holy awareness so that you may know the peace and joy of the Lord in your life! Amen.

VERSE 73

Jesus said, "The harvest is great but the laborers are few. Beseech the Lord, therefore, to send out laborers to the harvest."

You are not alone in the struggle of conscious evolution and the quest for enlightenment and liberation. The souls of the prophets and apostles of God, the spirits of the saints and sages, and the holy angels of the Lord are all present and willing to help you. The Spirit of the Messiah itself is present with you and within you. You are not alone, but rather you are in good company. You only need to invoke, ask for help, and open yourself to the presence of the luminous assembly, and the Lord will answer your prayer and send you the help you need. Anywhere, at any time, you can call upon the holy ones and divine assistance will be present for you. Praise the Lord for the holy ones who guide and protect the faithful and elect!

The adepts and masters of the Light-transmission work from within the inner planes and in the material world for the enlightenment and liberation of souls. They are servants of God and laborers in the fields of sentient existence, seeking the harvest of souls for the Lord. Along with the holy angels of the Lord, they labor for the refinement and evolution of souls toward God-consciousness. They are ever ready and willing to render assistance to anyone who invokes them and opens themselves to the presence of the Lord.

Very few are they who have the spiritual faculties actualized to see the more subtle and sublime manifestation of the holy ones and angels in glorified form. Although a holy one or angel might appear in the subtle dimension right before them, or an assembly of radiant holy ones might appear all around, they would not perceive nor be conscious of these holy ones. Thus, they could not directly receive the divine influence of these holy ones; they could only receive it unconsciously. The degree to which the holy ones and angels can influence and help most ordinary individuals from the inner dimension is often very limited. Therefore, the tzaddikim and maggidim incarnate in the physical world in order to have a more direct influence. Everyone can see and encounter an incarnate tzaddik or maggid, whether or not they are able to recognize the Divine presence of the holy one. Because of this, the holy ones may be able to render assistance, both visible and invisible, more effectively.

Now, compared to those in need and the souls ready for harvest, there are relatively few holy ones incarnate. While it is the sacred heart of compassion and the Will of the Lord that sends them into the world, it is also our own invocation and desire to receive them in the world that brings them into incarnation. Here, we might consider our Master's teachings regarding prayer. When we pray, we become channels or vehicles of the Divine presence and power in the world, making ourselves a link between heaven and earth so that the Divine powers may enter and accomplish the Divine Will. We are, in effect, the receivers and transmitters of the Divine powers. Only to the degree that the faithful and elect attune themselves and invoke the Divine powers, can the Divine powers enter into the physical world and act to bring about a greater good. So it is with the souls of the tzaddikim and maggidim—they also respond to our prayers and meditations, entering into the world dependent upon the balance of Divine providence we create. We must continually ask the Lord to send his holy ones into the world, inviting them, as it were, so that they may enter and labor with us in the great work on earth.

The Holy Scriptures and books of esoteric wisdom teach us that we determine the balance of Divine providence in the world. According to the degree to which human beings seek the Lord and cleave unto the Spirit of the Lord, the Divine presence and power is present with us and active in the world. Conversely, when human beings do not seek the Lord nor cleave unto the Spirit of the Lord in their lives, in effect they banish the holy Shekinah from the world and leave the world to the play of the cosmic forces of ignorance. Hence humanity plays an active role in the balance of the play of spiritual forces. Here, the Master is pointing to this truth and encouraging his disciples to consciously bring forth the Divine powers and the holy ones in the world.

The tzaddikim and maggidim are directly supported in their divine labor by the faithful and elect. The prophets and apostles of God do not labor alone, but labor together with their disciples, and the faithful and elect of their generation, to bring about the plan of God and to uplift humanity to God. Without their disciples and the matrix of the faithful and elect souls, they cannot accomplish the mission for which they are sent. We are all a part of the mystical body of Christ and have a role to play in the divine labor of the great transformation. The great work is a divine labor not only of individuals; it is a divine labor of collectives of individuals working together.

The Lord is not speaking of you as in any way separate or apart from the holy ones, but rather as intimately connected with the holy ones and a part of the same mystical body. The Lord is calling you, as a disciple, to the same ministry of the Word and Wisdom of God. Indeed, it is the intention of the Master not only that you should invoke the Divine powers and the holy ones, but that you also should bear forth the Divine powers as a holy one yourself. You also are a laborer of the Lord that, in your prayers, you call upon to help with the harvest of souls. This invocation is as much about your holy soul as any other soul of Light. You are needed in the great work. Many are the souls that need your help for their enlightenment and liberation. The need is great, and every soul among the faithful and elect is called upon to meet the need. The Lord is sending you out to the harvest of souls!

There is definite instruction in this verse regarding things we might pray for. We are to pray that the Lord sends prophets and apostles, saints and sages into the world and, likewise, for assistance of the holy ones and angels of the Lord for those we know are in need of assistance. So, too, we are to pray for the growth of our spiritual communities, that new companions come and labor with us in the great work. We are to pray for the holy ones and the faithful and elect, that they might be empowered by the Holy Spirit and have all that they need to accomplish the great work—hence, that the Lord go with his servants and glorify himself through them. The Lord is calling us to develop an active prayer life, not only for ourselves alone, but for the sake of all living souls. We are to pray for the health, happiness, and enlightenment of all living souls, and actively labor to assist in any way we can.

VERSE 74

*He said, "O Lord, there are many around the drinking
trough, but there is nothing in the cistern."*

The difficulty with dogmatic exoteric religion is that it
demands that we accept the beliefs and opinions of someone else about spiritual truth, without examining them ourselves. In so doing, many seek the Spirit of God in the broken
cistern of creeds, external ritual, dogma, and outer forms; thus,
they do not experience the Spirit of God directly.

There are many reasons for this. One that is central is that
dogmatic religion offers the security of clear black-and-white
answers and provides a clear, codified external structure—if
one believes in it and obeys, they will have no other obliga-
tion or responsibility. Basically, it is far less challenging than a
living spirituality in which one must think for themselves and
explore the mysteries, seeking their own spiritual experience.
Everything is made simple, defined clearly, and packaged
neatly. One really does not have to think or struggle or be
spiritually responsible for the development and evolution of
one's soul. This is certainly one of the main reasons individuals are attracted to fundamentalistic doctrines, although perhaps another reason is that many people do not know where
else to look and don't spend much time seeking. In any case,
fundamentalism, in many forms, is popular. Unfortunately, it
is unlikely to lead to Spirit-connectedness and evolution of

the soul to Messianic consciousness. Fundamentalism is an empty cistern, devoid of the living waters of the Spirit and Truth or, at best, holding only a precious little amount of the living waters.

Master Yeshua was not interested in the religions of his day nor in the creation of yet another dogmatic structure, any more than the prophets and apostles of God that came before him or after him. Like all messengers of God, he was a mystic and Spirit-filled person. His sole intention was that others should enter into the mystical experience of unity with God and know themselves Spirit-connected. This was the very essence and heart of his teachings—that the Spirit of God lives in you and that you can experience the indwelling Spirit and so worship God in Spirit and Truth. Life itself is this exact experience when delivered from our preconceptions, preconditions, and expectations. This very moment, we are a part of the Sacred Unity God is. We always have been and always will be part of the Sacred Unity. Everyone and everything in Creation is part of this Sacred Unity, and the Spirit of God dwells in the whole of Creation. At every level of our existence, we are experiencing something of God, though, indeed, God also transcends Creation entirely. The Lord our God is a Living God and every living soul can experience God first-hand.

Here is a prayer for Divine Grace so that all who seek might receive, regardless of the limitations or errors of their seeking. Although the Lord had no interest in the dogmatic religions of his day, he nevertheless prays that Divine Grace might flow through such religions to those whose faith is true so that they might receive the Holy Spirit according to their capacity. Likewise, it is a prayer that more mature souls might recognize the emptiness of outer religious forms and thus seek beyond the forms and inwardly for the Spirit and Truth. What is spoken in this verse, we have discussed at great length previously.

VERSE 75

Jesus said, "Many are standing at the door, but it is the soli-
tary and elect who will enter the bridal chamber."

Yes, you are called and you are chosen to enter into the
bridal chamber, my dear friend! The wedding feast has
been prepared and all the guests are gathered. Your wedding
gown is ready for you, the light-vesture that the Holy Spirit
has woven. She has made for you a rainbow Body of Light!
Many are standing at the door awaiting the day that they are
called and so chosen, but today it is you who are called to
unite with the Beloved. Gather yourself up, in behind your
heart, and arise above your head, meet the Lord in the space
above and so enter the embrace of the Beloved! You go in
beauty to your Lord and he receives you into his kingdom.
Blessed is the Lord and blessed are you, O soul of Light!
Light upon Light illuminates and transforms the world! Praise
the Lord!

Have you not directly experienced the Christ-Spirit within you? Exactly what do you think holy experience is—that
you think you are not experiencing Christ right here and
now? Are you really so lacking as you think, or is it simply all
this thinking itself that prevents your recognition of the inner
dimensions of the present experience? Let me share an open
secret with you. If you are alive and reading this, then you
obviously are experiencing the Life-power, and the Messiah is

the power of Life—the Light of awareness. Therefore, whether you know it or not, you are experiencing the Christ-Spirit right now!

Although we must speak often in terms of becoming within space-time-consciousness, do not forget the Truth of being and the infinite and eternal that is the source and self of your very being here and now. Recognize the being of the becoming and identify yourself with this Holy One of Being, and you will realize that there is nothing to attain that you do not already possess, nor anything to become that you are not already in the presence of the Lord. Indeed, you do not practice and entertain becoming in order to attain something you lack, but rather to draw out and directly experience who and what you most truly are—an Anointed One of God.

If there are many standing at the door who do not enter, perhaps it is only because they are seeking an experience outside of themselves and other than themselves, or an experience somehow different than the one they are having. Thus, they do not realize that they are the experience that they are seeking and they are having the experience of the Life-power they so deeply desire. They are waiting for an experience and do not know that they are having it! Let those who have ears listen and hear!

There is no other experience for you than the one you are having. The experience of the Christ-Spirit for you is within your present experience, and it is here, in your present experience, that you will find the Christ-Spirit and enter into the embrace of the Beloved. The fact of the matter is this: You are lacking nothing, for you are part of the Sacred Unity God is, and all sense of lack is an illusion in the mind.

Practice and live according to the Spirit and Truth and you will experience the Spirit and Light within yourself and your life. This is what the Master is saying. Remembering and practicing the Truth, we are greatly blessed! Put on your light-vestures, enter the bridal chamber, and praise the Lord! Let us rejoice in the Lord and praise the Holy Name of the Lord our God! Amen.

VERSE 76

Jesus said, "The kingdom of the Father is like a merchant
who had a consignment of merchandise and who discovered a
pearl. That merchant was shrewd. He sold the merchandise
and bought the pearl alone for himself. You, too, seek his un-
failing and enduring treasure where no moth comes near to
devour and no worm destroys."

How beautiful and delightful it is to behold the pearl
essence, white as snow, yet shining with every color in
the rainbow in a most sublime and subtle way. It is as Nothing, it is One-Without-End, it is Boundless Light, the inmost part of the soul, the holy Neshamah. There, in your
deepest center of being, the Spirit of the Lord dwells, that
pearl essence, which is no other than God itself. Listen and
hear, and receive the Word and Wisdom of God that is within you!

Bornless is your spiritual nature, your holy Neshamah.
Without father or mother, without genealogy, having neither
beginning of days nor end of life, but resembling the Sun of
God, she is inseparable from the Holy One of Being, abiding
ever in communion with the Most High God. She is Light
and Life and Love and Liberty. She is the one who is your Supernal Holiness, anointed in the Supernal Light.

The Lord has said, "No one has ascended into heaven ex-
cept the one who descended from heaven, the Son of Adam.

And just as Moses lifted up the serpent in the wilderness, so must the Son of Man be lifted up, that whoever has faith in the Anointed One of God may have Eternal Life" (Gospel of St. John 3:13–15).

So also the Lord has said, "Very truly, I tell you, no one can enter into the kingdom of God without being born from above. . . . Very truly, I tell you, no one can enter the kingdom of God without being born of water and born of Spirit" (Gospel of St. John 3:3 and 5).

Your holy Neshamah is the one who descends from heaven and therefore shall bring you in ascent with herself into heaven, taking your Ruach and Nefesh into herself and uniting you with the Lord. Receiving the holy baptism and chrism, Nefesh and Ruach are purified and consecrated unto the Lord, and you are redeemed in the holy blood of the Lamb of God, receiving your life, your living soul or holy Neshamah. She is the eternal life the Lord has prepared for you—the living temple of the indwelling presence of the Lord. Reborn of the water, the Holy Spirit descends and enters you and brings with herself your heavenly soul. It is Nefesh and Ruach that are redeemed by the body and blood of the Messiah, saved by the Grace of the Lord, who gives to you your heavenly soul.

For the refinement, evolution, and enlightenment of your Nefesh and Ruach you have come into the world. The Lord has given you your life, your talents and abilities, and all resources of your life, so that you might have the price to be paid for the pearl essence. Indeed! The Lord has given you this life so that you might discover and embody your holy Neshamah and give expression on earth to your heavenly soul and the Christ-Spirit that indwells that inmost part of your soul. Knowing that to receive and express your heavenly soul is to enter the kingdom of God and to attain life eternal, who would not give their life and all resources of their life over to this great work? It is not merely a matter of wisdom in the merchant, but common sense! Is there anything else you might purchase that will remain with you as your possession forever? Praise the Lord that we are given the sum of the ransom for the salvation of our soul and spirit!

Now here, the Master is speaking of the mystery of Neshamah and the indwelling Christ-Spirit. He is also speaking of the holy mystery of the soul of the Messiah as both Logos and Sophia. Receiving Logos (the Word), the Gnostic initiate must also seek to receive Sophia (the Wisdom), so that the Divine fullness of the Sun of God is revealed and received and the soul is made perfect and complete in the soul of the Anointed One of God.

The soul of the Messiah was incarnate as male and female in the world, although above the soul of the Anointed One is male and female in primordial unity. In Yeshua Messiah, we behold the incarnation of Logos and, in Lady Mary Magdalene, the incarnation of Sophia, the two together revealing the full mystery of the soul of Messiah. Although Logos was received and accepted in the matrix of the disciples, the reception of Sophia was only partial, and therefore the reception of the Christ-Spirit incomplete. Here, in a most subtle way, the Master alludes to this and encourages the disciples to seek to receive Sophia as well as Logos within themselves. The masters of our Gnostic Christian Tradition teach us that the next incarnation of the soul of the Messiah is to be in a woman's form, in order to complete the revelation of the holy mystery of the Spirit of the Messiah. There is a hint of this in the last verse of this gospel.

VERSE 77

Jesus said, "It is I who am the Light which is above them all. It is I who am the all. From me did the all come forth, and unto me did the all extend. Split a piece of wood, and I am there. Lift up the stone, and you will find me there."

N ow it is true that Yeshua Messiah made himself a holy sacrifice for the redemption of our soul and the soul of the world, the holy blood of the Lamb of God liberating us from bondage to sin and the karmic web. He who is without blemish of sin gave himself as an appeasement to the angel of death, and the Lord our God raised him from death to eternal life, giving him victory and dominion over the cosmic forces of ignorance. And so the Living Father has manifested the fullness of Divine Grace in Lord Yeshua, so that whoever has faith in the Anointed One of God shall not remain upon the wheel of life, death, and rebirth to perish on account of sin, but shall have their life in the Holy One of Being.

Indeed, under the old covenant, there was repeated sacrifice for the forgiveness of sin. In the new covenant, there is a holy sacrifice once and for all time for the forgiveness of sin and the liberation of the soul. The perfect Lamb of God is the perfect offering of salvation; his holy blood the perfect atonement and sacred sign of remembrance. To the righteous one with whom the Lord God founded the old covenant, God revealed his intention when he asked Abraham to go out and make the sacrifice of his only begotten son. When the Lord told Abraham to offer up his son Isaac, the Lord showed Abraham and Sarah the holy sacrifice God intended to make of his Anointed One, giving the promise of salvation—enlightenment and liberation—of an even better covenant than the first holy covenant. Although a magical link was made through the old covenant to the new covenant, enlightenment and liberation was not attained by way of the old covenant. Only the grace of a great soul embodying the soul of Messiah and entering the holy sacrifice, making himself a ransom for all souls, restores our soul to Life and Liberty.

All of this is certainly a mystery. Yet there is a deeper mystery in the crucifixion, mysteries within mysteries, to which the Master has given us the keys, so that we also might labor with him for God's plan on earth. While there is a sacrifice of blood given as an offering for sin, that is only the surface and outer level of the mystery of the crucifixion. On the inner level, the holy sacrifice is not a sin offering, but a vehicle for divine revelation that in no other way could transpire. Unless the perfect Master died and was resurrected, how would we know of the resurrection and the promise of Life? If the Lord did not show himself to us as the One Anointed in the Supernal Light and pour forth that Light upon us, how could we have remembered the Light, and so opened and surrendered ourselves to the Light, and thus received the Supernal Light? To openly and willingly embrace death and then to rise again was the only way to show us the Holy Light that is within our inmost part, our holy Neshamah, so that, having faith and gnosis of that Light, we might attain that Light presence and transform ourselves and our world with it. The outer mystery of the crucifixion alludes to the inner mystery, and prepares us to receive the inner initiation, just as the inner mystery alludes to an inmost secret mystery.

In the Transfiguration the revelation of the Supernal Light was given, but the revelation was complete through the death and resurrection of Lord Yeshua, his holy blood purifying our soul and spirit, so that we might be anointed and consecrated in the Supernal Light. The outer mystery is a preparation for the inner mystery and is a sign of the inner mystery, just as the inner mystery is preparation and a holy sign of the inmost secret mystery. Having spoken of the inner mystery of the crucifixion, we may now speak in such a way so as to perhaps glimpse something of the inmost secret mystery.

When the Lord says, "Split a piece of wood, and I am there. Lift up the stone, and you will find me," he is teaching a secret known among the elect. Keter is in Malkut and Malkut is in Keter; that is to say, the Supernal Light "above" is everywhere in Creation. The Supernal Light is hidden in matter itself. The secret center of every particle of matter is this spiritual nuclear force—this Light-force of supernal being. Not only did the soul of the Messiah incarnate to offer a perfect sacrifice and to bring down the Supernal Light into the world, but also to bring forth the Supernal Light from within Creation and matter itself, in order to bring all creatures to fruition in God. So the Lord brought down the Light from above; but in so doing, he brought forth the Light from within the Darkness below, liberating the Divine sparks of supernal holiness, as it were, through a perfect remembrance. For this reason, Lord Yeshua has said of the Holy Eucharist, "Do this in remembrance of me," that is to say, in remembrance of the Christ-Spirit and the primordial Light within yourself and all of Creation. It is this holy remembrance that is the redemption of our soul and the soul of the world.

Here, we are speaking of that which we have seen and heard and known, for every apostle of Christ has experienced the Transfiguration within themselves, and among their disciples are those who also bear witness of the Holy Light that can be seen to shine from a person, even from the physical body itself. As in the day of our Lord, today there are those who live and move among us in whom this Holy Spirit and Light is fully embodied, and who continue the divine labor begun in the Savior. It is the transmission of this Light that is our ministry in Christ, as we labor with the Lord for the Second Coming or advent of supernal consciousness on earth. The good news is alive!

St. John understood this mystery and so opened his Gospel of Christ, writing, "In the beginning was Logos, and Logos was with God, and Logos was God. He was in the beginning with God. All things came into being through him, and without him not one thing came into being. What has come into being in him was Life, and the

Life was the Light of all people. The Light shines in the darkness, and
the darkness did not overcome it . . . and Logos became flesh and lived
among us, and we have seen the Glory, the Glory of a father's only
son, full of Grace and Truth" (The Gospel of St. John 1:1–5 and 14).

There is great opposition to the Light in the world. The powers of
Darkness, ignorance, and forgetfulness reign with vast power, and re-
sist and oppose the Light. Yet to all who will receive the word of the
Lord, inviting and welcoming the Light into themselves and their
lives, and who labor for the advent of Light on earth, the Spirit and
Light is given freely. Through faith, they are established in the Light
and Truth, and through faith, they are fulfilled in gnosis according to
Grace.

On that day when you bowed yourself down before the Lord and
gave yourself and your life to the Lord, inviting and welcoming the
Christ-Spirit and Light into yourself and your life, you became as one
anointed with Light and the Spirit of Holiness came to dwell in you.
Remembering yourself as a child of Light and living according to that
Truth and Light, because you cleave unto the Lord, you are alive this
day and your soul is redeemed. Because of this, for you, there is the
ascension of Grace and hope in the resurrection and transformation of
the world. Having given yourself over to the Lord and inviting the
Lord into your life each and every day, you walk in holiness as an
Anointed One of God, and the Lord walks with you. What is the
promise of the Lord to one who walks with the Lord God? That they
should be taken up with him and united with him as Enoch was! This
is the promise the Lord has made to you, and the Lord shall not
change his mind regarding his promise. Knowing this, you are free to
abide in the peace and joy of the Lord, now, in this life and in the afterlife, for you are living the promise.

This we can say, remembering and practicing the Truth and Light
each day, we are greatly blessed, for to live according to the Way,
Truth, and Light is the enlightenment experience itself, and accordingly, we are saved, that is to say, we are set free. The Way itself is no
more or less than the fulfillment of God's promise—the attainment itself. How sweet it is! Let us rejoice in the Lord each and every day!
Praise the Lord! Amen.

VERSE 78

Jesus said, "Why have you gone out into the desert? To see a reed shaken by the wind? And to see a man clothed in fine garments (like your) kings and your great men? Upon them are fine garments, and they are unable to discern the truth."

Let it first be said that it is not the prophet of God who must seek you out and pursue you, but it is you who are to seek out and follow the holy prophet. If you seek, you will find. If you ask, you will ultimately receive the answer. If you knock at the gate of initiation, the way of the holy mysteries will be opened before you and you will be received in the Spirit of the Lord. But if you do not seek, how will you find? If you do not ask, how will the answer be given to you? If you do not knock at the gate of initiation, how shall it be said you were ready and willing to enter and be received? You must go out into the desert to meet with the prophet of God, for only when you enter into the world of the prophet can the prophet communicate the world of the Lord to you. As long as you remain in the city and in your own house, you cannot listen and hear the Word of the Lord in the prophet, for all of your self-concerns and worldly interests will not let you listen and hear the Holy Spirit that speaks within you. The God of Israel is the God of the wilderness, and you must go out into the wilderness in order to meet with him or her.

Why would you leave the comfort of your house and delights of the city? Why should you depart from the way of

242

the world to sojourn in the Way of the prophets and apostles of God? If the answer to this question is not within you, I cannot give it to you, for it is the Holy Spirit that calls a soul out into the desert and guides and protects the soul in the Way, and no one but God can impart such Grace. One is either given to a holy tzaddik in Spirit or one is not. If one is given in Spirit to the holy tzaddik, one must give oneself in Spirit in order to be received. Many are they who are given in Spirit, but few are they who give themselves; and so many are called, but few are so chosen.

Listen and hear, my dear brothers and sisters. When you are called to the interior church and the Spirit brings you into the mystical path, like the sons and daughters of the prophets before you, you are also a member of the assembly of prophets and apostles—a member of the mystical body of the Holy One. You also are called as conscious agents of the Word of the Lord and the great work, ordained by your calling as ministers of the Spirit and Truth. A companion in a mystical order is a conscious agent in a divine labor. He or she is a companion of a holy tzaddik on a mission from God, and yet more, he or she is a companion of the Holy Spirit herself, letting the Holy Spirit work within and through him- or herself according to the Will of God. Our calling is for a conscious participation, for that is the nature of a mystic and of mystical fellowships. We seek a direct communion in the Spirit of the Lord and to serve the Lord in Spirit and Truth.

Yes, a reed shaken in the wind! That is the very nature of the prophets. They are moved by the Spirit, and being empty of themselves, they are Spirit-filled. Consider the wind. You do not see the wind, save by way of those things that are blown by the wind. The wind is invisible and you do not see where it comes from or where it is going. It is only made visible to you by the things moved by it, and so you can discern the movement of the wind. So it is with those who are born of the Holy Spirit, the prophets and apostles of God. As the Spirit moves them, you are able to behold the Spirit and so, per chance, yourself be reborn of the Holy Spirit. Is that not why anyone would seek out a holy tzaddik, so that they might also be moved by the Spirit and follow in the Way of the Spirit?

The reed is hollow and therefore an open channel. And so the prophets and apostles of God are empty of themselves before the presence of the Lord and open to the Spirit of the Lord, so that they become as channels or vehicles of the Holy Spirit. Indeed, the Word of the Lord is conveyed through them, just as ink through a pen for the writing of the Word, and so the Word of the Lord is spoken. The Word of the Lord is fulfilled when it is received and imparted. "As it is spoken, so is it done." Vehayah—"And it shall come to pass." Surely, this is the perfection of faith!

Why do you go out into the desert? To participate in a mystery drama, so that, in your own experience, something of the holy mysteries is revealed. Why have you come into the wilderness of the world? So that you might bring about the civilization of Christ upon earth, that is to say, New Jerusalem. This is the point the Master is making, that you seek so that you might find and discern the Truth, and discerning the Truth, you might live according to it. In this way, the same Holy Spirit that speaks in the prophets and apostles of God shall speak in you also, and you shall be counted as a holy one in the presence of the Lord.

Listen and hear, right now the Spirit is speaking in you, there in the depths of your being, as in the one who is your brother and friend writing to you. What you are reading in this very moment is the Spirit speaking, and your own awareness and understanding is the Spirit speaking in you. Every time you listen and hear the Word of the Lord, the Holy Spirit is speaking before you and within you, and the Lord is present with you. Truly, this presence of awareness is the fruit of faith, for it is your intuition that informs you of the Spirit in such a sacred moment, and it is your intuition through which you recognize one in whom the Spirit is speaking. Faith is an intuition of an experience you have not yet had, but which is coming your way. Hence, indeed, faith is a manifestation of the prophetic Spirit. The Spirit of the prophets continues to speak! Praise God!

VERSE 79

*A woman from the crowd said to him, "Blessed are the womb
which bore you and the breast which nourished you."*

*He said to [her], "Blessed are those who have heard the
word of the Father and have truly kept it. For there will be
days when you will say, 'Blessed are the womb which has
not conceived and the breast which have not given milk.'"*

I will share with you a profound secret the Christian initiate
understands within him or herself. Whatever blessing the
Holy Mother has, it is our very own blessing, inasmuch as we
allow the Holy Spirit to enter and to give birth to the Word of
the Lord in us. The birth of the Messiah is not so much an
event of the past as an ever-present reality. Arising beyond
space-time-consciousness and entering into the consciousness
of the infinite and eternal, God's labor of ten thousand years
ago and God's labor of ten thousand years in the future are but
one and the same labor in Spirit. So the labor of the Lord God
here and now is the same labor; there is no difference.

To the degree that we are holy virgins unto the Lord, the
Word is born in us and through us, our body and life becoming the matrix of the Divine presence and power. But what is
this holy state of virginity in which all blessings of Mother
Mary are our own blessings? I tell you, it is the state of emptiness and openness to the Spirit of the Lord, so empty of oneself that there is no other desire than the holy desire of the

Lord, and so open to the Spirit of God that none can enter in but God itself. The holy virgin is one who is pure and pristine, natural and spontaneous in Spirit, as the Lord created her to be, having no desire but the desire of her Beloved, and opening herself to no other but the Beloved. She is completely transparent to her Beloved, therefore, she herself becomes the Beloved and is the Beloved, and there is no difference between herself and the self of the Beloved. When our soul abides in this way in its natural purity, it is the holy womb in which the Christ is born and our body itself is the holy womb that births our soul to eternal life.

So sweet and full of glory and Grace is the Holy Mother that she freely gives to her children everything they ask of her, and, indeed, she has everything to give. For the heavenly Father, who is the hidden cause of Creation, has put the Word in her. Therefore, all is hers to give to those who ask of her. Who is the Holy Mother? She is the personification of the upper Shekinah and primordial Wisdom. She is the speaking silence of the heavenly voice uttering the Word of Life, and so she, herself, is the Life and the Light of the world, inseparable from the Holy One who has come from within herself as the matrix of Creation. Who is the Mother of God but God herself?

Now this woman misses the mark, for in the presence of the Lord, she departs the present and falls into the past and personal history. She is not speaking of the Holy Mother, but of her own name and form, ignorant of the soul as both male and female, yet neither male nor female in its true essence. The holy mysteries are completely lost to her, as the moment of the Light-transmission is in the present always, but she departs the moment entering the dreamlike past. The Master, however, brings balance and speaks of the future, not to take her into fantasies of futures that do not yet exist but to bring her back into the present where the Living Word of God is, so that she might receive the real blessing in store for her. She speaks of a fond dream of the past and the Master speaks of the darkness and horror of the future. She speaks of the pleasure of conception and the Master speaks of the pains of labor in birthing. Until the pains of labor pass and Christ is born in oneself in full, the conception of Christ is as yet incomplete, for it is the birth that is the fruition of conception and surely the greater joy of the Mother.

What does it mean to hear the Word of the Lord and to truly keep it? Once again, the Master is saying that spiritual practice and spiritual living is the enlightenment experience itself. The true Christian will understand this; practicing and living the life of the Anointed One, he or she experiences and knows the Spirit of the Lord inwardly and therefore experiences the enlightenment of the Messiah in daily living. To remember and practice the Light and Truth is, itself, the great blessing the Lord has promised us. Let those who have ears to hear, listen and hear!

VERSE 80

Jesus said, "He who has recognized the world has found the body, but he who has found the body is superior to the world."

At another time, the Master speaks of one understanding the world as one who has discovered a corpse, yet here he says one who recognizes the world as having found the body. Therefore, we understand two distinct realizations indicated: one, an understanding of the profane world as something lifeless or dead, devoid of God's Spirit, and the other, a realization of the natural world as something filled with the Divine presence or as a manifestation of the Divine presence. The former realization precedes the latter, the first leading to the deeper awakening of the second.

Here, the Master is teaching a profound meditation. The truth is that your body and the world are completely interconnected and interdependent. It is an illusion that they are in any way separate from one another. In reality, your body and the world are unique and individual expressions of one underlying unity and are inherently united to one another. The body is a manifestation of the world in which the soul is incarnate. As the body is inseparable from the world, so the world is inseparable from the solar system in which it exists, and, likewise, the solar system is inseparable from the galaxy of which it is a part, and the galaxy is inseparable from the universe. All matter is star dust, and you and the world are stardust—solidified light!

The meditation is simple. One contemplates the Sacred Unity underlying the body and the world and, indeed, the entire universe, until a somewhat higher state of awareness dawns—an awareness of the Sacred Unity that God is. Merely contemplating the unity of the body and world and all that lives can bring about a higher state of consciousness. One who is able to live from this presence of awareness—the awareness of Sacred Unity—is superior to the world, in the sense that they see the whole rather than remaining in a fixation only on the parts.

In Hebrew, the word Achad, meaning "one" or "unity," and the word Ahavah, meaning "love," both equal the number thirteen. This indicates that an awareness of the Sacred Unity naturally leads to a universal and unconditional love, the love of others as oneself. In truth, all that lives is an expression of you and you are an expression of it—all is the expression of God. When this awareness is present, there can be no hatred or ill will, for one then knows that, whatever harm they might do to another, they ultimately have done to themselves. One can no longer consider oneself separate and apart from others and one's environment. One knows oneself completely interdependent and interconnected with the whole of Life and the universe. This, of course, naturally leads to the awareness of one's innate unity with God, the Life-power of which everyone and everything is an expression.

With this realization, the practitioner discovers many things. For example, with this knowledge comes the realization that there is no such thing as personal salvation apart from every other living soul. If we are so intimately interconnected and interdependent, how could you or I be saved without the rest of the world also experiencing salvation? Or, if enlightened, how could our own enlightenment be complete without the enlightenment of all living souls? Along the same lines, the initiate gains insight as to how the Lord took upon himself the sin and karma of the whole world in the crucifixion. For, in truth, the Lord is the world and the world is the Lord, just as you are the world and the world is you. Every individual who is awakened and liberated brings the whole world in ascent with him or herself, and every time another soul awakens, his or her own enlightenment increases.

There is a secret level of teaching here as well, a profound teaching from the holy Kabbalah. When there is an awareness of the Sacred Unity and one joins oneself consciously with the Holy One, then one discovers the world and universe as the body of Adam Kadmon in Asiah, that is to say, the body of the primordial human being in the world of making. On account of this realization, the Way of ascent toward the world of Adam Kadmon is open to the soul, and that soul is truly superior to the world in every respect.

If our body and the natural world can serve as an object of meditation, then so can anything in the natural world. A flame, wind, the ocean, a mountain, a flower, sunrise or sunset, the starry night sky, a living being—anything may be a focus of meditation and inspire conversation with God. The Master is suggesting this also. He himself was known to be inclined to meditations in Nature and upon Nature as the manifestation of God's glory, as were all of the prophets of God before him. Where did John the Baptist live, in a city born of human society or out in nature born of God?

You will understand from the above that Yeshua is actually speaking of many different forms of meditation in this one saying, all of which have the common ground of one's very own body and the natural world as the focus. Look and see the underlying unity within and behind all life and you will experience something of God's Spirit today! Lord give us sight! Amen.

VERSE 81

Jesus said, "Let him who has grown rich be king, and let him who possesses power renounce it."

There is a crown on the heads of the holy ones. It is a jeweled crown of Supernal Light, Truth-consciousness. They are wealthy ones, having knowledge, understanding and wisdom, compassion and right judgment, the beauty of their undying soul and body of light, dominion over all spiritual forces and the glory of the presence. Righteousness is theirs and, with it, the kingdom of heaven. The whole treasury of heaven and the esoteric wisdom is theirs, given to them by the Lord our God, through the agency of Divine Grace, and so they are ordained and established as holy priest-kings or priestess-queens of God most High, conscious agents of God's plan on earth. One who is wealthy in this way should serve the faithful and the Lord as a holy tzaddik, a king of righteousness and peace!

The enlightenment of which the Lord is speaking has many levels or degrees. Anyone who draws near and cleaves unto the Lord will experience one degree or another of enlightenment, though oftentimes the experience is a passing thing and one returns to ordinary consciousness following the experience. Yet, to whatever degree one is open and sensitive and surrenders oneself to one's experience of enlightenment, one is changed, and something of a gift is left from the treasury of secret wisdom. As a matter of fact, in the path of the holy Kabbalah, the initiate enters in and departs from enlightenment again and again, running and returning, as it were, ascending upward and bringing down something each time from above. The enlightenment of which the Master is speaking is not a fixed state, but a fluid and flowing spiritual life that moves as the Holy Spirit moves. In the journey, there are natural flows and ebbs. Having entered into one or another degree of the enlightenment experience, very frequently the initiate experiences a fall from grace, that is to say, a seeming loss of the enlightenment attained. This is often true, even of the adepts and masters who enter into higher degrees of enlightenment, although every falling out of grace proves the preparation for an ascent into an even higher level of the enlightenment experience. Ascent and descent, flows and ebbs, are all part of the process of awakening and liberation. There is no fixed state of enlightenment, but rather a constant flickering of the holy flame of consciousness between enlightenment and unenlightenment. With the masters, it is just that, the flickering occurs so rapidly, it appears as a constant Divine illumination.

Understanding this process of running and returning, ascending and descending, coming in and going out, you will realize why it is so very important that you do not grasp at any attainment or spiritual gift whatsoever, for just as swiftly as an attainment or gift comes, so also it can go, and it usually does. If you are grasping or thinking of it as a possession, then, in the midst of a natural ebb, you will surely suffer greatly and perhaps lose your way altogether. But if every experience is known to be given by Divine Grace and all spiritual gifts and experiences belong to the Holy Spirit of the Lord, then this ebb and flow will be known for what it is and your path will be all joy. The masters understand this and so always wait upon the Lord, seeking to move with the Spirit and abide with the Spirit in all things. This is exactly what spiritual mastery means.

Who has ever made themselves wealthy in the way the Lord is talking about? Indeed, no one has ever made themselves so wealthy, but rather the Grace of God, Divine providence, gives such wealth. It is a gift of the Lord, in the same way as the anointed kings of Israel were given the gift of royalty and rule over Israel from the blessing of

God. Whether a king in the material world or a holy priest-king, no one becomes a king save through the Will of God, hence, by way of Divine authority. All talents and gifts that make one a king, and the anointing itself, are all given by God. So it is with the faithful and elect; God has chosen them and made them members of the mystical body of Christ. It is the Divine presence and power that ordains them and bears witness of them, and it is by way of Divine authority that they impart the teachings and initiations, acting as a holy tzaddik. It is this way with all God's children.

While the Master is speaking here of everyone among the faithful and elect, calling them to act according to their individual capacity as a holy priest or priestess, he is also speaking specifically of those called to act as apostles of God or who will take up the service of the holy tzaddik among the elect. They must possess the talents and gifts needed and proceed only by Divine permission, receiving their instructions and guidance from the Holy Spirit. Hence, they must know clearly that the Divine power is not their own, but belongs solely to God. Every tzaddik is on a mission, and it is that sacred task they must accomplish in this life.

So it is with every soul. God sends the soul into the world for a purpose, and it is that purpose the soul must serve. Everything we might say of the perfect Master is a truth of ourselves, although perhaps the truth of a future self. That future self is our present self in Christ any time we are open to the Christ-Spirit that indwells us and surrender ourself and our life to the Spirit of the Lord. How wonderful! The Lord calls each and every one of us as his own, and ordains us as holy priests or priestesses of his kingdom. Our Holy Mother rebirths us as royal heirs to the throne on high. Hallelujah! Praise the Lord! Amen.

VERSE 82

Jesus said, "He who is near me is near the fire, and he who is far from me is far from the kingdom."

In the Holy Scriptures, we read that "the Lord is a consuming fire," fire consuming fire making all like unto itself. The burning bush that the prophet beholds is on fire with the presence of the Lord and is not consumed. Likewise, in another place it is written, "You who cleave unto the Lord are alive this day." In the secret books of wisdom, the Lord is called "the Radiant One," "Ain Sof Aur," "the Endless Light." Outwardly, it would seem there is a contradiction here, or else that there are three fires of the Lord, but the masters teach that there is one holy fire of the Lord, a threefold fire of the Divine presence. Hence, there is one holy fire (Divine power) that manifests in three distinct modes or at three different levels.

Now, rightly it can be said that fire is fire. It both burns and illuminates and, in every case, transforms. Although we would speak of one holy fire, we can also see that there are different forms of fire. For example, in nature, we find the typical fire we call "fire" or "flame," but we also find chemical fire, electrical fire, and nuclear fire. Each form of fire is a moment of transformation from one state to another, a change in the form of energy by way of a release of energy from its former state into another. Here, we have the secret of fire and the Master speaking of himself as the holy fire. Lord Yeshua is a transforming and liberating agent and, by nature, illuminating. That is to say, this is the very nature of Logos, a transforming and illuminating Divine power.

Yet consider the nature of fire. Can anyone draw near unto fire who is not like unto the fire? If any form of fire comes too close to anything that is not like unto itself, the fire burns and consumes it. Indeed, the Lord teaches of a baptism by fire, the holy fire of the Spirit, saying of this baptism that it is Life and Light to all who receive it. The masters also teach us that the fire of hell is the fire of the same Holy Spirit purifying the souls of the wicked and unclean spirits. What this holy fire is depends upon the present condition of the one to whom it draws near or who would seek to draw near it. To one who is like unto this holy fire, it is a great blessing of Light and Life and Divine fulfillment. To one who is not like unto this holy fire, it burns utterly and consumes, appearing as a curse and wrath. It is the same fire, yet to one it is life and to the other it is death. This is one way in which the different manifestations of the holy fire are understood. Thus we know, to draw near unto the Lord, we must fashion ourselves in the image of the Lord, becoming like the Anointed One of God.

We understand in the Lord a threefold baptism—of water, of fire, and of the Holy Spirit—that is to say, of the life, death, and resurrection of the Lord. Before the initiation of fire, we must receive the initiation of water, for first we must be purified and receive our life in the Christ-Spirit, becoming like unto the Holy One, before drawing near unto the Holy One. Being purified by water, we must then be consecrated by fire, transformed into the likeness of the One Anointed in the Supernal Light. Only then can we receive in full the baptism of the Holy Spirit and the Divine resurrection that she brings.

I will tell you plainly, to pass through the holy gate of the kingdom of heaven, you cannot be lukewarm, but must be hot, on fire with the Lord, filled with divine passion. No one knows the presence of the Lord and the Lord himself who is not passionate for the holy Shekinah as he himself was passionate. Such holy passion burns oneself utterly away and there is only the Beloved. At the same time, holy passion itself is transforming and illuminating and is, itself, the Divine Life, for what passion comes is the passion of the inner self or Christ-self, a new and Divine consciousness and being filled with Light and Life. Once again, you must understand that to live in the Way, Truth, and Light is, itself, the enlightenment experience, the reward promised to us in Yeshua Messiah. He lived according to the righteousness of Logos in him and so was called the Way, the Truth, and the Light, and so also are we the Light when we take up our cross daily and follow him, living the Divine Life.

There is a deeper mystery in this saying, for, in truth, there are different forms of the holy fire or Divine power to be awakened in us. First, there is a digestive fire that must be kindled that allows us to take in and integrate the energy-intelligence of teachings and initiations we receive. It appears as a passionate desire to receive for the sake of heaven, although there is a fiery energy inwardly that produces this radiant and holy passion. This fire becomes the passionate desire for mystical union with the presence of the Lord, and so transforms from a digestive and consuming fire to an illuminating and spiritual fire. On fire with the Lord, one not only receives and digests the secret Wisdom, but one gives of oneself to others and shares what one receives. On account of this divine passion, the Holy Spirit can enter and awaken her holy fire in us and bring down the most secret holy fire, the spiritual nuclear fire of the supernal consciousness.

I will tell you a secret, a holy mystery. This holy fire is the same fire transforming into one form of fire, then another, and yet again another. The spiritual nuclear fire is the secret source of every other form of fire, each form of the Divine power being a mode of operation of this one holy fire on different levels. This is reflected in the Tetragrammaton (YHVH), which is the same Divine presence and power manifesting through the four universes. The threefold fire is reflected in the three holy letters composing this four-lettered name of God.

Perhaps this experience seems far away from you; yet, in truth, it is very near to you. The Light-force of the soul of the Messiah is within you and all around you this day. If it seems distant, it is only because, as yet, you live on the surface of yourself and have not gone within to live within to bring forth the Light that is within you. Nevertheless, in potential, this holy fire is within you, ever near and awaiting ignition, hence initiation.

There is a meditation in the tradition through which initiates gain knowledge and understanding of this holy threefold fire of Melchizedek. It is a holy meditation upon a lamp or candle flame. With proper blessings, the practitioner kindles the flame and, praying to the Lord, then meditates upon the body of the flame, looking to see the threefold fire in the single flame. Near the wick, there is a black fire, the consuming fire, that at times changes color, becoming red or blue, each state of this lower fire having a certain meaning in contemplation. Then above this lower fire, and resting upon it, is the white fire. At first, this upper fire appears as a golden flame, but looking and seeing this upper fire, the practitioner sees that it is, in fact, white fire that never changes. The fire below changes, but the upper fire never changes. The lower fire corresponds to the Lord as a consuming fire and the upper fire corresponds to the Light of Life that never changes and gives life to all who cleave unto the Lord. Having looked to see the lower and upper fire, the practitioner looks to see another secret fire, represented as the radiance around the flame, within, all around, and yet beyond it. This is the representation of the transparent Light of Supernal Holiness. Receiving instruction on this holy meditation, initiates then have a method of gaining insight into the holy fire of the presence of the Lord. Here, in this saying, the Master is alluding to this secret practice and several others that use fire as a focus.

VERSE 83

Jesus said, "The images are manifest to man, but the light in them remains concealed in the image of the light of the father. He will become manifest, but his image will remain concealed by his light."

You have looked upon the sun and seen the light of the sun. Yet never have you seen the sun itself, only the glory or light of the sun. You have seen the river of light flowing from the sun, but never have you actually seen the sun. The sun is hidden by the glory and light that streams forth from it. In the same way, no one has ever seen the heavenly Father. The glory or Light of the image of the Lord conceals the holy image. How much more the very essence of God itself? Beholding the presence of the Lord and gazing upon the image of Light, no one has ever seen the Living God, only the glory of God, the Light and Life that pours forth from the image of the holy Father-Mother.

Ain Sof, the One-Without-End, is the concealed of the concealed, the nameless and unknowable, ever hidden within and beyond the streams of Light and glory that continually pour forth from it. Indeed, it is this aspect of the Lord our God that we call the hidden God, while the holy Sefirot that span the four universes are the manifestation of the attributes or images through which God reveals something of itself. Yet the holy images or attributes that are manifest cannot be confused with Ain Sof, the One-Without-End, for although Ain

Sof is within them and they emerge from and exist within Ain Sof, they do not define or limit Ain Sof in any way. Ain Sof remains totally transcendent of all images or attributes through which it is revealed.

For the elect who would receive the teachings and initiations of the secret wisdom and embark upon the mystical journey of Ma'aseh Merkavah, understanding this becomes very important so that, when entering into the Palace of Lights and the prophetic states of consciousness, the initiate should not be confused by the nature of their experience but rather gain true knowledge, understanding, and wisdom. The images beheld are not God itself. They are the Light and glory of the Lord God in the process of self-revelation. While the holy Sefirot or spiritual flows of the Divine powers reveal God, at the same time they completely veil or conceal the Lord. Just as we can use the analogy of the sun, so we can use the analogy of garments a person might wear. The garments reveal something of the person wearing them; yet they are not the person, let alone the soul and inner self of the person. It is the same with the holy Sefirot and image of the Lord. They are like garments of Ain Sof, which reveal something of Ain Sof, although Ain Sof is completely beyond.

The very term, the "Lord our God," reflects the holy mystery of which the Master is speaking. For the "Lord" is the impersonal and hidden aspect of the Divine, and "our God" is the revealed and personal aspect; the Lord the transcendental aspect, and our God the immanent aspect. In the singing of the Shema, we affirm the truth of these two aspects of the Lord God, the transcendental and immanent as one and the same in nature and essence—hence, an essential and mysterious unity. Save through the production of images or forms of self-revelation, God could not make itself known to the human being and likewise the human being would have no way to link him or herself consciously with God. Such forms or images represent a self-limitation upon God, thereby concealing more than they reveal.

As this is true of the holy Sefirot and images beheld in prophetic states of consciousness, it is also true of the personalities of Divine incarnation. It is a confusion regarding this very mystery that lies at the core of orthodox Christianity and its grave misunderstanding of the nature of the Messiah, a confusion of the image or person (*partzuf*) that acts as the vehicle of revelation and transmission and that which is revealed and transmitted. Here the Lord Yeshua is warning against this mistake. Just as we can say God is love, but love is not God, so we can say the Messiah is Lord Yeshua, but Yeshua is not the soul of Messiah. It is a subtle and sublime distinction, yet necessary for a greater understanding of the holy mystery of the Messiah. Lord Yeshua and the Spirit of the Messiah are one, yet the fullness of the soul of the Messiah is beyond the person of the perfect Master.

Now, having said this, we may also speak of an inner level of this saying, for the Master is giving instruction to his disciples concerning an ascent of Merkavah through the holy Sefirot of Asiyah, Yetzirah and Beriyah into Atzilut. The images manifest to the human being are the holy Sefirot of the three lower universes, while the Light of the image of the Father is the upper universe of Atzilut, and the image of the Father is the universe of Adam Kadmon or the Human One. The Light and Life-power of the holy Sefirot of the lower universes is contained in the universe of Atzilut (the world of emanation or nearness). When the initiate enters into Atzilut, the Lord will reveal himself directly, yet the image of the Lord, the universe of the primordial human being, will be concealed.

In the preceding saying, when Yeshua speaks of one being near to him as being near to the fire, he plays upon the meaning of the word Atzilut, "nearness." Atzilut is the universe of holy fire or Light. Thus the Master alludes to the soul of the Messiah embodied in himself as something of the Light of Adam Kadmon brought down through these various levels or dimensions into the physical or material dimension. With the statement that one who is far from him is far from Malkut (the Kingdom), he alludes to both the perfection and fulfillment of Malkut in the universe of Adam Kadmon, as well as an understanding of the physical universe and all creatures as the body of Adam Kadmon or the mystical body of the Messiah.

Here, I cannot go any further into these holy mysteries but can only give some gates through which one might pass into a deeper insight and understanding in their own sacred quest of contemplation and meditation. In fact, what the Master teaches in this one saying could easily fill volumes, and, indeed, already has. Verses 82 to 88 are among the most esoteric sayings in the Gospel of St. Thomas, containing the inmost secret teachings of the Master. They are intended to be contemplated independently and collectively according to the masters of the tradition.

VERSE 84

Jesus said, "When you see your likeness, you rejoice. But when you see your images which came into being before you, and which neither die nor become manifest, how much will you have to bear!"

When you have experienced your subtle body or astral body, you truly have a cause to rejoice, for in that very experience of consciousness beyond the physical form, you know that death is not the end, but only the transition of your soul into another state of existence. You know your soul is not dependent upon the body and you know the purpose and meaning of this life is different than you previously might have imagined. Not only do you know that you do not cease to exist after death, but the inner dimensions of the reality-truth-continuum open to you, and you know that there are invisible realms and worlds within worlds. Yet the experience of the astral body is only a beginning to the development of the consciousness beyond the body, which is the practical realization of the resurrection and eternal life. Having experienced it to some degree, the initiate must then develop the ability to transfer his or her consciousness at will into the subtle body and awaken the faculties of the subtle body and soul. Through the Christ-Spirit, the Supernal Light must be brought down into this body, transforming the subtle body into the Body of Light.

This development is an appearance from within the space-time-consciousness continuum, that is to say, a perception of time-eternity. From the perception of timeless-eternity, this solar body of supernal consciousness-force already exists. It is the real idea of your true self, the Christ-self, which has no beginning or end, is never born and therefore never dies, but abides ever in perfect unity with the Lord God above. To see this supernal and Divine image of yourself is a greater attainment than the experience of the astral body, and the bliss is far more intense. Not only do you know you will never die, but you know the Divine fullness God intends for you. Yet the attainment of that Divine fullness is dependent upon your own labor in the great work, your own struggle to consciously evolve into that holy image of the Lord and to embody that Truth and Light. When the Master says, "How much you will have to bear," on the one hand, he is speaking of the intense bliss of this self-realization, and on the other hand, he is speaking of the personal responsibility for the great work that such knowledge brings. Once we behold this Divine ideal in Messianic consciousness, we become partners with the Lord, sharing the responsibility of bringing about the fulfillment of the Divine vision.

This solar body is the holy threefold body of Melchizedek—the body of Truth, the nature of which is Ain; the body of delight, the nature of which is Ain Sof; and the body of emanation, the nature of which is Ain Sof Aur. The totality of this holy threefold body of Melchizedek is what is known as the solar body or Body of Light in our tradition, the mystical or spiritual body of enlightenment and liberation.

How can you come to understand this Body of Light? You may begin your contemplation in this way: The emanation body is a material or physical manifestation that can be seen, touched, and felt, experienced by physical senses. A tzaddik who has entered into Messianic consciousness or a high degree of the enlightenment experience can manifest such a body or dissolve such a body at will, magically appearing and disappearing. This body can be experienced by anyone in the environment, although most who encounter a master in this form would not know the nature of this emanation body.

The physical body of an incarnation may be considered an emanation body, but perfect Masters are capable of manifesting and dissolving the emanation body at will, in which case it is understood as a magical body somewhat different from a typical physical body of incarnation. The maggidim and tzaddikim appear in the material dimension in order to reach out and contact those who otherwise would not be able to encounter or perceive them in the subtle dimensions.

Those who can perceive the presence of the tzaddikim and maggidim in the subtle dimensions do not need to assume an appearance in the emanation body, but can manifest to the faithful and elect in the subtle dimension through the body of delight or glorified body. Most ordinary individuals cannot perceive the appearance of a tzaddik or maggid in the glorified body; only those who have the gift of more subtle perception can see them.

You might contemplate the emanation body and the body of glory in this way: Imagine you are present with Yeshua when he takes a few of his inmost disciples up the mountain to let them experience the Transfiguration. Before he is transfigured, you see a human being like yourself with a physical and material body, appearing as anyone else. You are experiencing the emanation or manifestation body of the Master. However, in the Transfiguration, when the body of the Master shines with light, as though made of sunlight, yet becomes translucent like a rainbow, then you are experiencing the glorified body or body of delight. The body of Truth is the enlightenment experience, Messianic consciousness. Only the holy ones experience this mystical body.

How do we know that the Master is speaking of the holy threefold body of Melchizedek? When the apostle writing the Letter to the Hebrews spoke of Yeshua Messiah having come from the order of Melchizedek, he says of the holy priest-king that one who is of that holy order is "(w)ithout father, without mother, without genealogy, having neither beginning of days nor end of life, but resembling the Son of God, remains a priest forever" (Hebrews 7:3).

Just as the holy ones presently labor in the great work, both within the world through emanation bodies and from within the inner planes through glorified bodies, so also are we to become conscious agents of God's will, destined to attain this body of the resurrection and ascension. In Christ, this is the truth of ourselves—a Divine potential we are to actualize. What wonderful news! Praise the Lord!

VERSE 85

Jesus said, "Adam came into being from a great power and a great wealth, but he did not become worthy of you. For had he been worthy, [he would] not [have experienced] death."

The body has evolved through the agency of a great power and great wealth, Mother Nature. She has labored long and hard, slowly savoring the progress of evolution toward the development of these bodies capable of serving as vehicles of a higher intelligence—life-forms that have the self-awareness through which she might become conscious of herself and enact a conscious evolution. Nature is in no way separate from God, but in fact, she is the operation of God's Spirit here below, within and all around us. As one righteous person wrote, "The earth is filled with the glory of God." We would go so far as to say that the whole world and physical universe is the material glory of God and that matter itself is a most dense manifestation of God's Spirit.

As yet, however, Nature remains for the most part unregenerated and unredeemed on account of the cosmic forces of ignorance that still dominate her. Although Nature is becoming conscious of herself through the agency of the human being, as humanity itself, as yet, she is not fully awake and aware of herself, and the fullness of the Divine power in her has not been actualized. Much still remains in potential, and Nature remains for the most part asleep and dreaming, enacting evolution through the deep unconscious rather than the conscious intelligence.

When we ask exactly what the ongoing divine revelation through the prophets and apostles of God is all about, the answer is an awakening and call for humanity to exercise its God-given power to consciously evolve, to unite heaven and earth, and to act, with the Lord, as conscious co-creators of a new heaven and new earth. Indeed, we are being called to bring forth a new and Divine humanity and an enlightened society upon the earth, and to bring down that Divine presence and power from above that will transform our consciousness and the world. If you examine the Holy Scriptures, you will see a steady progress in the divine revelation toward an enlightened and liberated humanity that exists in a conscious unity with the Lord God and acts to fulfill God's plan on earth. The old and new covenants represent an ascending level of spiritual teachings and initiation, from outward signs and obligations to a completely inward spiritual life no longer dependent upon outward things.

Now in this process, as we have said previously, something from deep within and above is necessary for a progress to a more advanced state of consciousness and being—our Neshamah and the Christ-Spirit that brings with itself the supernal consciousness-force. This Light-force has the power to radically accelerate the progress of evolution of life on earth, and even the development and evolution of the physical body. When, in any world, Nature develops from within herself self-aware and intelligent lifeforms, those lifeforms must then make a choice for conscious evolution and bring down the Divine presence and power that takes up and completes her labor. It is this that is the regeneration and redemption of Nature of which the masters of our tradition speak.

There is within us this Divine power from above. Nature has fashioned bodies that can receive the fullness of our Divine soul, but she does not generate our soul and self. Rather, our soul and Divine self come from above, from the Lord our God, and this holy living soul is far more noble and precious than the mortal body. In fact, it is this Divine soul and self that potentially can give the material form immortality. In this sense, the true and faithful disciple who brings his or her Divine soul into incarnation is more worthy than the animal human being. The soul is more worthy than the body and bestial nature, for it is the Divine soul that redeems both the human personality and the body with eternal life. The one who is more worthy is your secret and undying soul and the Christ-self that indwells it. In the prehistoric past, the early human beings, more animal-like than God-like, did not attain this, but in the progress of human history, we see more and more individuals attaining something of this enlightenment and liberation. They are worthy of praise, as is the Lord whose Holy Spirit brings them to perfection in Christ.

VERSE 86

Jesus said, "[The foxes have their holes] and the birds have their nests, but the son of man has no place to lay his head and rest."

If the foxes are foxes and the birds are birds in this saying of the Master, then he is speaking of the difference between the animal kingdom and human kingdom. God's creatures of the animal kingdom are content in their station and have no impulse to conscious evolution and self-perfection. They are satisfied and know no other existence beyond their own, and therefore are happy and at home exactly where they are, just as they are. This is not so for the human being. Within us is an impulse to growth, development, and evolution, a deep need toward mastery of ourselves and Nature, and thus toward self-perfection. Our soul-being is not inclined to rest and be satisfied until self-realization and self-perfection is manifest.

Just as we might speak of this distinction between the animal and human kingdoms, this difference exists within the human kingdom, between the animal human being and the Divine human being. In humanity, there are many levels of evolution, as we have previously said, and not everyone possessing a human form has yet cultivated their humanity and become fully human. The distinguishing factor between animal humanity and divine humanity is the impulse to conscious evolution and seeking a conscious unity with God—

hence, the higher purpose for which humanity has been created. In the masses, there is little difference between the animal and human existence. Although the human life is naturally more complex and sophisticated, nevertheless, the fundamental drives, intentions, and desires are all the same, the rituals of life are the same: finding a mate, breeding, making a den, establishing a station in the pack or herd, gathering food, and so forth. For much of humanity, this is the whole of life and there is little or nothing more, yet as the soul-being evolves, the human being begins to reach beyond the animal level of existence, seeking to cultivate its humanity and, yet more, the Divine potential within its humanity. In so doing, one becomes a son or daughter of the human spirit, Adam, seeking conscious evolution and self-perfection. The awakening soul is no longer satisfied with living only in surface consciousness and a purely mundane or worldly existence, but seeks the development of a greater intelligence and a spiritual life. Here, the Master clearly speaks of the difference between two realms of humanity.

But there is another level in what the Master is saying, which points to the same truth of the human being as a transitional being evolving toward a higher state of consciousness. The foxes represent the demonic forces or forces of cosmic ignorance and the birds represent the angelic forces of the Divine power. According to teachings of the holy Kabbalah, neither angels nor demons evolve during a cosmic cycle, but remain what they are for the duration of the life of the universe. These forces-beings do not evolve, but remain what they are, as they are. This points to a central difference between the human soul and the soul of an angel or demon: the human soul-being is destined to grow, develop, and evolve beyond even the level of the archangels— hence to evolve to the likeness of the soul of Messiah.

Let it be said that our dissatisfaction, our hunger and thirst for a higher, more noble existence, is a blessing of the Holy Spirit. There is within us a consciousness-force that impels and compels us to evolve—the Logos and Sophia of God in our soul. It is present at every level of consciousness, including in our physical bodies. It is the Holy Spirit seeking our redemption and perfection in God. It is this consciousness-force awakening in us that makes us truly human—one who is created in the image of God.

VERSE 87

Jesus said, "Wretched is the body that is dependent upon a body, and wretched is the soul that is dependent upon these two."

You are more than the physical body and the name and form of this present life. Your personality and life-display, your Nefesh, is but the surface of your being. Deeper within you, and higher than the Nefesh, there is your Ruach (human spirit), and yet deeper and higher than your Ruach is your holy Neshamah, your supernal and heavenly soul. It is through your higher intelligence (Ruach) and within your heavenly soul that you will discover your true self and find fulfillment. Although this body and world may be a vehicle of expression and experience of that Divine fullness, neither the physical body nor material world, in and of themselves, have in them the perfect joy you seek. Rather, the peace, joy, and fulfillment you seek comes from deep within yourself—from the Christ-self that is the secret and Divine center of your consciousness and being.

It is not a question of whether or not there is the potential of the holy Neshamah and Christ-self in you, or whether or not your holy Neshamah exists in the world of Supernal Light. It is the Truth of every living soul that this Divine potential exists within it, just as the potential of a whole life exists within the fertilized embryo. It is a question of drawing out what is within you, giving expression to your true and inner self, so that you actualize and experience the enlightenment and liberation of that Christ-self. Until there is the activity of growth, development, and evolution, a life come into being and lived, the fullness of the Life-power in the embryo remains unmanifest and unknown. What is inherently within it must be drawn out and come into substantial being, must transpire, in order to be. Only having transpired and passed by is the Life-power actualized and realized and fulfillment attained. It is the same with regard to your higher intelligence and heavenly soul. You must draw out what is within you. In this way, you will find your fulfillment.

The right order of our consciousness is manifest when the Nefesh is dependent upon Ruach, Ruach upon Neshamah, and the holy Neshamah is dependent upon the Lord, the lower is linked to the higher, forming the Sacred Unity of an authentic individual. Your fulfillment lies within your individuality, individuality being the gate to universal and transcendental consciousness. In order to be an authentic individual, you must go within yourself and live within, from the Divine center of your being. Here, the Master is indicating this attainment of Divine fullness through a contemplation of how such fulfillment is hindered or obstructed.

Let me share a basic truth with you. If I live dependent upon my present name and form and the world for my fulfillment, living only on the surface and shaping myself by images of an unenlightened society, then I do not live as myself and am not myself, but live as the idea or image of someone or something other than who and what I most truly am. Surely, there is great pain and suffering in such falsehood and any true fulfillment or satisfaction becomes impossible for me. Not only is my life unfulfilling to me, it is identified with an existence that is by nature transitional and temporary; the end can only be sorrow and suffering. I can only attain a true state of health and happiness being the individual I am in Spirit and Truth. I must depend upon that which is within me if I am to experience a lasting peace and joy—real satisfaction.

If you look and see and understand this, you will realize why the Master would speak of the lost soul, dependent upon name and form and the material world for satisfaction, as "wretched," that is to say, in bondage to great pain and suffering. Such a soul, lost to its true self, and therefore lost to God, can only invoke compassion in one who knows and lives according to the Spirit and Truth.

While the Master is giving a teaching regarding living from within and the necessity of it for our fulfillment, he is also giving a teaching on the birth of love and compassion in ourselves, which is the sacred heart of enlightenment. Basically, he is saying, having awakened to something of the mystery within you, let compassion for those as yet unawakened dawn in you and live in such a way as to manifest a Spirit-connectedness for yourself and others, and so be satisfied in the Spirit.

VERSE 88

Jesus said, "The angels and the prophets will come to you
and give you those things you (already) have. And you too,
give them those things which you have, and say to yourselves, 'When will they come and take what is theirs?'"

The very nature of the holy Kabbalah and Gnostic spiritual practice is the direct contact and experience of the Divine powers and God itself. The methods of mystical prayer
and prophetic meditation taught and practiced tend to invoke a luminous assembly of the Divine powers into the environment of the initiate—angels of the Lord that minister to
the initiate and assist in the divine labor of the great work;
spirits of saints, sages, and prophets who bring the Word of
the Lord to the initiate and instruction in the Way of the
Holy Spirit; and along with the holy ones, spiritual flows of
the Divine power, the holy Sefirot.

Now the angels and spirits of the prophets do not come to
give you something outside or foreign to yourself, but rather
to educate you in the esoteric wisdom and the path of righteousness. That is to say, the holy ones come and minister to
you in order to draw out that Truth and Light from within
you. In your holy Neshamah, you have all knowledge, understanding and wisdom, all attributes of the image of Messiah
and the fullness of the Divine presence and power. In Christ,
you are lacking nothing whatsoever, but that Divine potential

must progressively become realized and actualized. Therefore, the holy ones come to help you in this education of self-realization.

Here, the Master makes it clear that this reception is not a one-way street. Just as the ministering angels and saints come to share and give to you, so also do they come to receive from you. Hence, the luminous assembly manifests as an exchange of holy sparks. In life, various individuals carry holy sparks of your soul, and likewise, you carry the holy sparks of others' souls. When you encounter one another in this world, you exchange the holy sparks you have carried for one another. Just as this is true with visible and incarnate beings or souls, so also is it true with invisible and disincarnate beings or souls. In essence, we are giving to one another what is already our own, giving of ourselves to each other in an infinite matrix of complete interdependence and interconnectedness.

The Master is not only speaking of an awareness of giving and receiving and the combination of spiritual humility and divine pride with which we should enter into the Holy Communion of the Saints. He is also indicating that, while the experience of salvation, on the one hand, is a personal and individual experience, on the other hand, there ultimately is no such thing as personal salvation of oneself apart from every other soul and the whole of Creation. We are intimately bound together with every other living soul and all that God has created, and our salvation is completely interwoven with the redemption of others and the resurrection of the world.

Perhaps most important is the element of faith that the Master alludes to in this saying, for only through faith will the sacred awareness emerge that makes us open and sensitive to higher mystical experiences of this kind. One must cultivate faith in the Divine possibility of contact and communion with the Divine presence and power in all forms. This faith must then become the activity of spiritual practice and spiritual living that creates the conditions necessary for mystical and magical experiences to occur—hence, for a manifestation of Divine Grace. One must know that, with God, nothing is impossible and act according to that knowledge. The nature of this Gnostic Christian faith is active, bold, and confident in the Spirit, a dynamic aspiration with complete trust of the Christ-self within oneself.

VERSE 89

Jesus said, "Why do you wash the outside of the cup? Do you not realize that he who made the inside is the same one who made the outside?"

God brings forth Creation from within him-herself, and we bring forth our lives from within ourselves. In so doing, the inside and the outside must match. It is not enough to sound spiritual or to appear spiritual on the outside. Rather one needs to be genuinely spiritual inwardly, so that the outward appearance is authentic or real. In essence, the Master is asking us to be real in our spirituality.

One can convert to this or that religion, but an outward conversion will not bring about any real change within oneself or benefit the soul if there is not a corresponding inward spiritual conversion. Likewise, one can enter into an esoteric order and receive the teachings and ceremonial initiations of the various grades, but unless there is an actual change in one's consciousness and one embodies something of a higher consciousness, it is really meaningless. Whether exoteric religion or an esoteric spirituality, it is only through an inner spiritual conversion or change in consciousness that we progress toward enlightenment.

A radical change in consciousness is necessary to enter into Christ-consciousness. In truth, Christ-consciousness is something more than a change of mental concepts and emotions and the like. It is a transcendence of the mental and vital being altogether; the transformation of the mental, vital, and even physical consciousness through the Divine power that comes with self-realization in Christ. One must actually be reborn and transfigured by the supernal force that comes from above.

The truth is that it is not enough to have spiritual or mystical experiences. One does not acquire gnosis merely by having an experience. Like any other form of experience in life, one must learn and grow from one's spiritual experiences. The experience must be integrated and bring about a change in oneself—a change in one's consciousness that leads to corresponding changes in one's personality and life-display. Otherwise, a spiritual or psychic experience has no more or less value than watching a movie on television or reading a fantasy-fiction book. Authentic mystical experiences change those who have them. Where there is no change, the experience remains, at best, a glimpse of a possible future and nothing more.

We see this in the process of initiation as we pass from one grade to another. Although ceremonies of various grades may be performed and may even facilitate something of the spiritual experience corresponding to that grade, we have not attained that initiatory grade until we can embody and live according to the higher state of consciousness that corresponds to it. The real grades of initiation are degrees of enlightenment and liberation. Unless the corresponding degree of self-realization transpires inwardly, we are not, as yet, a true initiate of that grade.

Initiation means "a beginning." It is the recognition of something that one must then labor to realize. It is an experience that reveals a new level of the Spirit and Light that one must then seek to embody. Recognition is one thing; realization is another. The initial experience of a new state of consciousness is one thing; embodying the higher state of consciousness is another. The experience of recognition must not be confused with the experience of realization, just as information must not be confused with knowledge, understanding, and wisdom.

We have said that faith is an intuition of an experience not yet had. However, there is another definition of faith that is equally true. Faith is also living according to the Truth and Light revealed in our experience. In this sense, we can say that one must have faith in one's experience and faith in one's ability to evolve toward the new level of enlightenment and liberation revealed in one's experience. When there is an appearance on the outside that is different from the appearance on the inside, then there is typically an imperfection in one's faith, and certainly an impurity in one's gnosis.

To speak of washing or cleaning something is to speak of the process of self-purification. My teacher was fond of saying, "The path to Christ-consciousness is self-purification and self-consecration. It is nothing more or less than this!" To say that the path is primarily one of self-purification at first sounds rather negative. However, the truth is that it is an affirmation of the goodness that is in us—the indwelling Christ, for to say that the path is primarily a work of self-purification means that the attainment is already present in us; we only have to remove whatever may be obstructing our recognition and realization of that Holy Being.

We might liken our unenlightened condition to that of a window that has not been cleaned for so many years that it has become totally opaque. Whether dirty or clean, the window is still a window, though while dirty, one cannot see through it. When it is cleaned, it is suddenly transparent and one can see through it. The same is fundamentally true of our consciousness. Any time our consciousness is allowed to abide in its innate purity—whenever we are clear—the Light of Christ shines through us, for Christ is the Truth of our soul of Light and our Divine self. We need only make ourselves transparent to the Lord!

I pray the Holy Spirit empowers you to a true spiritual conversion and that you receive your initiation from the Holy Spirit and, through her grace, bring it to fruition! Amen.

VERSE 90

Jesus said, "Come unto me, for my yoke is easy and my lord-
ship is mild, and you will find repose for yourselves."

Not I, but Christ in me, accomplishes everything. Of myself, I can do nothing, but the Holy Spirit fulfills and perfects my soul and liberates my spirit. Even the emergence of faith in me and my yearning for the Truth, for union with God, is the operation of Divine Grace. Grace sets me on the path, leads me in the Way, and labors for the advancement of my soul from one holy rung of the Ladder of Lights to the next. On my part, I must only surrender myself in faith, becoming open and sensitive to the Spirit of the Lord, and actively aspire with the power of free will God has given me. Making myself the channel or vehicle of the Christ-Spirit in this way, it is the power of the Holy Spirit that accomplishes the great work within and through me. This is the yoga of Christ, the yoga of Divine Grace.

How could I not give thanks and praise the Lord for his grace and mercy? The holy spark having been ignited, and faith and righteousness conceived in a virgin birth, surely holy awe and wonder lead the soul, reborn in the Spirit of the Messiah, to thanksgiving and praise. This very act of sacred awareness is the inspiration of the Holy Spirit leading the soul in ascent to the next rung above. In this way, every development coming from within is the operation of the Holy

Spirit elevating the soul yet higher, and so the path to enlightenment unfolds in the yoga of Christ. God is gracious and compassionate, Rachum Ve-Hanun! Praise the Lord!

There are many rungs upon which souls stand, some higher and some lower. Not every soul is able to attain perfect *devekut*—that is to say, to attain the highest rung on the Ladder of Lights and so cleave to the Lord our God directly. Therefore, there must be a mediation between God and humanity, between heaven and earth. For this reason, God sends the Spirit of the Messiah into the world and ordains prophets, apostles, saints, and sages, so that something of God's Word and Wisdom might reach the souls upon every rung. By cleaving to the person of a holy tzaddik or maggid who cleaves directly unto the Lord, a soul also might be elevated with the holy man or woman and united to the Lord God above.

Indeed, something of heaven is brought down on earth through the person of the holy apostle, and likewise, something of earth is raised up into heaven to repose. In the person of a tzaddik or maggid, God in some way takes on a name and form and becomes a holy person so that the people might have some link or connection directly with him. Through the person of the prophets, apostles, saints, and sages, God establishes an intimate personal relationship with us, if only we are able to recognize, accept, and draw near to the Spirit of God manifest in the holy tzaddik.

Now, it is true that the holy man or woman could more easily live in seclusion and abide continually in the communion of the higher rung to which his or her soul has attained. There are certainly those adepts who choose to do this, and that is well and good. Yet there is a greater good the masters know and serve—the Will of God who is merciful and compassionate and who reaches out to the living souls of his Creation, the children of her womb. Reaching ever higher upon the Ladder of Lights, love and compassion dawn and the illusion of personal salvation for oneself alone naturally falls away. So the holy souls of the tzaddikim and maggidim have the impulse to descend from their lofty rungs to come among the people of God, seeking to make a connection with them, to minister to them and elevate them, and to win the freedom of their souls in the Spirit of the Messiah.

Ascending, they descend to bring others in ascent into perfect repose in God. For one who cleaves unto a holy one, a prophet or apostle of God, a saint or a sage, it is as though one cleaves and unites oneself directly with God. This is the mystery of true discipleship in the Spirit, and we are invited into it.

As we learn in the verse that follows this one in the Gospel of St. Thomas, we must come to recognize the holy Shekinah resting upon the tzaddik or maggid who is to be our spiritual guide and guardian. You cannot ask a spiritual master if they are a spiritual master and expect them to say, "Yes, dear child, I am a spiritual master." Spiritual humility, which is a central part of the constitution of an authentic adept or master, does not allow them to answer such a question. Rather, they will hide themselves and direct your attention to God, knowing your own capacity to recognize who and what they are in the Spirit is the awakening of that same Spirit of enlightenment within you. It is the Holy Spirit that will answer your question if you are willing to look and see and listen and hear, and to cultivate spiritual humility within yourself. Only through a recognition and love of the holy tzaddik born within ourselves, through the agency of the Holy Spirit, can we cleave unto the tzaddik and fully receive teachings and initiation from him or her.

Becoming a disciple, we must surrender ourselves to the spiritual and moral guidance of the tzaddik. The spiritual teacher and guide, our holy tzaddik, will not place on us too great a burden. Rather, he or she will seek to guide us from the rung upon which we presently stand in a gradual and gentle way toward the next rung in our own ascent. They will ask us to do whatever we can do for ourselves. When we reach the limit of our capacity, they will reach out and help us. To guide and to protect is their mission among the people, to bridge the gap between God and the people, between heaven and earth, and so fulfill the Will of God in creation. We also are called to this Divine labor to the extent of our own capacity, like the holy tzaddik or maggid, to become a conscious channel or vehicle of the Divine presence and power, the holy Shekinah.

Understand that, ultimately, there is no separation between the holy tzaddik and his or her companions. The tzaddik is a disciple and companion of the Holy Spirit, as is every companion in the mystical Body of Christ, the interior church. He or she is fully human, striving and struggling for conscious evolution like everyone else, learning through trial and error. He or she is not to hold him or herself in seclusion or in separation from the people, but rather to be a person among the people of God, the faithful and elect, reaching out to the souls of the righteous and wicked, alike. The tzaddik is a Holy Light that must shine and illuminate the world, and as the Master has previously taught, so also are we. Hence, we come to understand the perfect Master himself, and all of the holy ones, as the image and reflection of our own inner and Divine self. In cleaving to them, we come to cleave to that Christ-self within us and to draw out something of that Light and Life. In so doing, we discover a spiritual life that is effortless and a true and lasting repose or peace.

VERSE 91

They said to him, "Tell us who you are so that we may believe in you."

He said to them, "You read the face of the sky and of the earth, but you have not recognized the one who is before you, and you do not know how to read this moment."

First, I must say that it is a blessing that we hear of the struggles to understand and to receive the teachings and initiation of the Master among his direct disciples. It affirms our own struggle and striving to receive and understand, and encourages us to continue the good fight in the face of our own trials and errors, until at last we are able to fully receive and understand. Likewise, when we hear that, at certain times, there is greater receptivity, insight, and understanding and, at others, there is far less, we come to realize the ebbs and flows in our own experience as something natural and to be expected. At times, through the grace of the master and the power of the moment, the disciples are elevated to higher rungs of the Ladder of Lights (higher levels of consciousness). In early development, however, just as with ourselves, the disciples cannot maintain their stance upon the higher rungs, falling back down to lower rungs and experiencing the confusion and uncertainty that is all part and parcel with the running and returning throughout much of the path. Through the disciples we get a realistic picture of what we can expect in our own journey. It is a blessing we are given these insights, for they can serve to encourage and guide us through similar conditions.

Recognition of the divine presence and power with a holy tzaddik must come from within ourself. It really would do no good if a spiritual adept or master were to announce themselves to us and tell us what rung of the Ladder of Lights they worked from. First, it would mean nothing to us; second, whatever they said of themselves would not penetrate and transform us; and third, information gained from the outside in such a way cannot lead us toward our own self-realization in Christ. Assuming we even believed them, coming from the outside and not as a realization from within a deeper part of ourselves, the information could only be an obstruction. The whole process of discipleship is about the elevation of our soul and the unfoldment of self-realization. This holy recognition is a stage in our own development and the beginning of our own self-realization, and must come in its own timing. Any other way could easily lead to one or another perversion of the truth. This is the case with the false doctrine of the exclusionary status of Yeshua Messiah as the only manifestation of the soul of Messiah, which is the result of a holy mystery distorted by spiritual immaturity in those hearing it before reaching a certain degree of personal spiritual growth and experience.

The moment of recognition is a special moment of receptivity, and there is a natural and spontaneous transmission that comes with it. Something penetrates and transforms us in a way that cannot be explained outside of the experience. It is as if something awakens in us that has long been asleep, as though a most important and deep memory suddenly emerges. The nature of spiritual recognition is not so much a single moment, but a series of moments that gradually reveal a larger recognition, a recognition at various levels. In truth, the full recognition of the soul of an adept or master occurs only in the dawning of our own self-realization, when the capacity comes into being through which we might directly know the fullness of the Divine soul, both within ourselves and the person of the holy tzaddik.

Here, the Master points to forms of recognition of the body, saying basically, "just as you are able to recognize things of the earth through your body, so you must learn to recognize the things of heaven through your soul, and thus embody your Divine soul, your holy Neshamah. You are looking with your body and finite reason; look and see with your soul! Look with eyes remade for awe and wonder!"

As much as speaking about the holy recognition of the soul of the tzaddik, the Master is also speaking of the necessity of the development of our ability to discern between good and evil. The same capacity that comes into operation in this holy recognition manifests also as the discerning or discriminating awareness of good and evil—hence, our sense of direction on the path and sense of right and wrong in our own lives. Without the awakening and development of this capacity, an individual would certainly not last long upon the path before being deceived by the enemy. This reflects even more the importance of inner recognition. We must awaken and cultivate the faculties of our soul, among which is the power of recognition. What is recognized we must then cultivate to full realization within ourselves. This is the process of the path.

VERSE 92

Jesus said, "Seek and you will find. Yet, what you asked me about in former times and which I did not tell you then, now I do desire to tell, but you do not inquire after it."

The mystical journey and spiritual life is, by nature, a sacred quest to which there is no final answer. Rather, it is a continuum of self-expression and experience through which the soul advances and evolves consciously. It is an on-going gradual and organic process of exploration and penetration of the holy mysteries of God and Creation, and thus the unfoldment of one's own self-realization. Those who seek will discover, and continuing to seek beyond discovery, God will continue to reveal itself without end, for God is Ain Sof, the One-Without-End, the infinite and eternal. This continual self-revelation of God and communion in God is the reward of the righteous and elect, a reward inherent in living the Divine Life.

True discipleship is not a casual or brief affair. It is a lifetime relationship. It grows and naturally evolves and changes over time, just as any living relationship does, unfolding as both the holy tzaddik and the disciple unfold and advance together in their spiritual evolution. Although a disciple may be carried a great distance from one's tzaddik by life, nevertheless one remains the faithful disciple, intimately connected both psychically and spiritually to one's teacher. Even though the tzaddik should pass out of this world or the disciple becomes an apostle of God, succeeding the teacher as a lineage-holder of the Light-transmission, nevertheless the disciple remains always a disciple of his or her holy tzaddik, the teacher is his or her teacher for all time. Thus, the assembly of the elect is a community of disciples—a continuum of discipleship that flows through the ages and generations of initiates from the original Master of the tradition. In our own tradition, the lineage goes back to Yeshua Messiah and the assembly of prophets of ancient Israel, and yet further to the predawn of human history and the first conscious contact and communion of a human being with the Creator.

Discipleship is a microcosm of the ongoing divine revelation of God that has evolved over the ages of human history. Just as we see the revelation of God grow, evolve, and become more and more refined, subtle, and sublime, as humanity itself has grown and evolved, so it is with the teachings and initiations the tzaddik imparts to the disciple. At the outset of discipleship, it is not the inner and secret teachings that are imparted, but the outer teachings and initiations that form the foundation for the revelation of the greater and supreme mysteries.

There are many levels of teachings, practices, and initiations, each level unfolding from the one that came before it. With each gradation comes the increase of knowledge and experience that makes it possible for the initiate to receive, integrate, and understand the next cycle of teachings and initiations. It is not that, at any time, the master is keeping any secrets from the disciple or withholding teachings and initiations, but rather that the conditions necessary for transmission must be created by the disciple, the receptivity of the disciple being the real key of transmission. Early on, the disciple's receptivity and ability to understand is limited, and therefore there are many things the tzaddik cannot share. As the disciple matures in spiritual practice and spiritual living, growing in experience and knowledge, he or she is able to perceive things he or she was not previously able to perceive. The disciple is able to receive levels of teachings and initiation he or she formerly could not have understood.

As discipleship spans long periods of time, the disciple must keep the vigil of pursuing the holy mysteries and seeking. One actively invokes teachings and initiations from one's tzaddik, along with maintaining one's own continuum of spiritual practice, through which direct spiritual experience comes. The questions and receptivity of the disciple invoke the response of the tzaddik. Hence, the Master reminds his disciples that it is the disciple who initiates the continuum of transmission through his or her active desire to receive.

Above, we have said that the holy tzaddik, like his or her disciples, is also a disciple of a teacher. The spiritual adept or master and his or her disciples are not separate from one another, but, in truth, are completely interconnected and interdependent. They fulfill and complete each other, and between them, the conditions necessary for the Light-transmission and divine revelation are manifest. They need each other for their continued development and evolution. The mystic understands that, just as the master and disciple need one another for fulfillment and completion, so God needs a divine humanity for fulfillment and completion. Discipleship in Christ is the cornerstone of ongoing divine revelation and the great work toward the Second Coming.

Not only is the Lord speaking to his disciples of some two thousand years ago, but to his disciples today. There is more to be revealed of the holy mystery of the Messiah and God's plan for humanity and the earth; neither the succession of the prophets nor the succession of the apostles has ceased—the divine revelation continues. So we are to continue our seeking into the mysteries of God and Creation, and to inquire of God regarding those things the generations of initiates preceding us could not inquire about. All that can be revealed is not yet revealed; the divine revelation remains incomplete. We are part of an organic, ongoing process of physical, psychic, and spiritual evolution and we are called by God to be conscious agents of that great work. May the Lord make us fit servants and channels of Divine Grace! Amen.

VERSE 93

Jesus said, "Do not give what is holy to dogs, lest they throw them on the dung heap. Do not throw the pearls [to] swine, lest they ... it [...]"

The disciple and apostle of the Anointed One bears a threefold ordination and ministry. First, to exorcise and drive out dark and hostile forces wherever they are found, from both the people and the land; second, to minister to the people and heal them, restoring them to a Spirit-connected-ness; and third, to bear forth the Word of the Lord and the good news of the dawn of Messianic consciousness. Hence, it is the ministry of the exorcist, the healer, and the preacher-prophet to which the elect in Christ are called—a holy priesthood in which the initiate is a conscious agent and ve-hicle of God's Will on earth. This calling is, by nature, both mystical and magical.

We are called to actively bear forth the Divine presence and power. Receiving, we are called to share and give of our-selves and what we have received, that the Light might be in extension and others might also receive and so be joined to the mystical body of Christ. We do not seek to receive for ourselves alone, but in order to be empowered and have something to share and give to others. Our aim as initiates in the Christ-Spirit is to be channels of God's Grace, vehicles of his continual outpouring of blessings. Yet in the process of sharing and giving of ourselves and what we have received, we must be alert and act with awareness, seeking the guidance of the Holy Spirit regarding God's Will. Every individual is unique and different, and their needs are different. Likewise, everyone has a different capacity to receive and can only receive within their capacity. In terms of spiritual matters and esoteric wisdom, some individuals have no desire to receive and therefore no capacity of reception. In the activity of the ministry to which we are called, we must learn to pray, meditate, and seek in Spirit when and what to share with each individual. Like the tzaddik, we must act only with Divine permission and authority.

Here, the Master makes it clear that the esoteric wisdom, the inner and secret teachings, are not for everyone. While outer teachings may be more freely shared, the inner and secret level of the teachings must be shared only under the guidance of the Holy Spirit with those who are ready to receive them and who will not profane them. We are charged to share and give what we have received, for only in this way is our reception fulfilled, but we must impart the transmission consciously, with discernment and with skillful methods, giving to each person what the Spirit would have us give and what is good for them.

We are, indeed, spiritual warriors in a battle of cosmic forces, seeking to win the enlightenment and liberation of as many souls as we possibly can for the sake of heaven. Yet only those souls ripe for redemption can be won over. We must understand that there shall be many not ripe as yet, some actually perverse, for whom we can do nothing at all, save pray for them and offer them up before the Lord. As much as we are to extend the Light here below, so are we to accomplish a balance, harmony, and unification in the Upper World. Hence, in the midst of our ministry, we must be conscious of that which is transpiring behind that which appears and respond accordingly. Not by way of a judgment based upon external appearance are we to respond, but by way of an interior discernment of what is transpiring within and behind appearances. For such interior discrimination, we must rely upon the Holy Spirit to instruct, inspire, and guide us.

Now this is true of the teachings and initiations we receive from our holy tzaddik, and the knowledge and wisdom we gather from our studies and contemplations. It is even more true of our personal spiritual experiences. Knowledge of our experiences and the experiences themselves should be shared only with the greatest level of discrimination and only when there is a clear good to be accomplished in so doing. We speak freely with our tzaddik regarding experiences in prayer, meditation, and ritual, as well as the dreams and visions that may come, for our tzaddik is our spiritual mentor and there must be an open and honest exchange for our tzaddik to accomplish his or her mission with us. Yet outside of this sacred friendship, we must be very careful with whom we share our spiritual experiences. It is possible that we might taint the experience ourselves through the wrong motivation in sharing it, or in sharing it with the wrong person, we might form a link to a dark or hostile force and so bring unwholesome influences into our continuum. This forms a deeper level of understanding of what the Master is saying.

Do not be selfish and withhold yourself from sharing, nor be afraid to share and give of the Light you receive, but be awake and alert as you share and follow the guidance of the holy Shekinah. When she is present, share freely; when she departs, be silent and go on your way. If you remain always open and sensitive to her, you will always know where she leads you. Although there may be some trial and error along the way, nevertheless, learn from your mistakes and continue as her companion, letting your Light shine to illuminate the world. Lord, guide us as we let our Light shine! Amen.

VERSE 94

Jesus [said], "He who seeks will find, and [he who knocks]
will be let in."

We have the promise of our Lord and Savior, our very
own Christ-self, that, if we seek, we will find and experience the Christ-Spirit and penetrate the holy mysteries of
God and Creation. Likewise, we have the promise that, if we
knock on the door of the holy sanctuary seeking initiation,
we will be let in and initiated in by the Holy Spirit. This very
promise is a part of our faith and our spiritual hope.

Let us begin with the secret level of the teaching that we
might consider the outer level of the teaching and perceive
what is behind it. Knock on the first gate, and entering, you
will behold the universe filled with angels; knock on the second gate, and entering, you will behold the dominion of the
Divine powers; knock on the third gate, and you will draw
near unto the Lord, beholding the image of the glory of the
Lord our God. Seeking, you will find that the Lord God is an
awesome and wonderful God. Now, here is the teaching by
the number three, but we might also give the same teaching
by the numbers ten, twenty-two, thirty-two, and fifty, speaking of the same holy mystery of running and returning and
the great ascension.

The seeking of which the Master is speaking is receptivity,
but this receptivity is not an inactive and passive state, rather

it is active and dynamic. It is a surrender to the Holy Spirit in an active aspiration of faith and hope, cultivating in oneself an openness and sensitivity to the Holy Spirit and the holy mysteries she reveals. The nature of this aspiration is active questioning and exploration of the holy mysteries, in which we seek to receive teachings and initiations from the holy apostle of God, and likewise, through our own continuum of spiritual study and practice, seek to receive instruction and revelation from the Holy Spirit directly. Openness and sensitivity is the first part of this seeking; active exploration the second part.

A passive surrender will accomplish nothing, for the Spirit of God will not do for you what God has empowered you to do for yourself. Created in the image of God, you are a co-creator with God and a partner in the divine labor of the Holy Spirit. The surrender is a working upon yourself to purify and perfect yourself as a channel of the Divine presence and power, thus creating the conditions in which the Holy Spirit can fully work within you and through you to accomplish God's Will (the great work). An active surrender is called for that continually offers up every aspect and part of yourself to the Lord and invites the Spirit of the Lord to work within and through you each day. The natural expression of this surrender is spiritual practice and spiritual living, an active questioning and exploration in Spirit and Truth. We come to understand what "seeking" means—an active receptivity. With an active and dynamic receptivity, you will discover!

VERSE 95

[Jesus said], "If you have money, do not lend it at interest,
but give [it] to one from whom you will not get it back."

In the midst of a capitalistic society, undoubtedly such a saying falls upon deaf ears. To the mind-set of selfishness and
greed, it seems completely insane, but such a mind-set is exactly what the Master is intending to shatter with this saying, for
selfishness and greed are a total obstruction to the flow of Divine Grace and self-realization. They are, in fact, the basis of a
poverty consciousness in which, no matter how much one may
have, it is never enough and there can be no satisfaction.

Merely in terms of the material world, consideration of the
inner dimensions and spiritual world set aside, as part of collective humanity and the world, we are part of an abundant and
universal supply of energy-intelligence. We are connected to
an inexhaustible supply of energy, resources, and opportunity
of every kind, but as long as we are bound to the selfishness of
greed or a siege mentality, we sorely limit our ability to draw
upon the abundant supply and to actually experience abundance in our lives. To freely give away money, lands, or other
possessions can prove to have a healing effect upon the one
who gives, along with uplifting and benefiting those who receive. It is a remedy to greed and poverty consciousness.

The teaching given here is perhaps most important to the
initiate of the Christian mysteries living in this present generation and society, as the subject of material resources is natu-

rally an area of the greatest resistance and obstruction to a holistic spiritual consecration. It is not only the heart, soul, mind, and body that the initiate offers up to the Lord for the sake of heaven and the great work, but their whole life, including the resources God has given into their care. Fundamentally, advanced initiates know the resources of their life, not as personal possessions, but as a sacred trust given to them by God to accomplish the upliftment of themselves and humanity. Whatever resources they may have, whatever powers in the world, whether it be money power, fame power, sex power, social-political power, and so on, they know it is their mission to redeem and restore these to God's Will. They consider whatever resources they have been given by the Life-power, God, to be their offering to the Lord.

The question of the initiate in the assembly of the elect is, "How do I skillfully use my talents, abilities, and all that I have for advancement of my soul in conscious evolution and elevation of the collective soul of humanity? How do I serve the Lord with who and what I am and what I have in my life?" Such a question is the difference between the profane individual and the true initiate in the world. For the would-be truth seeker and spiritual aspirant in this generation, the offering of material resources and active charity prove among the most significant stumbling blocks on the path.

This is reflected in the issue of tithing to churches or spiritual communities. Tithing is the practice of giving 10 percent of one's income to the service of the spiritual community and God. This is an issue of duty to the spiritual practitioner, and is itself a spiritual practice. To tithe is not charity, but duty. Charity includes those material contributions, as a free elective, that go beyond duty. Among both the faithful and elect today, it is more common that less than 10 percent is given to the service of the Lord. On account of this grave resistance, ministers and spiritual teachers are reduced to beggars, or worse, fall into the sin of selling teachings and initiation in order to ensure support for spiritual work. If this is true of tithing, one can only imagine the plight of charity in the spiritual life of the faithful and elect!

Obviously, this was as great an issue in the time of our Lord as in our own time, although our own ability and resources in this society are undoubtedly greater among common peoples. The Master is speaking here of money, yet it can be any power in the material world that can be placed in the service of an active compassion or charity. Behind what he is saying is the awareness of Sacred Unity and universal consciousness on a material level. Cosmic or universal consciousness is the threshold of supernal or messianic consciousness. Our consciousness must be universalized in order for Messianic consciousness to dawn, and we must actively live with an awareness of Sacred Unity underlying all life. While mental and vital-emotional consciousness must be universalized and transformed, so also must the physical and material consciousness. Charity is the active expression of that transformation, the active response of recognition and realization of our complete interdependence and interconnection with all that lives, with everyone and everything. The Master is calling for a practice of this Truth on a practical level.

As long as strong resistance and obstruction remains on the material level of sharing and giving, there are aspects and levels of our consciousness that cannot be universalized and transformed. Understanding this, the Master is encouraging us to actively seek to address and dispel the withholding of ourselves on practical levels, as well as on the more subtle levels of mind, heart, and soul. With all levels of our consciousness and being, we are to serve the Lord and act as vehicles of God's Will and Grace. Material gifts, psychic gifts, spiritual gifts, all are gifts of the Spirit—and whatever gifts we may have, we are to share and give of ourselves through them. How will you use the Divine energy as it is manifest with you—to what end? This is the question the Master is asking us and that we are to ask and answer ourselves as disciples of Christ.

Considering that we are spiritual beings having a material experience, it might rightly be said that practical and material assistance may be most important in the great work, certainly as important as the invisible assistance we may render to others. Without material and practical support, the more subtle and sublime modes of assistance have no ground in the world. Thus, in the Holy Scriptures, we hear the Lord speaking through the prophets about true sacrifice not being in the religious services of the temple, as much as in acts of charity, providing for the orphan and widow, defending the oppressed and seeking justice, active compassion, kindness, love, and all manner of material and practical things through which the human spirit is cultivated and uplifted. Here the Master reflects this fundamental Truth.

VERSE 96

Jesus said, "The kingdom of the Father is like [a certain]
woman. She took a little leaven, [concealed] it in some dough,
and made it into large loaves. Let him who has ears hear."

This holy woman is your Neshamah; you and your life are
the dough. The yeast is the Holy Spirit that she brings
into you and your life. On account of her, your Nefesh grows
and evolves, and your Ruach comes to perfection. The kingdom of the Father is the reality of your secret and undying
soul. The kingdom is within you and all around you when
you bring it forth from within you.

In truth, every level and manifestation of consciousness-
force or energy-intelligence is a secret operation of the Holy
Spirit. Even matter itself is a dense manifestation of the Spirit
of God, and Nature also is the manifestation of God's Spirit
continuing his creative self-expression and revelation. She
works within everyone and everything to enact God's Will.
She is the consciousness-force within and behind all of Creation and the evolutionary impulse in Creation and all God's
creatures. Her aim in the human being and Creation is the
manifestation of the kingdom of God—the fruition of God's
Creation in conscious union with him.

The sense of the mystery, the impulse to seek and find, to
search and discover, to strive and struggle for a greater good
and more noble existence, the yearning to unite oneself with
one's source and Creator, this is the Holy Spirit within the

individual and Creation, seeking to reunite herself with her Beloved, the Holy One of Being. She is the desire to receive and the desire to impart, the active agent of God's Will.

Like her Beloved, the One-Without-End (Ain Sof), she is mysterious and invisible. You will never see her at any time, but drawing near to the Lord, receiving your higher intelligence (Ruach), your heavenly soul (Neshamah), and the Holy Spirit who comes with these, her companions, you will experience her presence and power. Even before you have attained the holy rungs of Ruach and Neshamah, you will experience her presence and power, for she is the presence and power of life and consciousness itself, and you live and are self-aware on account of her.

She is the virgin mother of the soul of the Messiah, the holy mother and bride of the God. It is she who will give birth to Christ in you, and to Christ-consciousness in the world. The soul of the Messiah has come into the world to pour forth the Holy Spirit upon the world, imparting her presence and power to the elect, that, through the faithful and elect, she might labor for the Second Coming and the manifestation of the kingdom of God. The Holy One has ascended into the heavens, to sit at the right hand of the heavenly Father and enter into the repose. She has remained below with the earthly mother as her midwife in birthing Messianic consciousness, living in exile among us until the day of be-with-us. She is the yeast of the bread of heaven, something small, within and hidden, that makes something great and glorious. She is the active power of redemption and she will lift you up with herself into the bridal chamber.

The Spirit who lives in me, she will accomplish everything. The promise of God is assured through faith and fulfilled through Grace. Praise God! Praise the Lord! Thanks be unto the Lord our God for mercy and Grace! Amen.

VERSE 97

Jesus said, "The kingdom of the [father] is like a certain woman who was carrying a [jar] full of meal. While she was walking [on the] road, still some distance from home, the handle of the jar broke and the meal emptied out behind her [on] the road. She did not realize it; she had noticed no accident. When she reached her house she set the jar down and found it empty."

This woman is the Nefesh who, without her Ruach (higher intelligence) and Neshamah (heavenly soul), becomes distracted in her journey through the world and therefore departs from this world empty. She will then have to acquire another jar (physical body), again make the journey to get meal (merit for heaven), and bring it home (entering the kingdom of heaven with merit). How sorrowful it must be for those souls who depart this life empty, only coming before the Holy One in the afterlife to realize the vanity and futility of the life they have lived. Surely, it must be a great anguish in the soul! We pray for the comforting of such souls and for their awakening while in this life so that they do not have to endure this suffering!

There is more here than the tale of the soul of a profane individual who accomplishes nothing in this life, who departs the world empty, having only attended to vanity. There is also the allusion to one who has acquired something of the true faith and gnosis, yet becoming distracted and unmindful, loses what they have gained. We understand this through our own experience with a continuum of spiritual practice, for when we are as yet immature in the spiritual life and go on and off with our spiritual studies and practice, we see that it is often as though we must begin all over again, having lost the greater part of what we had formerly gained in terms of energy-intelligence, knowledge, and so forth. To keep what is given to us by the Spirit and to increase what we have, to grow and evolve, we must keep holy vigil with the Spirit of the Lord, maintaining a continuum of spiritual practice and spiritual living. We must continue to feed our soul so that she remains present and strong with us. If we become distracted and mindless in this matter, although we have sojourned in the Spirit for many years, all that we have generated and gathered could swiftly dissipate and depart from us. It is a fundamental truth of how life works.

Consider a beautiful garden filled with all manner of flowers and plants, a garden someone has cultivated for many years, perhaps twenty or more, until it has become a virtual paradise and haven, a sanctuary of natural glory and splendor. Now suppose the person who cultivated and tended this garden stopped doing so, no longer watering and fertilizing it, pruning and weeding it, and daily tending it. The longer this went on, the more their garden would shift from what it once was. Eventually, if a long period were allowed to pass, say some years, it would go completely wild and no longer be the garden it was. It is the same with your spiritual practice through which an authentic spiritual life is cultivated and tended. If left unattended, it is ruined with the passage of time.

We cannot forget in our spirituality that we are organic living beings and that the same laws apply to our spiritual life as to any other expression of life and nature. Without a dedication of time and energy, attention and activity, without continued conscious movement, our spiritual life can easily wither away and cease to be. Consistent dedication, mindfulness, and alertness are absolutely necessary. While in this world, we must maintain the holy continuum actively. We must actively live the Divine life, so that we might depart with the Divine fullness. Let us pray our jar is not found empty when we return home! Lord, help us to remember and to keep vigil! Amen.

VERSE 98

Jesus said, "The kingdom of the father is like a certain man who wanted to kill a powerful man. In his own home he drew his sword and struck the wall in order to find out whether his hand could carry through. Then he slew the strong man."

In the Talmud, the rabbis tell us that one must first purify oneself and only then can one purify others. It is the same for the holy tzaddik, acting as the preacher or prophet of the Word of God, giving *musar* (a message of reprove or rebuke) to the circle of companions. First, the holy tzaddik must rebuke him- or herself and repent of the sin being rebuked. Only then can he or she give musar to the assembly, having first purified him- or herself of the klippot to be shattered and driven out. In this way, the holy one is bound to the assembly and inseparable from the people, and so can act to purify and elevate them along with him or herself.

Is not the Master speaking here of the disciple becoming a spiritual warrior? Indeed, he is. But the first and foremost battle to be won is within our own house, within our own heart, soul, mind, and body, severing all links with the dark and hostile forces and driving out the enemy from within us—hence, cutting off the sitra ahara, the inclination to evil. Only to the degree we are victorious in Christ within our own consciousness, against the enemy, and against the inner demons that are the subjective expression of evil, can we then combat the objective evil in our environment and the world.

This is a most important matter for everyone chosen to be a disciple of Christ and ordained through the Christ-Spirit as a holy priest and apostle. Central to the mission of every disciple and apostle is the ministry of exorcism, that is to say, dispelling and driving out the dark and hostile forces wherever they are found. If one is not strong in one's own faith, having cultivated the ability to distinguish good from evil, and purifying oneself of the inclination to evil, how could one possibly combat an outwardly manifest evil or demonic spirit? How could one render assistance to another in order to drive out darkness?

Dear child of Light, do not be ignorant in such matters. Pay close attention to the teachings and example of the perfect Master. Every true adept or master has spoken of the enemy and his hordes. Without exception, spiritual teachers of every Wisdom Tradition of the world affirm the relative reality of evil and the enemy. Let us not be so foolish as to disregard the Word of God in the holy ones, or to write off a central part of their teachings as something fanciful and unreal. Quite the contrary! Every authentic spiritual practitioner will affirm in his or her own experience the reality of opposing cosmic forces and the truth of dark and hostile powers that seek to prevent, for whatever reason, the ascent of humanity to its fulfillment in enlightenment or God.

You must know and understand that, whatever power or dominion such beings-forces might have over you, it is on account of an inner affinity in vibration within your own thoughts and emotions, your own desires and fears. Through these psychic complexes, they have a link and influence upon you. If you purify yourself of dark and negative thoughts and emotions, perverted desires and fears, and the root of all of these evils—namely selfishness or self-grasping—no dark or hostile force can ultimately have any power or dominion over you. Rather, in the holy name of the Lord and the Divine powers, all such beings-forces will be subject unto you, according to the Will of God and the power of the Holy Spirit dwelling in you.

If you ask me of evil, I must tell you that every action that breaks down faith and trust between human beings, and breaks down faith in goodness and God, is the work of evil. The man who beats a dog, so that the dog cowers in his presence, no longer trusting in him or feeling safe, has committed an act of evil. How much more so are any of our actions evil that break down the trust between our brothers and sisters in humanity and our faith in God? Are not such actions the meaning of sin or missing the mark? We must say of evil that most of its manifestations are not so gross and obvious as with a character, such as a Hitler, Charles Manson, Jeffrey Dahmer, and the like, who embodies demonic forces. Evil typically lurks in the shadows and hides itself. It perverts and acts in more subtle and sublime ways, through thousands of little and seemingly harmless actions, all of which serve to erode any bond of solidarity and unity among ourselves and with God. Consider the little nothing of mere gossip. Whether it is true or not, there is injury to all parties involved. The one of whom it is spoken, the one to whom it is spoken, and the one who speaks it are all harmed. If nothing else, there is less trust and less positive thought and emotion between everyone involved following the gossip than before the evil was committed. Goodness is eroded by evil actions.

Now, consider what sacrifice (or means of drawing near to God) the Lord has spoken of through his prophets and apostles. God calls us to look after one another, to build up and uplift one another, to consider our individual and collective welfare. God calls for compassion and kindness, social justice, charity, care for the poor, the orphan and the widow, defense of the oppressed, genuine and active concern for others—the love of our neighbors as ourselves. We are called to evolve individually, to cultivate our humanity and the Divine potential within us, and together, to develop enlightened societies that act in harmony and unity with God. Here is the practical sacrifice, our means of drawing near.

Bear in mind that the root of what opposes this is selfishness, greed, and fear. Moreover, the opposition occurs first within our own thoughts and vital emotions. Therefore, the place to make a change is in our own consciousness. Only in this way shall we transform the world and bring about the resurrection of the world. With this knowledge, you possess the key to the defeat of the enemy and the victory of the Anointed One of God.

VERSE 99

The disciples said to him, "Your brothers and your mother are standing outside."

He said to them, "Those here who do the will of my father are my brothers and my mother. It is they who will enter into the kingdom of my father."

There is a more important bond than that of mere flesh and blood to be discovered and honored. It is a bond and connection of the soul in Spirit. While the family with which you share a blood tie is your family for a lifetime, with the family of your soul you share a bond forever—a connection that spans many lives. On account of this, it may rightly be said that our spiritual family or our soul's family is primary to us, and our temporary family of physical birth secondary, although in some cases it may be that these two families are interwoven, as in the case of Lord Yeshua. Recognition of this truth comes more and more as we let go of our strong self-identity with name and form and generate a new self-identity with our soul and Christ-self. Then we realize the purpose and meaning of this life to be far more than we might at first have imagined.

The masters of the holy Kabbalah teach us that living souls come forth from different spiritual roots and that, according to the root from which a given soul comes, it has a corresponding root essence and an intimate and special connection to other souls with which it shares the same holy root. The masters speak of this in terms of the organs of the body of Adam Kadmon, teaching that souls come from different parts of the body of the primordial human being and that one's nature, temperament, and function corresponds to the organ of the Divine body from which one's soul is derived. The closest bonds we share with others in this life are with those who have the same soul-root as our own, being drawn together in order to accomplish certain mutual tasks in this world. This is said to be especially true of the spiritual community we are attracted to and enter, becoming a member. Those who gather together in spiritual communities share something of the same root-essence in their soul, and thus have a special soul connection. Hence, in a mystical fellowship, it is said that a holy tzaddik and his or her companions share the same holy root-essence and come together for a specific mission. While this can be true of gatherings of souls other than those of spiritual communities, here the Master is speaking specifically of a mystical and spiritual community. Thus, on one level, the Master is giving a teaching on soul-roots and connections between souls, while, on another level, speaking about the importance of the spiritual community in the great work.

Not only is our own individual spiritual practice important, our collective work together in spiritual communities is also crucial. Working spiritually in seclusion and isolation will not accomplish the greatest good nor facilitate the highest advancement of the soul. To actually accomplish a greater good and for a higher level of attainment, we need a spiritual teacher and the spiritual community that naturally forms around the teacher. They are our soul's family, and like our physical family, we cannot ultimately be severed from them. Rather, our spiritual community is our spiritual family for our lifetime and, according to the esoteric wisdom, far beyond that.

This teaching reveals why it is very important that we seek out and participate in a spiritual community and not make the mistake of bouncing around from one to another. Moreover, it reveals why, once we find an authentic teacher and community we have a true connection with, it is important that we remain with that community and labor with our spiritual community in the great work. An organic connection must be developed. The transmission that passes through a community to the individual member transpires only after due time. Likewise, whatever the work of our particular spiritual teacher and community, it is our work also. Fundamentally, we have a need for others and community for our greater fulfillment.

Here, it must be said, as we have before, that it will be through many small collectives of the faithful and elect working together that the advent of the supernal consciousness will ultimately occur, not merely through isolate individual efforts.

In terms of spiritual communities, their bond is deep within us, within our soul, and the ultimate unity is in God. Every individual has a unique role to play in the life of the community. Every community has its own task or mission in the great work. Thus, we find among the tzaddikim different modes and forms of the teachings, each lineage developing upon unique lines, even within the same Wisdom Tradition. Their own emphasis reflects something of their mission, the specific purpose for that manifestation of the Light-transmission reaching out to souls of certain levels and root-essences. Just as the individual is part of the greater body of the particular spiritual community, any given spiritual community is part of the greater community of the Wisdom Tradition followed, and ultimately, is part of the universal spiritual community worldwide, composed of all faiths and Wisdom Traditions—all who, in their own unique way, do the Will of God and so enter into the kingdom of God.

There is a basic truth underlying this teaching. We are all brothers and sisters, every living creature is part of our family, and God is our Father-Mother. May we remember to love and bring to unity. Amen.

VERSE 100

They showed Jesus a gold coin and said to him, " Caesar's men demand taxes from us."

He said to them, "Give to Caesar what belongs to Caesar, give to God what belongs to God, and give me what is mine."

As mental beings, we are prone to extremes. Creating dualism in our minds, we tend to go to one pole or the other, denying what appears to us as the opposite and contradictory side. Many people abandon God, spiritual practice, and spiritual community for the sake of worldly things, but just the same, many spiritual aspirants attempt to deny and escape the world for the sake of spirituality and God. Neither of these two extremes represents the enlightenment about which the perfect Master is speaking in his teachings. In either case, there remains an immaturity and imperfection in the soul and an incomplete enlightenment.

I certainly cannot betray my soul and my God for the things of this world, for nothing of this world will give me my soul nor the enlightenment that leads to resurrection and eternal life. I know what the pearl of great price is, and it is that alone which is worthy of purchase. If I do not have contact with my Neshamah, my Divine nature, I am not myself and I live apart from God. It is also true that the Lord my God has placed me in this world for a reason, that God has created the world and all who dwell in it. Just as I cannot deny or abandon God, neither can I abandon his Creation or

seek to escape involvement in the world by hiding behind my spirituality and faith in heaven. In truth, as a human being, created in the
image of God as a co-creator and partner with him, it is my role in
Creation to uplift Creation to God and to bring God down into Creation—to live in such a way as to unite heaven and earth.

If I establish myself in a Spirit-connectedness and take up the Divine
Life, but deny the world and retreat from it, seeking escape from my responsibilities in the world, how shall I practically bear forth the Word
of God and extend the Light? If I do not live in the world, how shall I
labor effectively to win souls for heaven's sake or for the resurrection of
the world? It is just the same with the person who does not labor for the
sake of heaven—how shall they expect to enter into heaven when they
have made no place for themselves there while in this life?

More profoundly, there is this point: Who is it that makes a separation and division between heaven and earth, between the human
soul and God, and thus would divide spiritual and material life? Whatever separation or division there appears to be, it is only in the mind,
a product of mental being as yet incomplete in evolution. For the real
truth is this: there is no separation between the earth and the heavens,
nor between the living soul and God. Where there is division, it is the
creation of the human being on account of fundamental ignorance.
Hence, both extremes of seeking only the world or seeking only God
are the product of ignorance, the domain of the evil one.

If I realize the unity underlying all of Creation, both the heavens
and the earth, there is no more delusion that a choice is to be made
between one or the other. I come to understand the interconnection
and interdependence of heaven and earth, the Creator and creature,
and seek the fulfillment of both creature and Creator in conscious
union. It is this very unity the Master is speaking about in this teaching, suggesting that duty in the world, duty to God, and duty to the
holy tzaddik are, in fact, one unified duty or responsibility—a duty to
life, light, love, and liberty.

God abides in heaven above, and above the heavens, transcendent
of Creation, yet the Spirit of God is also in Creation and all creatures.
My duty and responsibility to God's creatures is equally my duty and
responsibility to God. There is no separation or division whatsoever.

Just as all direct activities of Gnostic worship, such as prayer, meditation, and so on, are a duty or responsibility of my soul to God and serve as vehicles for the Holy Spirit, so also are my mundane activities and responsibilities potential vehicles of God's Spirit and are as important to my spiritual evolution. The whole of my life is a vehicle for the Truth and Light, including matters of work, family, and the community at large. In the midst of the mundane world and my daily living, not only through my words but through my behavior and actions, I must bear forth the Light and the Word of God. How I respond in any given situation or go about any given activity directly reflects upon my faith, all of the faithful, and upon God to anyone who is watching. This I must bear in mind each day and so live in such a way as to bring light and hope among the people. And surely to live in the way of righteousness is its own reward on earth and in heaven.

Whether in spiritual community or in the midst of unenlightened society, the duty of the faithful and elect is always to reflect the Spirit and Truth, and moreover, to utilize every circumstance, situation, event, or activity of life as a vehicle of the Holy Spirit. While a yearning for mystical experience is good, which illuminates the individual, so also is the yearning and labor for historical and social justice, which is the illumination of a whole society of individuals. I am placed here, in this world, by God for this divine labor. As long as I am in this world, it is the duty of my soul to act as a conscious agent of God in both the mundane and supramundane dimensions of life. Save that I am fully in the world while maintaining a higher rung of enlightenment, I cannot labor for the upliftment of humanity and the transformation of the world. We have a duty to our society and to God, and it is the same sacred task—the Divine Life.

VERSE 101

Jesus said, "Whoever does not hate his [father] and his mother as I do cannot become a [disciple] to me. And whoever does [not] love his [father and] his mother as I do cannot become a [disciple to] me. For my mother (of this world gave me death) . . . but [my] true [mother) gave me life."

As we have said before, the word translated as "hate" may also be translated as "detachment" or "to put aside." The Anointed One, teaching the doctrine of Divine love, surely would not encourage us toward any form of hatred. For fear, leading to anger, which in turn leads to hatred, is the path that leads to the dominion of the evil one and place of anguish. No, indeed, the Lord is not speaking about hatred, but rather about self-cherishing and liberation from such ignorance. Your material mother and father represent the foundation of your self-identity with name and form, and thus the root of your self-cherishing. Hence, putting aside your grasping onto your physical family in an egoistic way reflects the loosening of your grasping at name and form so that you might cleave to your heavenly soul and to the Lord as your refuge.

More than this, the Master is speaking about striving for a love that manifests equality, an equalizing wisdom. The nature of the love of the Messiah is such that apostles of God do not love their mother more than they love the stranger in the street. They do not love their father more than even their enemy, but they love every living soul equally with the love of Christ. Now I shall not say that I, or anyone, can love in this way. Rather, the Christ-Spirit in me and in you can love in this way—a love that is perfect and true, knowing every living soul as mother and father, brother and sister equally, and seeking a greater good for one and for all. It is a love that comes through the Grace of the Holy Spirit and is perfected in the Holy Spirit, although on my part, I must let go of self-cherishing and favoritism in order to let this holy love of God shine through me.

Lord Yeshua did not give his life as a sacrifice only for his family. He did not live his life only for his own benefit and the benefit of his family. Nor did he make himself a sacrifice only for the faithful and righteous, but also for the unrighteous and his enemies. The Anointed One made himself a holy sacrifice for one and all, so that all who would seek their heavenly soul and cleave unto him might share in his resurrection and have eternal life. He has given his love, his life, in obedience to the Lord our God, for the salvation of every living soul. His love and his salvation are universal, and such Divine love is our noble ideal as his disciples. It is the only way to live.

VERSE 102

Jesus said, "Woe to the Pharisees, for they are like a dog sleeping in the manger of oxen, for neither does he eat nor does he [let] the oxen eat."

The names and titles have changed, different human institutions of religious authority have arisen, and other dogmatic doctrines and creeds have been formed, yet the inherent ignorance remains the same. Any person or organization that claims an exclusive representation of the Spirit of Truth or claims to be the sole authority of the Word of God is a modern pharisee. That this should happen in the "name of Jesus" is something of an oxymoron, considering that Yeshua was a spiritual revolutionary who spoke out against the conventional wisdom of his day and all exclusive claims of religious authority.

Lord Yeshua was a spiritual revolutionary and so is everyone who is reborn of the Holy Spirit, for the Holy Spirit is a living presence and power. God is a Living God. The Divine revelation is constantly ongoing. We ourselves are constantly growing and changing. In the Holy Spirit, there is a constant spiritual revolution. How could any fixed or dogmatic doctrine or creed ever contain this living presence and power? Can the conventional wisdom of any age be anything more than a dim reflection of God's Wisdom?

Let us consider the meaning of the Cosmic Christ and be clear about the Gnostic view. The Cosmic Christ means an

awareness of Christ within everyone and everything—a living presence and power that is inclusive, not exclusive. Likewise, "Cosmic
Christ" is a term for the universal Logos and Sophia of God that is the
source of all divine revelation, and thus of all world Wisdom Traditions inspired by the Spirit of Truth. The soul of the Messiah is the
great World Teacher and is as present in other prophets and apostles
of God as in Yeshua Messiah. Thus, in the Gnostic view, something of
the Cosmic Christ is manifest in all of the sages, prophets, and apostles of every Wisdom Tradition. What is meant by Christ is something more than "Christian."

It is often forgotten that Lord Yeshua and his disciples were not
"Christian," but were Jewish. Although Jewish, Lord Yeshua was something more than a Jew. He was a Spirit-filled person and an incarnation of the great World Teacher. In truth, he transcended Judaism and
all human institutions of religious authority. To say that he came to
found yet another human institution of religious authority is to miss
the mark entirely as to the real message of the Gospel and the meaning of Christ. It may correctly be said that he came to restore us to a
Spirit-connectedness and to deliver us from bondage to the establishment, whether the conventional wisdom of an unenlightened society
or the ignorance of religious authority.

I speak in the mystical or symbolic language of Gnostic Christianity and the holy Kabbalah, upon which the tradition I received is
founded, but the Wisdom Traditions are only that—a spiritual language and a vehicle for spiritual or mystical experience, nothing more.
The language is not the Truth expressed by it, nor is the vehicle of the
spiritual or mystical journey the experience itself. On spiritual matters,
I speak in Gnostic Christian language. One might say it is my spiritual
mother tongue. On mundane matters, I speak English because that is
my mundane mother tongue. If I were to speak or write in French or
German or Spanish, the same truth would be spoken as in English,
though the language would be different. It is the same with regards to
a mystical or symbolic language of a Wisdom Tradition. From one tradition to another, although the language is different, the Spirit of
Truth being expressed is the same. Fundamentalism and dogmatic religion tends to forget this and thus loses sight of the Spirit of Truth.

The opposite problem occurs in much of what is called "modern spirituality." Taking words from diverse mystical or symbolic languages, without ever becoming adept in any single language, many people think this enables them to entertain a full communion in the Spirit or to communicate the Spirit. However, without a complete language and larger vocabulary, it is impossible to receive or impart anything of a deeper knowledge, understanding, and wisdom. Their communication with the Spirit is sorely impaired. Merely consider a person forming their mundane language out of many different languages and having no complete knowledge of any single language. Perhaps he or she takes fifty Arabic words, sixty German words, twenty French words, a hundred Greek words, and so forth. Now imagine that person trying to communicate in this way. It would be ridiculous! When a spiritual language is formed in this way, it represents the opposite side of the same ignorance a religious fundamentalist suffers—a failure to understand that a Wisdom Tradition is a spiritual language and the function of that language!

Thus, it is important that one does not confuse the spiritual language or vehicle of experience with the truth of the experience itself. Likewise, it is important that one has at least one spiritual language in which they are completely fluent. Anything less is to fall into the trap of the pharisees.

The Christos is the Word and Wisdom of God, and thus is the source of all language through which the Spirit of Truth is communicated. This is not only true of spiritual truths but of all Truth; so we can include such languages as science, mathematics, art, music, and such in our contemplation of this verse. The whole of Creation and the whole of Life is the communication of the creative Spirit of God. The idea that there is a conflict between science and spirituality, or between any one expression of Truth and another, so that one expression of the Spirit of Truth should deny another, is also what is meant by "pharisees."

We often speak of worldliness versus spirituality in the teachings. What is meant by worldliness is the tendency toward denial of or ignoring the holistic dimension of our experience of the Life power. Thus, the religious person who denies good science and the scientific person who denies good spirituality are equally "worldly" in this sense. The way of the world is always a partial truth mixed with falsehood; it is something admixed, impure and imperfect. The Christos is the purity and perfection of all-Truth or what may be called Truth-consciousness. Authentic spirituality is a conscious evolution toward Truth-consciousness, and it integrates the Truth in every form it is discovered.

In the midst of this contemplation, one cannot help but remember the words of St. Paul: "For now we see in a mirror, dimly, but then we will see face to face. Now I know only in part; then I will know fully, even as I have been fully known" (1 Corinthians 13:12). This is the true Gnosis that is the aim of the Gnostic initiate.

VERSE 103

Jesus said, "Fortunate is the man who knows where the brigands will enter, so that [he] may get up, muster his domain,
and arm himself before they invade."

First, we may understand the Master as speaking of the
virtue and necessity of self-knowledge, which among
other things includes the knowledge of personal strength and
weakness. Knowing areas of personal weakness, we can then
work on those aspects of ourselves to overcome whatever
weakness, impurity, or imperfection may be present. We can
work to strengthen what is weak, purify what is impure, and
work out the imperfections we find. In order to consciously
evolve, we must acquire self-knowledge through the agency
of the silent witness, being awake and alert in our daily living,
for only with self-knowledge can we work with the Holy
Spirit to refine and shape ourselves in the image of Christ.

Suppose I find in myself a strong tendency toward anger
and see that I tend to lose my temper far too often. Knowing
this, I can then pray about it and look into it more deeply,
seeking to discern the deeper causes of the anger in me and to
heal the dis-ease in my consciousness. Fundamentally, I begin
to pay more attention to my angry outbursts, first to understand the complex of thoughts and emotions behind them,
and to observe my nature and temperament that contribute.
Then I begin to become more alert to the indications before
my anger arises, the types of thought, feeling/emotion, and

sensations that herald the coming into being of anger. Identifying these, I can then practice shifting the matrix of consciousness through which anger is born and learn how to use the energy-intelligence consciously and constructively, rather than the destructive form of anger that plagues me. Now throughout this process, I continue to pray about it, using methods of prayer and meditation adapted to work on those contributing factors I discover, as well as to empower me to control my temper. I may use many different things creatively in order to combat the inner demon of anger and rage, ultimately relying upon the Lord to heal my spirit and soul of this mental-emotional dis-ease. I consistently apply the right antidotes to the poison I recognize. This is what working on oneself spiritually means.

Working out such areas of personal weakness, impurities, and imperfections, is not only the dissolution of one's own internal demon, but a banishing from one's life of the external influences of dark and hostile forces that use one's weakness as a way of forming a link to influence and enter one's life. In effect, driving darkness out of oneself, one is assisting to drive darkness out of the world and becoming increasingly more empowered to help others do the same. It cannot be said often enough how important it is to cut off and dispel every link or connection to demonic forces. It is only through incarnate and physical beings that the dark and hostile powers influence and enter into the world.

It is written, "Sin crouches at the door." This indicates the second meaning of this verse, one level of understanding being the gates of the senses: eyes, ears, nose, mouth, and flesh. These are the gates of sin, and watching these gates mindfully allows one to withhold oneself from missing the mark. These are points through which the "brigands" will attempt to enter. By purifying each sense consciousness and keeping vigilant watch over it, one will prevent oneself from falling to the assaults of the klippotic forces. Thus self-knowledge is spiritual self-defense against dark and hostile forces.

If I know that I am going to encounter a person whose heart is bad and who tends toward negativity and draws in demonic influences, or if I must go to a place I know is pervaded by negative energy and the presence of evil spirits, then before going I am wise to consciously prepare and fortify myself and go as a spiritual warrior and exorcist. Prior to going, I may use the middle pillar, the lesser banishing, or some other method, along with prayer, to prepare myself. I will put the holy fire of the Spirit in my sphere of sensation and turn my aura into the diamond light through which no dark or demonic force can enter. In this way, I walk in a mindful fashion and, through Grace, may be empowered to drive out darkness in the situation I find myself in. I walk as a spiritual warrior, which is the meaning of the Master's teaching in this saying.

VERSE 104

They said to Jesus, "Come, let us pray today and let us fast."
Jesus said, "What is the sin I have committed, or wherein
have I been defeated? But when the bridegroom leaves the
bridal chamber, then let them fast and pray."

Here, fasting implies a need for self-purification of some impurity, imperfection, distortion, perversion, hindrance, or obstruction that prevents one's unification with God's presence. The idea of prayer is of a similar meaning in this verse, in that prayer implies some degree of separation from God's presence, whether gross or subtle, and thus a dualistic condition. One who is in a conscious union with the presence of God has no need of fasting or prayer. The purpose of fasting and prayer and all other forms of spiritual practice is unification with God. While there is a conscious communion and unity in God's presence, the need for the spiritual practice is no longer present. For this reason, when Lord Yeshua raises Lazarus from the dead, according to the Gospel of St. John, he says, "Father, I thank you for having heard me. I knew that you always hear me, but I have said this for the sake of the crowd standing here, so that they may believe that you sent me."

In the state of Christ-consciousness, everything transpires by way of a silent and conscious volition, without need for thoughts or words or any outward act. Everything comes into being from within oneself, according to a silent will. This supernal consciousness is beyond the mental, vital, and physical being, though hidden within them, and thus operates by way of the silent will of the Divine I am or supernal being, which is a state of pure radiant awareness. In this state, one's holy soul is inseparable from God and the Godhead that indwells it; one's will is God's Will, and God's Will is one's own. Thus, one's own silent will is God's Will and whatever one wills comes to pass the very instant one wills it. This complete unification of oneself with God is the state of the perfect tzaddik or Master and is called the Realm of No Difference, or the Realm of No More Practice.

This reflects a common mistake of aspirants concerning spiritual practice. Often aspirants grasp onto spiritual practices as though they were the enlightenment experience itself, not understanding that the practices are but methods of entering into the spiritual or mystical experience to which they correspond. While authentic spiritual practices, whether of a mystical or magical nature, are founded upon the enlightenment experience and reflect the experience of an adept or master who has fashioned it, the spiritual practice, in and of itself, is not the enlightenment experience. Thus, engaging in a spiritual practice, one is to use the practice until the experience to which it corresponds dawns for oneself. Once the enlightenment experience dawns, one must let go of the practice and let the experience unfold. It is much like rockets blasting a payload beyond the earth's atmosphere into outer space. As the rocket rises up, the boosters are shed, and, once orbit is attained, the vehicle that launched the payload is completely shed. So it is with the various spiritual practices of our tradition. Once the experience the practice facilitates transpires, the vehicle of the practice is shed. One would only take up the practice again if one finds that one has fallen out of the higher state of consciousness that dawned.

There is another way to say the same thing. An authentic spiritual practice that has been generated from the enlightenment experience transpiring with an adept or master is an expression of that spiritual or mystical experience. However, when the actual experience dawns, the practice is no longer a "practice" but has become the experience itself. In that instant, the practice is shed as the experience occurs. If one clings too tightly to the practice, then the experience it represents cannot unfold. Although this might seem to contradict the former point of the practice not being the experience itself, in truth it is another way of saying the same thing and is equally true. Yeshua makes this point perfectly clear in this verse.

The bridegroom and the bridal chamber imply the bride. These three terms have different levels of meaning. On one level, the bride is the Nefesh, the earthly soul, which is to be united with the bridegroom, which is the Neshamah, the heavenly soul. Ruach is the Spirit or Divine intelligence in us through which the Nefesh and Neshamah are joined together—hence the bridal chamber. On another level, however, the bridal chamber is the holy Neshamah, which here represents the inmost part of the soul in which God and Godhead indwell and through which we are joined to God and the Godhead. The aim of spiritual practice is this unification. As long as the bridegroom is in the bridal chamber united with the bride, there is no need for practice. Only when the bridegroom departs and a sense of separation occurs is there a need for typical spiritual practice.

This verse also suggests the presence of a holy tzaddik with his or her disciples. While the holy tzaddik remains alive and among them, there is a distinct Grace of the living presence and power of which the holy tzaddik serves as a vehicle or channel. While the holy tzaddik is among the disciples, the spiritual life and practice has the quality of a celebration and love-play between the lover and the Beloved. When the holy tzaddik departs, as the life of the tzaddik comes to an end, the texture and nature of the spiritual practice of the disciples changes. It is no longer the celebration and love-play it once was, at least not in the experience of the disciple. There is something quite special about spiritual practice and spiritual life while one's holy tzaddik is alive and with oneself in the physical world—something that cannot be described outside of the experience, any more than the delight of a love affair can be explained outside of the experience. Yeshua is also indicating this state of Grace that exists while the tzaddik remains with the disciples.

I pray that you might know the delight of a love-play with the Beloved, and yet more, the delight of the embrace and mystical union with the Beloved! Amen.

VERSE 105

Jesus said, "He who knows the father and the mother will be called the son of a harlot."

According to conventional wisdom, legitimacy in spiritual matters is determined by academic and religious institutions. Unless one has the right credentials, one will be considered illegitimate and thus will not be recognized as an authority. While sometimes individuals who have the right credentials are taken up and inspired by the Holy Spirit, and are reborn of Mother Wisdom, more often than not those whom the Holy Spirit chooses as her messengers are not individuals of the establishment. Thus, in the eyes of the establishment, they are children of a harlot—illegitimate.

Yeshua himself faced persecution on account of this. He did not receive teachings and initiations from the recognized authorities of his day, the pharisees and scribes, but from elders of an esoteric order and the prophet John the Baptist, who were outside of the establishment. Ultimately, it was the Mother Spirit, the Holy Spirit, from whom he received his education, and from visitation by the spirits of the prophets and holy angels; hence a true and invisible Divine order. In the eyes of the establishment, the Master came out of nowhere. He was accused of being a drunkard, of keeping bad company, of being illegitimate, of heresy, blasphemy, and being demon possessed. So great was the persecution of the establishment that it led to his crucifixion.

The religious institutions of today would tell us that the time of the prophets and apostles of God is long since past, and they teach nothing of mystical prayer, prophetic meditation, or magical ceremony as used by the prophets and apostles. The foolish man who proclaimed "God is dead!" merely echoed the ignorance of the outer and unspiritual church. The spiritual disease of atheism is the product of fundamentalism and dogmatic religion that has lost the keys of the mysteries and true Gnosis of Yeshua Messiah.

Lord Yeshua led a spiritual revolution in his day and, as disciples of the Christos, so too must we be willing to lead a spiritual revolution—a mystical and magical revival of the true faith. It is not from the establishment that we must seek our validation or recognition; it is from the Living Father and Mother Spirit that we must receive our authority. It is not from the outer and unspiritual church that we must seek to receive teachings and initiation, but from the true and invisible Divine order—the interior and Gnostic Church of the Christos. As Lord Yeshua himself and the first apostles, we must seek our empowerment from the Holy Spirit and be willing to face whatever challenge or persecution may arise as we follow in the Way of the Mother Spirit.

Our Father is God Most High, the One Being-consciousness-force, and our Mother is the Holy Spirit, the One Life-power. It is she who reveals to us the face of our Father, and who leads us into all-Truth. It is she who rebirths us according to our supernal and heavenly image and who makes us perfect as our Living Father is perfect. The Father is God and the Godhead transcendent and the Mother is God in creature and Creation. Through her, we know the Father, and knowing our Mother and our Father, Yahweh Elohim (Lord God), we are children of the Light, having true Gnosis. Mother Wisdom, who manifests as understanding, is the virgin mother of all the Christed or enlightened ones.

Now the masters of the tradition tell us the virgin is a whore! It is a proclamation meant to shock us into a deeper understanding of Mother Wisdom. Hearing this, we say, "No! That cannot be! What does this mean?" The meaning is simple: Mother Wisdom is ever virgin, and every time there is gnosis of her, it is as for the first time. Whenever another soul attains enlightenment, it is as though it is the first time enlightenment has dawned in Creation and as though all of the enlightened ones of the past, present, and future have attained in that instant, the one who is an enlightened being inseparable from all the enlightened ones of the past, present, and future. For he or she has recognized and realized Yahweh—that which was, is, and forever shall be—who delivers (Yeheshuah, Yeshua, or Jesus). Yet, Mother Wisdom is a whore, for she refuses no one who seeks to know her or who desires to be intimate with her. To anyone who seeks to know her and who seeks her company (the company of heaven), she unveils herself. So, indeed, she is a virgin and a whore! The one who says the Gnostic is the son or daughter of a whore speaks truth!

There is something more within this saying, for Abba (Father) and Aima (Mother) are the Partzufim of the supernal Sefirot of Hokmah and Binah, wisdom and understanding, respectively. These are the Divine parents of Da'at, the Sefirot of knowledge or true Gnosis. So the Master is saying, "One who has wisdom and understanding will be a true Gnostic."

There is a suggestion of the bridal chamber in this, for as the Zohar teaches us, "a stirring below creates a stirring above." Thus Abba and Aima are united above when the bridegroom and bride are united below. In this instant, the image of the male and female above and the image of the male and female below are joined—hence the generation of Adam Kadmon, the highest of all Partzufim. If the Divine Mother gives birth to this Human One, but the Father is nameless and unknown, is not this Holy Child the child of a harlot?

This alludes to the state of the attainment of supernal being—the second Adam—which is the union of Christ the Logos and Christ the Sophia in One Body of Light. The holy soul entering into this supreme attainment has united the male and female within itself, so that it brings forth everything good from within itself and, thus, gives birth without need of anything outside of itself (hence, without need of an external partner). This is a great mystery that cannot be explained; yet through meditation on this Divine idea, many things are revealed.

This state of supernal being directly relates to the mastery of the three supernal Divine names: Eheieh (I am or I shall be), Yahweh (the force or Life-power; that which was, is, and forever shall be), and Elohim (the one and many, the matrix of Creation or form principle)—

hence, the Gnosis of Creator and Creation. Meditation on these three Divine names, specifically the holy letters composing them, reveals a great deal concerning the supreme mystery of supernal being.

The supreme mystery of supernal being is the recognition and realization of the inmost part of your soul, which is ever at-one and inseparable from God and the Godhead that indwells it. Thus, it is the mystery of Yechidah (the Divine spark or Divine I am) and the Hayyah (Life-power) within the holy Neshamah (supernal or heavenly soul). This is the knowledge that will set you free and through which you will attain the power of the resurrection and ascension—the inmost secret revealed through the person of Yeshua Messiah.

Although I am speaking of the ultimate and supreme attainment of Christ-consciousness, do not be put off or think it something so removed or distant from you. It is not distant at all. Through the Divine incarnation of the soul of the Messiah, this fiery intelligence has been brought down to earth and the Light-seed sown in the human life-wave. To anyone who believes in the Divine incarnation and who makes him or herself open to the baptism of this supernal consciousness-force, the fiery intelligence of the Holy Spirit is granted through the Grace of Yeshua Messiah. Opening and becoming sensitive to the Holy Spirit, she will work within you and through you to accomplish this great transformation.

We receive this Light-transmission through the agency of a holy tzaddik, whether in the physical plane or through the inner planes, but this word "receive" is deceptive. The tzaddik is not giving to us anything that is not already within us. Rather, he or she is like a mirror in which we behold the Light presence that is within us, and thus recognize and realize the Divine presence and power that is our true self. What we receive comes from the inmost part of our holy soul— our spiritual guide, serving to remind us who and what we really are.

In speaking about the Father and the Mother, the Master makes it clear that this is a creative affair and that we ourselves must be creative in the process. No one is going to come and give us anything that we are unwilling to seek and find within ourselves, nor is anyone going to work out our enlightenment and liberation other than ourselves. The Holy Spirit is a creative spirit and this creative power is within us. In the prophetic experience, we have a creative role to play.

When the Holy Spirit moves, she manifests as a creative flow and we must move with her. Only to the degree that we move with her does the prophetic experience unfold. The same is true in the process of unfolding self-realization.

Consider what has been said of the supreme and ultimate attainment of Christ-consciousness. It is a state of supernal being in which one is able to know the truth of things inwardly and to bring forth from within oneself everything good. This means that creativity plays a central role in the enlightenment experience and that enlightenment is not a fixed or static state as one might first conceive it to be. Because, in part, it is a creative affair, one might feel oneself unauthentic or deluded, knowing that to some degree one has conjured something out of nowhere; also, others outside of oneself may well view the creative aspect illegitimate, as though, in the speaking of the Holy Spirit, it is not a two-way conversation in which oneself does not have a part. In the actual experience of a communion with the Christ presence (the Communion of the Saints), one's mind becomes the mind of Christ, one's heart becomes the sacred heart of Christ, and thus one's speech and actions become an expression of the Christ-Spirit or Holy Spirit.

Perhaps, at first, much of our experience is little more than a flight of fantasy, something we ourselves have visualized and created apart from the Holy Spirit. However, it is our creative acts that form a vehicle for the Holy Spirit, and ultimately she will enter into that vehicle and bring it to life if we are willing to cooperate with her. As for the test of what is true or what is false, that really remains to be seen in the fruition of the creative process.

There is a playful and creative element in the prophetic experience, as well as in the process of self-realization. This is a key that is often overlooked, and it would seem that, on one level, the Master is reminding us of this key. How shall I ever evolve to the state of supernal being without a spiritual practice of creatively bringing forth what is within me—hence, living as a creative person in the Spirit? Isn't that a revolutionary idea?!

I pray that you might be empowered as a conscious co-creator and know your validation in the Holy Spirit and, yet more, that you might overcome the dominion of the establishment and experience the delight of freedom in Christ-consciousness! Amen.

VERSE 106

Jesus said, "When you make the two one, you will become the sons of man, and when you say, 'Mountain, move away,' it will move away."

There is a Divine power in us to be awakened, our soul and Divine self. That Divine potential is not far removed from us. It exists within our humanity, and cultivating our humanity, we naturally and spontaneously awaken it. For this reason, we hear the Word of the Lord in the prophets calling us to a worship in Spirit and Truth in a practical way through ethical and moral behavior; for submitting ourselves to ethical and moral behavior, living with sincerity, integrity, and a good heart, is the cultivation of our human spirit. We are called to have concern for and to help the orphan, the widow, and the oppressed; to reach out to the outcast in love and compassion and to seek social justice and freedom for one and all; to concern ourselves with all living souls and to act as caretakers of all creatures, the environment, and the earth— to actively labor for an enlightened human society. All mystical and spiritual practices aside, such cultivation of our humanity for heaven's sake, with faith in God or the potential of enlightenment, naturally serves to awaken the Divine power of our soul and Christ-self. It is this practical spiritual living, coupled with spiritual practices of mystical prayer and prophetic meditation, that Yeshua Messiah taught his disciple as the Way.

The inside and outside must be brought into an integral union, the male and female aspects of ourselves made co-equal and complete in one another, the earthly and heavenly part of our soul united, all fragments of consciousness integrated with the indwelling Christ-self, our authentic individuality in God. The Divine power that flows through us when this unification occurs is unimaginable and beyond description, and so here the Master uses an analogy that indicates something of the incredible power that actually exists in potential within each and every one of us—a power that can do the seemingly impossible.

From other sayings in the gospels, we understand the active agent of this Divine power as faith. It is faith that opens us to Divine possibilities we otherwise might not imagine; it is faith that makes us increasingly more sensitive to the Spirit of God in our lives; and it is faith that creates the conditions necessary for miracles to happen. Faith is the intuition of an experience we have not yet had, and therefore the invocation of that spiritual or mystical experience. Faith is the certainty of things not seen and the awareness that, with God, nothing is impossible. It is a great and awesome magic-power, and a most significant part of what makes us truly human. By nature, a human being is a creature of faith and worship, and until faith is born in us, as with certain other innately human qualities, it may be rightly said that we are not yet human beings in the fullest possible sense. A little faith can move mountains and make great wonders transpire, and through faith, we are redeemed from our ignorance and forgetfulness. One might say that faith is the holy remembrance that we are children of the Light, sons and daughters of the Living God. The Master is speaking of the power of faith to make us authentic individuals and heal every dis-ease—hence, that which gives both peace and joy. Let us keep the faith that we might cleave to life! Amen.

VERSE 107

Jesus said, "The kingdom is like a shepherd who had a hundred sheep. One of them, the largest, went astray. He left the ninety-nine and looked for that one until he found it. When he had gone to such trouble, he said to the sheep, 'I care for you more than the ninety-nine.'"

First, the Holy One is saying that nothing of creation shall be lost. No living soul shall be lost or separated from God forever, but one and all ultimately shall be gathered into the Lord and fulfilled and made complete in the Spirit and Truth. The salvation of Christ is universal; it is inclusive and not exclusive. Every living soul will receive the redemption of the blood of the Lamb of God, although, indeed, many souls will pass through the fires of hell before their redemption comes. The Lord loves the souls that must pass through the purifying forces of hell no less than those of the saints who go straight into heaven. In fact, being moved with boundless compassion for their great suffering, in effect, the Lord's love is yet greater for them than for the saints who never knew such darkness and horror.

Imagine that! No matter how far you go astray or how great your sin, God loves you just as you are—and loving you, God will seek you out and find you and redeem you. Whatever your sin or the darkness that is in you, God loves you and has already forgiven you. You must only turn to God, let go and let be, and so forgive yourself and others as

God forgives you. This is the covenant Christ offers to you, a covenant of forgiveness from sin and liberation from the cosmic forces of ignorance. Whenever you are ready and willing to receive it, the Lord is there waiting for you, to give himself to you and to receive you into himself. This very saying is this promise of redemption the Lord has made to you and to all living souls. What wonderful good news!

While in our mortal folly we might want the enemy, the evil one, to burn in hell for all eternity, it is only our ignorance that thinks like that or would put such words in the mouth of God. Our God is gracious and merciful, and has said through his prophet that even the fallen angels and Lucifer himself shall ultimately be redeemed. Indeed! When the evil inclination passes away into oblivion, the goodness in the fallen will be revealed and the holy sparks restored to their rightful place. It is all a matter of time and evolution from our perspective, yet in the infinite and eternal, it is a present reality, now and always. In the soul of the Messiah, one and all are redeemed!

Perhaps at times you feel there is so much darkness in you that you will never be able to draw close to God and stand in the Light of the presence of God. Nothing could be further from the truth! Let me share a simple secret with you that my teacher shared with me when I confessed such feelings. Your capacity for Darkness is your capacity for the Light. The greater your capacity for the Darkness, the greater your capacity for the Light. It is one and the same capacity, and the moment you turn to God and empty yourself, you will be filled with God's Light and Spirit.

Perhaps you feel you do not have the strength and ability to seek and find the Lord, or that you are so far away from the Lord that you will never reach him, even though you should travel countless lifetimes toward him, but there is another part to this secret. Not only is the Lord ever near to you, as near as the beat of your heart and very breath, it is not you who will find the Lord, but the Lord that will find you. Ask any soul who has found the Lord and they will tell you that it was the Lord who found them and revealed himself to them! We need only have faith in the Holy One of Being and the indwelling Spirit of the Holy One within us.

The Lord is seeking you out and will find you. The Holy Spirit is laboring for your enlightenment and she will lead you to your freedom. This very instant, the Lord is with you, all around you and within you as this Life-power, the living presence. This is the faith the Lord has called us to. Praise the Lord who is ever with us! Amen.

VERSE 108

Jesus said, "He who will drink from my mouth will become like me. I myself will become he, and the things that are hidden will be revealed to him."

To drink from the mouth of the Anointed One implies two things. First, a very deep intimacy, as though the intimacy of a lover to their beloved; and second, an active living and experiencing of the teachings given—hence, living the Word of the Lord. These two things are, in fact, one and the same, for the lover of the Lord will draw near unto the Lord by living his teachings and practicing righteousness, thus becoming more and more like unto the Anointed One. The natural result and climax of such nearness or likeness is that the Anointed One manifests as you. To live the teachings of Christ is to become Christ-like and, yet more, to embody Christ, the Spirit of Christ manifesting through your person. This is the aim of the Gnostic Christian initiate.

The things that are hidden are revealed as one enters ever more deeply into the mystical experience of Christ; this is an obvious truth. Many things can only be revealed through direct spiritual experience. Save within the context of the experience itself (hence, with another person sharing the same experience), these things cannot be communicated. Thus, experience is the basis of initiation. Here, the Master is speaking of the inmost secret initiations that transpire through direct experience of Messianic or supernal consciousness.

This emphasis upon direct personal spiritual experience is the foundation of Gnostic Christianity. By "Gnostic" is meant knowledge acquired through personal and direct spiritual experience. Because of this emphasis, central to the teachings of Gnostic Christianity are methods of spiritual practice, mystical prayer, and prophetic meditation, through which the aspirant may attain some degree of direct experience and so bring their faith to fruit in gnosis of the Christ-Spirit.

VERSE 109

*Jesus said, "The kingdom is like a man who had a [hidden]
treasure in his field without knowing it. And [after] he died he
left it to his [son]. The son [did] not know (about the treasure). He inherited the field and sold [it]. And the one who
bought it went plowing and [found] the treasure. He began to
lend money at interest to whomever he wished."*

One who finds a buried treasure in a field he purchases
will seem to the onlooker to have become wealthy out
of nowhere. It will seem as though, from poverty or an aver-
age state, great wealth has arisen by way of some miracle. Yet
he will know how he has come into his wealth. It is the same
with a holy tzaddik. He or she seems to come out of nowhere
and to bring forth a wealth of wisdom, understanding, and
knowledge of the Holy Scriptures and spiritual matters from
thin air. Yet that treasure from which they draw is within him
or herself from the indwelling presence and power of God.

It is amazing and seems like a miracle only so long as that
same treasure remains hidden within ourselves and we have
not discovered it. What we see with the tzaddikim and maggidim is within each and everyone of us. We need only bring
it forth from within ourselves, as they have brought it forward, in order to experience the spiritual wealth.

A holy tzaddik, one who has brought forward his or her
soul and Divine self, can share something of that wealth with

us. Under the right conditions, they can demonstrate something of the Divine presence and power and even facilitate a direct spiritual experience, but such blessings are like a loan that we must pay back. We must integrate and actualize what we have received to the extent that we also can share and give of that Light to others, not only being elevated by our tzaddik, but also elevating our holy tzaddik and others. This is the interest we owe to the holy one who teaches and initiates us so that the Light-transmission remains alive and continues beyond our teacher.

Let us bear in mind that in the fruit of a tree are the seeds of the next generation. Receiving, may we be empowered to share and give what we have received and so fulfill the cycle of initiation. Amen.

VERSE 110

Jesus said, "Whoever finds the world and becomes rich, let him renounce the world."

Renunciation of the world means very little to one who has had no success in the world and desires to escape living life on account of his or her perceived poverty, failings, and inadequacy, but renunciation on the basis of such self-consciousness and insecurity has little or no meaning and cannot lead to anything noble or good. In fact, much of what motivates renunciation of the world could easily be called cowardice! However, the authentic spiritual aspirant seeking to become a servant of the Lord and spiritual warrior is anything but a coward. Rather, the soul that seeks the mystical path must be strong, courageous, and driven to success, whether in mundane or supramundane pursuits.

"I renounce the presidency of the United States of America in order to seek God for the sake of heaven!" How can I renounce what I do not have and never have had a real chance to obtain? Indeed, I can renounce nothing that I do not have in my own experience. Just the same, I must have a life to surrender it to God. It is as though the Master is saying, "Get a life so that you have something to offer up to God."

Let us consider more closely the meaning of renunciation. It does not mean that we avoid, abandon, escape, or deny anything. It is not a self-denial of any sort, at least not of the kind that considers the denial of the enjoyment of life somehow more holy. No. Renunciation simply means letting go and no longer viewing things as one's own personal possessions. It means no longer grasping at whatever is renounced as a means of feeding and sustaining egotism. It is about renouncing the false claim of ownership over people, places, and things—and even more, renouncing ownership of subtle objects such as thoughts and feelings and so forth. In this sense, whatever we have is to be renounced, and what must be renounced is different for each individual. Everyone has different things in life to let go of and offer up.

Interestingly enough, such renunciation leads to greater enjoyment of everything in one's experience of life and increased freedom to be oneself.

We may also speak of renunciation in terms of letting go of our limited world view, cherished beliefs, preconceptions, preconditions, and expectations, all the things that obstruct us from seeing reality or God as it is. Hence, renunciation is a term for the emptying of oneself so that one might be Spirit-filled. These are the two ways we understand renunciation in the teachings.

VERSE 111

Jesus said, "The heavens and the earth will be rolled up in your presence. And the one who lives from the living one will not see death." Does not Jesus say, "Whoever finds himself is superior to the world"?

I s it apocalyptic horror or apocalyptic delight that I will experience at the hour of my departing from this world? Bear in mind that the word apocalypse means "revelation." It all depends upon that with which I have identified myself and from which I have lived my life. At the time of death, in the experience of dying, during one stage apocalyptic visions arise in consciousness of the heavens and earth being destroyed and devoured by fire, and for the individual, it is as though the whole world is passing away. In that one's Nefesh is departing the world, for oneself the world is actually ceasing to exist. In death, the world one has known no longer exists for one's soul. If one is attached to anything of this world, or one's self-identity is based only on things of this world, then such a vision could only be a dread and horrible thing. Yet for one who is not attached to this world or anything in it, that same vision could be a blissful experience of liberation. It would all depend on one's point of view, whether founded on ignorance or on the enlightenment experience of one's Neshamah (Divine nature).

I cannot say what my experience in the hour of my death will be. I do not know, any more than I know when that hour will come for me, but I can labor now to dissolve my self-identity with name and form and things of the world and to generate a new self-identity with my Neshamah (bornless Divine nature) and the Christ-Spirit. I can engage in spiritual practice to develop a continuity of consciousness throughout all states of consciousness in my present experience. In other words, consciously living in Christ, I can prepare myself to consciously die in Christ-consciousness. If I die in Christ while I am alive, then death will not be death to me, but rather a transition to a higher plane of existence that is experienced as an awakening and liberation. It is this possibility the Master is pointing out, as he often does in his teachings. If we come to understand the deeper levels of the mystery of crucifixion, we will realize that death never existed, but rather that what we call death is a divine revelation—the revelation of the Divine presence and power of God within and beyond us. I would have to say that this is good news, considering how deeply we dread death! Praise the Lord for the divine revelation!

VERSE 112

Jesus said, "Woe to the flesh that depends upon the soul, woe to the soul that depends on the flesh."

The soul of which the Master is speaking is the Nefesh, the bestial or earthly soul. This part of the soul is the personality and life display, and it is the astral matrix within and behind the body and life. Unless the Nefesh is joined to Neshamah through the agency of Ruach (higher intelligence), just as the material body decomposes following death, so also does the Nefesh disintegrate and return to the basic elements of which it was formed. The body, which depends upon Nefesh, decomposes, and the Nefesh, which is dependent on the body, disintegrates at the time of death.

At the outset of this holy gospel, it was said, "Whoever finds the interpretation of these sayings will not experience death." That is to say that they will acquire the knowledge of how to unite their Nefesh with their Neshamah so that, at the time of death, they will experience a continuity of conscious existence and be empowered to rise into a higher plane of existence—hence attain one degree or another of the kingdom of heaven. However, to not experience death has a greater implication than the attainment of one of the heavens. It is written, "The heavens and the earth will pass away . . ." Thus, the ultimate attainment of Christ-consciousness is beyond the heavens. It is the attainment of the world of Supernal Light, which marks the end of the need for incarnation in the material world, the true attainment of eternal life.

Understanding this, the term "salvation" takes on its true meaning, for one understands that it is one's Nefesh and Ruach that is in need of salvation from the endless cycles of transmigration, which, until these are joined to the holy Neshamah, remain in bondage. This also reveals the meaning of Divine rapture, for when one joins one's Nefesh and Ruach to one's Neshamah, embodying the holy Neshamah in full, then at the conclusion of that life the Nefesh and Ruach are taken up and integrated into the Neshamah, essentially attaining an eternal existence. Neshamah is the bornless and Divine nature—the secret and undying soul—and when Neshamah is attained there is no more death; hence no more breaks in the continuity of one's conscious existence.

There are many grades of the Neshamah corresponding to the four universes (Atzilut, Beriyah, Yetzirah and Asiyah) and the universe of Adam Kadmon, which is the unity of the four. At the highest level, the holy Neshamah is at-one with the soul of the Messiah, and thus is an individual manifestation of the Messiah, which is to say supernal being. When the teachings speak of salvation through the Grace of Yeshua Messiah, what is meant is this: through the mystery of the Divine incarnation, the truth of our holy Neshamah and the Christ-self is revealed, so that, in the person of Yeshua Messiah, one has an image of one's supernal self. Living according to that Divine image or Divine idea, the grasp of cosmic ignorance is dispelled and one is empowered to consciously evolve toward that noble ideal and thus work out one's salvation. If this image was not revealed through the person of the holy Master, one would not know to direct the creative Spirit in oneself toward that holy fruition, but would remain ignorant of one's soul of Light and thus bound to aimless wandering through countless cycles of transmigration. The Grace imparted through Yeshua Messiah is the gnosis of the soul of Light and Christ-self.

Belief in the Divine incarnation takes on new meaning once we understand this, for it is more than merely belief in the incarnation of the Christos in Yeshua; it is faith in one's own soul of Light and Christ-self. To believe and be baptized means a progressive shedding of one's old and unenlightened self-identity, and putting on a new self in Christ—hence the generation of a self-identity with one's holy soul and Christ-self. One's soul of Light and Christ-self is, indeed, the only Way, Truth, and Life, and without it, one's Nefesh and Ruach cannot be delivered from their bondage.

In the gnostic view, while this material universe is the matrix through which we realize our soul of Light, the holy soul has not come from the material universe nor this world but from the universe of Supernal Light, which is "nearness to God" (Atzilut). The root-essence of that holy soul comes from a universe beyond Atzilut, called Adam Kadmon (primordial human being or soul of Messiah). While life-forms through which this soul of Light and Divine spark is realized come from the natural order, the soul of Light comes from a Divine order.

An esoteric teaching in Gnosticism proposes that the soul of Light only descends upon an earthly soul when the earthly soul has refined itself to a sufficient degree so as to be a holy vessel that is capable of receiving the influx of Supernal Light—hence, the terms "profane," "faithful," and "elect." The profane or ordinary individual represents an earthly soul that has not evolved to the point of receiving the soul of Light destined for it, and thus lives devoid of the influence of the soul of Light, often being referred to as a "child of Darkness" on account of this. The faithful person is an earthly soul who is beginning to receive something of the influence of the holy soul—one in whom the Divine spark is awakening and who is actualizing this Divine potential. The elect person is one who has received the fiery intelligence of his or her holy soul and embodies one grade or another of the holy soul. Those who have the influence of their holy soul or who embody something of their holy soul are called the "sons and daughters of Light."

By these terms, the Gnostic is not preaching a doctrine of elitism, but rather acknowledges three distinct realms of the development and evolution of souls. These three realms in the evolution of souls are clearly reflected in the world by those who have no inclination or interest to spiritually seek, those who seek only on the outer or exoteric level, and those who seek on the inner or esoteric level—one's own desire to receive reflecting the development and evolution of one's soul-being. The elect are, thus, individuals in whom something of the mystical inclination has sparked and are naturally drawn to the inner tradition in one form or another.

While we speak of a labor of the soul through which development and evolution has taken place, one has merely created the conditions for the reception of a gift of the fiery intelligence (influence of the soul of Light). In truth, this gift is a manifestation of Divine Grace and, in the experience of the Gnostic initiate, is not the product of anything he or she has done. It is something that naturally and spontaneously happens in the development and evolution of the soul-being, and thus appears as a gift from above or something of a Divine election, hence, the terms "elect" or "chosen."

Here, the Master speaks of the state of the profane individual and alludes to the blessing upon the faithful and elect. Far from being elite, the elect, as elder brothers and sisters, are responsible for their younger siblings; more than a personal salvation, the labor of the elect in the great work is to help others create the conditions through which they also will receive the Divine gift of the fiery intelligence. Thus, the Master is speaking of the need for the faithful and the elect to act as Light-bearers, sowing seeds of Light in the collective human consciousness. A saying such as this is not meant to create elitism, but rather is meant to remind one of the plight of souls who are as yet in bondage, and to invoke compassion. If one were to see a person trapped, suffering, and in danger of losing their life, would one look down on that person or would one do everything possible to comfort that person and preserve his or her life?

This awareness is very important to anyone who is venturing into the study of esoteric teachings or who seeks to be an initiate. All too often, the realization of various levels or grades of spiritual evolution is allowed to create an egoistic elitism, which is something arrogant, prideful, and self-righteous. It can go so far as a disdain or hatred of others whom the would-be initiate considers inferior to him or herself. One must recognize this tendency as a falling to the other side or the dark side and not allow it. The principle of an elitism of the "elect" represents the path of those who are dark magicians, and not the path of the mystics and magicians of the Light, as Yeshua Messiah.

I pray that you receive the gift of the fiery intelligence of the Holy Spirit and your soul of Light, and that you are empowered in your journey by the sacred heart of Christ! Amen.

VERSE 113

His disciples said to him, "When will the kingdom come?"

Jesus said, "It will not come by waiting for it. It will not
be a matter of saying 'here it is' or 'there it is'. Rather the
kingdom of the father is spread out upon the earth, and men
do not see it."

Unenlightened humanity talks about longing for peace
and yet is always preparing to go to war, talks about a
desire for social justice and then oppresses the poor and fa-
vors the wealthy, talks about the need for more consciousness
with regard to the environment but then continues to exploit
and poison it, talks about an interest in a change in human
consciousness and yet refuses to actually labor to bring about
a change in consciousness—and so it is with so many things.
It is as though we do not really understand that, if we want a
greater good in the world, it is we who must bring it about.
This is even reflected in many religious teachings concerning
the kingdom of heaven and the Second Coming. We want to
see the kingdom of heaven upon earth and are waiting for
Jesus to bring it, but do little or nothing to bring forth the
Divine kingdom from within ourselves!

Many good Christians actually believe that the kingdom
of heaven will come without any effort on humanity's part to
manifest it, but this could not be further from the truth! All
one has to do is study the prophets and the stories of attempts to bring about a more enlightened society in the form

of the Promised Land and Jerusalem. While God had one thing in mind, humankind had something else in mind, and so Jerusalem (the City of Peace) could not stand. God had one intention; human beings had another. Therefore, God's intention could not be fully manifest. Should we then assume that the kingdom of heaven and New Jerusalem will manifest without some human effort and cooperation? There is a saying, "Continuing to do the same thing, but expecting a different result, is insanity!"

"The kingdom of heaven is spread out upon the earth," which is to say it is possible in this world. "But men do not see it," which is to say that human beings do not envision it and labor to bring it into substantial being. "It will *not* come by waiting for it;" hence, unless the Divine vision is recognized as possible, envisioned, and enacted, it will not come to pass. On the literal level, the teaching could not be any clearer!

One cannot go out and change the world or save the world or heal the world all by oneself. Even Yeshua Messiah could not instantly transform the entire collective consciousness of humanity. However, the truth is that the collective consciousness can be and is influenced by individuals, and when it is transformed, it is through the transformation of the consciousness of the individuals that compose the collective. This means that, if you bring about a transformation within your own consciousness, it contributes to the transformation of the collective consciousness. When a sufficient number of individuals transform their own consciousness and labor together for the sake of the kingdom of heaven, the Divine kingdom is manifest among them. If this were to transpire in a larger segment of humanity, the collective human consciousness would be transformed. This is the aim of the great work in this world.

One cannot simply go out and change the world, but one can labor for a radical change in one's own consciousness, and one can work with others to bring about such a change. Here, we find the need for both the spiritual individual and the spiritual community in the great work. There is a real power in the individual, and there is a greater power in a group of individuals. This verse suggests that it is important that we understand this creative power and consciously direct it according to a noble ideal, specifically, a Divine humanity and Divine kingdom.

There are layers of esoteric teachings behind this practical teaching. There is a clear statement that the kingdom of heaven exists and is present in the same space as this world—which suggests worlds within worlds, universes within universes, all existing in the same space at the same time, although in different dimensions. This is exactly what teachings of the four universes and inner planes in the Gnostic Kabbalah is proposing. The world or universe of Supernal Light is within and all around us, as are all universes, worlds, or realms of sentient existence. The heavens, the earths, and the hells are all right here, whether or not we are conscious of them! To experience a higher plane of existence, one merely needs to generate a body of consciousness that corresponds to it.

Lord Yeshua is essentially saying, "When you have a body of consciousness that corresponds to the Divine kingdom, you will see that the kingdom exists in the same space as this good earth." In this regard, you will recall the sixth Beatitude, "Blessed are the pure in heart, for they will see God" (Matthew 5:8). The experience of unification with God and the experience of the kingdom of heaven is a state of consciousness—a state of mind and heart and life. In terms of the world of Supernal Light, it is an experience of a state of consciousness beyond the physical, vital, or mental levels, hence, a metamind or supramental state.

Human society or the world directly reflect the state of consciousness of the individuals forming the collective. Thus, in effect, the world that we experience is the radiance of our own consciousness or is created by our state of consciousness. In truth, the reality we experience and our state of consciousness are completely interconnected. Therefore, to change the reality of our experience, we need to bring about a corresponding change in our consciousness. Mystical attainment means a conscious unification with God; magical attainment means a change in consciousness, which brings about a corresponding change in reality or manifestation. Obviously, one cannot exactly separate the mystical attainment from the magical attainment, or speak of divine acts of magic devoid of mystical aspiration. A divine magic is inherently mystical—the prophet or apostle is a Divine magician.

Here, in this saying, the Master is encouraging his disciples, not only in a mystical attainment, but also is teaching them fundamental principles of a divine magic and encouraging them in the magical act. He is essentially saying that, by nature, consciousness is magical and that, if one understands the principles of consciousness, which are the principles of magic, one will be empowered to transform the reality of one's life into something of the Divine kingdom. One may wonder at the use of the terms "magic" or "magical," yet one need only consider the various miracles performed by Yeshua Messiah and by his disciples. These miracles reflect the knowledge of a magical science or art in his teachings, and rather than belief in miracles, Gnostic initiates believe in a science and art of divine magic through which radical changes in the matrix of reality are possible. As much as a mystic or prophet, Yeshua was a highly skilled magician. Thus, Gnostics seek to develop a magical art as part of their process of self-realization. The power of the Holy Spirit is a magic-power!

What is the nature of a divine magic? It is having the same intention in one's own mind as God, and thus an invocation of the Divine powers through which the Divine kingdom is manifest.

VERSE 114

Simon Peter said to them, "Let Mary leave us, for women are
not worthy of life."

Jesus said, "I myself shall lead her, so that she too may
become a living spirit resembling you males. For every woman
who will make herself male will enter into the kingdom of
heaven."

Those few who have reached out to comment on the
Gospel of St. Thomas have typically explained this verse
away, essentially denying its value and authenticity as an essential part of these wisdom teachings. However, they have
not studied the esoteric wisdom deeply or received the esoteric teachings from an initiate that would reveal the inner
meaning of this verse, and thus they speak in ignorance regarding it. The very fact that the apostle who wrote these
sayings down used this saying to close the Gospel should
make it clear that its inclusion was purposeful and that the
inner meaning is important to the overall teachings presented
in the Gospel.

First, this saying reveals the tension and opposition that always exists between the conventional wisdom of unenlightened society and the transcendental Wisdom of God. In the
days of the Master, society held women in low esteem, to
such a severe point that we might say that women were held
in contempt. Women of ancient Palestine, as in many Middle

Eastern countries to this day, had no legal rights of their own apart
from men and, likewise, had no authority in public or state domain.
Thus, if the spiritual and religious domain was greater than the social
and state domain, then women certainly could not have any spiritual
or religious authority either. Therefore, it was unheard of that women
should study the inner tradition of esoteric wisdom, let alone be received as a disciple and receive teachings and initiation directly from
a holy master. Conventional wisdom of the day forbade it. Yet there is
clear evidence that the Master nevertheless taught and initiated women—the Samaritan woman whom he met at the well and to whom
he taught the Gospel being a fine example.

Spiritually, however, the argument against women has no basis. In
reality, the holy soul has no gender association or distinction. Within
the holy soul, there is the potential of male and female alike; yet the
holy soul is neither male nor female. Thus, spiritually, there is no difference between men and women, as they are fundamentally the same
in the inmost part of their holy soul and are co-equal in Spirit. As our
life comes from our soul, it stands to reason that this equality plays itself out on spiritual, psychic, and physical levels. What differences
there may be complement one another, and underlying our differences, there is a sameness, and thus a co-equality, both on earth and
in heaven. Although the Master understood this, the society in which
he lived did not, and many of his disciples did not either. The conventional wisdom of his time contradicted the Wisdom of God.
Therefore, the teachings of the Master contradicted those of the society in which he lived.

Only now, in some of our modern societies, are we seeing a slow
change in this area of conventional wisdom. If we want to understand
how fierce an opposition there would have been to this change in the
time of Master Yeshua, we might merely consider the fierce opposition against equal rights for gay and lesbian peoples in our societies
and spiritual communities today—an opposition that often goes so far
as grave persecution, and even murder, to which no real justice is typically rendered. Hence, conventional wisdom remains ignorant and
unenlightened. On this level, the Master is saying to his disciples that
they cannot follow in the way of the conventional wisdom of society

and seek a true enlightenment. Rather, they must generate more enlightened spiritual communities founded upon the greater Wisdom of God—the Divine Wisdom of love and compassion.

The Way of enlightenment is opposite to the way of unenlightened society. You must separate yourself from herd consciousness and sojourn in the opposite direction of unenlightened society in order to realize Christ-consciousness in yourself. Once having realized something of a higher consciousness, you must then labor to enlighten your society and to bring about a greater good.

In regard to making the female male, one must understand that, in the holy Kabbalah, terms of gender have a different meaning and intent than they do in mundane terminology. In the Kabbalah, female means receptivity and receiving, and male means sharing, imparting, or giving. Obviously, the two are interdependent and interconnected to the extent that one cannot exist without the other. In fact, they represent two distinct operations of the same capacity.

The novice disciple or initiate, according to the Kabbalah, is female. In the beginning of the path, he or she has only the desire to receive for him or herself alone and is not yet capable of imparting the teachings and initiations. The novice must first receive the teachings and initiations, and then bringing forth the Light and Spirit from within him or herself, he or she will become male, which is to say, able to share and impart what he or she has received. Thus, every novice disciple or initiate is female, and, as he or she progresses in the path, becomes male. This statement of Master Yeshua applies to both men and women and, in this light, takes on whole new levels of meaning.

In terms of Christian Gnosticism, there is much more to be said of this saying of the Master. The Christian Gnostic initiate of the Sophian Tradition believes that St. Mary Magdalene was more than a disciple, that she was the consort and wife of Lord Yeshua. Not only does the Sophian Tradition view her as a spiritual consort and wife, but views her as the holy bride, co-equal and co-divine with Lord Yeshua (the bridegroom). He embodies Christ the Logos (Word) and she embodies Christ the Sophia (Wisdom). The holy mother is the personification of primordial or uncreated Wisdom; the holy bride is the personification of created Wisdom. Hence, they are representations of the holy Shekinah above and below, respectively. Through Sophia (Mother and Daughter Wisdom), Logos (Son of God) is revealed and made known.

In the same way that one's holy soul is neither male or female and yet has the potential of both male and female within it, so is the soul of the Messiah neither male or female, yet has within it the capacity of the male and the female—hence, Logos and Sophia, the Spiritual Sun of God. Thus, in the Gnostic view, save that the soul of the Messiah is revealed through both male and female form, the revelation of the soul of the Anointed is incomplete. Although the embodiment of Logos in Yeshua Messiah was accepted by all the disciples, the embodiment of Sophia in St. Mary Magdalene was accepted by only a few of the disciples. Thus, in the First Coming of the Messiah, the Logos was accepted and the Sophia was rejected, so that the full revelation of the Christos is as yet incomplete in the gnostic view. Christ must come again in a woman's form to complete the divine revelation.

In the Gnostic Tradition, it is believed that redemption of humanity as a whole will not be complete until womanhood is also fully redeemed, and man and woman stand as co-equal in the Spirit—a possibility that only now in our own times is beginning to be realized. As much as having faith in Lord Yeshua, Gnostic initiates feel that faith in Lady Mary is equally important. According to the tradition, the incarnation of the soul of the Messiah in a woman will be central to the Second Coming of Christ in glory—specifically, a reincarnation of the soul of St. Mary Magdalene.

The soul of Yeshua Messiah ascended into repose in the Living Father, but it is said that the soul of Kallah Messiah (Mary Magdalene) remains with us in the world. As yet not having been accepted and received in full, she continues to incarnate in a woman's form from one generation to another, and will continue to do so until the time of the Second Coming. She will embody the soul of the Messiah, and she will unite herself with the bridegroom in one Body of Light, perfecting the manifestation of the second Adam, male and female restored to primordial unity. When the Lord speaks of our becoming "like unto the angels," it is this state of union of the male and female within ourselves that he alludes to. Such is the nature of a supernal state of being.

The true nature of the Second Coming is something more than the incarnation of the Christos in a woman. It is a dawn of Christ-consciousness in a sufficient number of individuals to effect a radical transformation in the collective human consciousness. The association of the true Church of Christ with the Holy Bride alludes to this, and it is through Christ the Sophia that it will come to pass. By nature, true womanhood is the matrix of Christ-consciousness; the enlightened woman has the innate power to spontaneously transmit the Spirit and Light to others, thus bringing about the dawn of Christ-consciousness in a larger segment of humanity. Whereas, with Christ the Logos, select individuals receive the Light-transmission, with Christ the Sophia, groups of individuals will receive the Light-transmission. With the presence of the Holy Bride, they will have the Divine power to bring about the great transformation.

Outside of a relatively few esoteric circles, the mysteries of the Holy Bride are not known. Very few are aware of she who is the apostle of the apostles, let alone know of her role in the holy gospel and the ultimate fruition of the divine revelation. As this saying indicates, even among the disciples of Master Yeshua, many did not believe in the co-divinity of the Bridegroom and Holy Bride or understand the greater and supreme mystery of the bridal chamber in the Second Coming. Here began the division between the orthodox and Gnostic Christians, which continues to this very day.

If reception is only complete in imparting, then the incarnation of Christ the Sophia in St. Mary Magdalene was incomplete. A sufficient number of individuals receiving the Sophian aspect of the Light-transmission is integral to the full embodiment of the soul of the Messiah in a woman's form. Christ the Sophia waits the holy day of her full reception when she will be able to complete her divine labor in humanity and bring the divine revelation of the Christos to fruition. Believing in her, as we believe in Yeshua Messiah, inviting her and welcoming her, we labor with the Holy Bride to bring about the holy day of her reception when the mystery of the bridal chamber shall be fully disclosed in Divine rapture.

Many would listen and hear these teachings on St. Mary Magdalene and consider them blasphemy or as something inspired by the devil. Isn't that exactly the accusations that the pharisees made of Lord Yeshua, and why they sought to put him to death? The only real devil is ignorance, and it is clear that ignorance still dominates this world. How else could it be that so many believe in Christ incarnate as a man, but are not able to accept Christ incarnate as a woman? Tokenism abounds in some churches that include the Holy Mother in their worship! It is fine to pray to the Holy Mother, but to consider her equal to Lord Yeshua is unacceptable, let alone to consider Christ the Sophia incarnate in the person of Lady Mary Magdalene. Our gospel must address this disbalance between the Divine masculine and Divine feminine and restore God the Mother and the Holy Bride to their rightful place as co-equals with God the Father and the Son. How else shall we ever come into the Gnosis of God Most High, beyond all duality such as gender, or attain a state of non-dual Gnostic awareness without first realizing an equality of male and female? In the view of Gnostic preachers, the point of this necessity cannot be made strongly enough!

Many books could be written imparting the teachings of the holy bride, which are present in the Sophian Tradition of Gnosticism, but what has been said should suffice to open this saying of Yeshua to you and give you some insight of the inner levels of meaning Gnostic initiates find within it. Contemplation along these lines will bring you more insight. Through meditation upon the Holy Bride herself, you may well find that she comes to you in dreams and visions and inspirations.

May the Divine fullness of the Messiah grow and increase, and may the advent of the Second Coming be swift in arriving! Let us all pray that more and more women enter into the living apostolic succession, so that, as co-equals, male and female apostles might invoke the new dispensation of the Holy Spirit and truly bring about a new age! Amen.

GLOSSARY

Adam Kadmon: Primordial human being; the fifth Kabbalistic universe; the union of the four Kabbalistic universes; the source of the essence of human souls; associated with the soul of the Messiah.

Ain: No-Thing or No-Thingness; a term for God in the Kabbalah; an indication of the nature of God; the emptiness which is at the same time Divine fullness; the transcendence of God and Godhead.

Ain Sof: The infinite; a term for God in the Kabbalah; an indication of the nature of God; the infinite and eternal potential; the unmanifest; another aspect of the transcendence of God and Godhead.

Ain Sof Aur: Endless Light; a term for God in the Kabbalah; an indication of the nature of God; the One Being-consciousness-force transcendent.

Apostle: One in whom the Light presence dwells and who is able to initiate others. See Tau and Tzaddik.

Archon or Ruler: A Titanic cosmic force; sometimes refers to what could be called arch demons.

Asiyah: Universe of making; the fourth Kabbalistic universe following Yetzirah; the physical or material universe and manifestation of cosmic forces in it.

Atzilut: Universe of nearness or emanation; the highest of the four Kabbalistic universes; associated with the Divine names of God, the element of fire and archetypes.

Baptism: A specific Gnostic ceremony of initiation; the experience of mystical death and rebirth—hence, ultimately, an inner event in consciousness. There is a baptism of water, fire, and the Holy Spirit, and each is distinct, having a correspondence to the three grades of Christ-consciousness.

Beriyah: Universe of Creation; the second Kabbalistic universe following Atzilut; associated with the archangels and cosmic forces of Creation.

Binah: Understanding; the third Sefirah; corresponds to God's principle of Life-form; the Holy Mother (Aima); the Divine name Elohim or Yahweh Elohim (God or Lord God); the archangel Tzaphkiel and the angelic order of thrones.

Bridal Chamber: A specific Gnostic ceremony of initiation; a Gnostic mass; the holy soul through which one is united with God and Godhead; the mystical body of the bridegroom and holy bride in union; a certain form of spiritual practice in Gnostic Christianity involving the mysteries of the Arayot; a term in Gnosticism for the attainment through which true Gnosis comes. See True Gnosis.

Chrism: Anointing; a specific Gnostic ceremony of initiation; a ceremony of anointing through which healing and spiritual power is conveyed.

Christ-Consciousness: A metamind or supramental state of consciousness; a state of consciousness beyond cosmic consciousness which is supernal; a state of non-dual Gnostic awareness or pure radiant awareness or primordial awareness. While cosmic consciousness is a gradation of Christ-consciousness, the full attainment of Christ-consciousness is something more according to the experience of the masters of the tradition.

Cosmic Consciousness: The state of universal mind; the peak of mental being; the threshold to the attainment of Messianic or Christ-consciousness, which is beyond mental being, hence, supramental or supernal.

Cosmic Forces of Ignorance: Most common terms for Archons in Sophian Tradition; cosmic forces manifest through ignorance or partial or imperfect knowledge—includes both titanic forces and demonic forces.

Cosmic Ignorance: Most common term for the Demiurgos in Sophian Tradition; a power in Creation through which involution and gradation comes into being; the principle of cosmic restriction and death; the principles through which evil comes into being in Creation; the cause of dualistic consciousness and the appearance of a dualistic universe.

Da'at: Knowledge; this holy Sefirah appears when Keter is absorbed into Ain Sof Aur; maintaining the number ten, and represents a hidden dimension of Tiferet. It is also said to be Yesod in another dimension than the Tree of Life immediately appears—hence the next higher universe from the one in which it is experienced. It is a mysterious Sefirah that would require too great a space to properly explain; however, here we can say it is the Sefirah of Gnosis.

Day of Reckoning: The day of one's death; but also the time of the advent of Messianic consciousness on earth.

Demiurgos or **Demiurge:** Cosmic ignorance; cosmic illusion power; the great beast; false creator (false conceptions of God); cosmic egotism. Sometimes this term is used synonymously with Samael or Satan (the "evil one," the "enemy," "adversary," or "opponent"), but often cosmic evil is seen as a product of the Demiurge having a relative reality of its own.

Divine Mother (Aima): The immanent aspect of God.

Divine Order of Melchizedek: The universal order from which all Wisdom Traditions derive their inspiration—the source of all enlightenment teachings.

Elect: This term applies to one who has received the gift of the fiery intelligence; the baptism of the Holy Spirit and who has acquired some gnosis through the Grace of the Spirit (inner initiates).

Esoteric: Something understood only by a few or something secret; hence, esoteric wisdom.

Eucharist: A specific Gnostic ceremony of initiation; a talisman of bread and wine representing the Divine presence and power and consumed in Gnostic worship.

Evil: Denotes negative thoughts, feelings/emotions, or dark imaginings that are enacted in speech and deed (actions performed in ignorance).

Faithful: This term applies to both the religious person and to the spiritual person in whom something of the mystical inclination has sparked (outer initiates).

Gevurah: Severity; rigor or judgment; the fifth Sefirah; corresponds to God's power of purification and revelation; the Divine name Elohim Givor (God of strength or power or might); the archangels Kamael and Samael, and the angelic order of Seraphim (fiery serpents).

Gnostic: One who has acquired some degree of gnosis or who is an aspirant seeking gnosis—hence, one who knows or seeks to know through direct spiritual or mystical experience. Specifically, one who seeks enlightenment and liberation through a conscious unification with God.

Gospel: Literally, "good news." Esoterically, it is the path to self-realization or enlightenment—the enlightenment teaching and experience.

Hayyah: Life-force or Life-power; the glory or power of the Yechidah. See Yechidah.

Heavenly or **Living Father** (Abba): The transcendental aspect of God.

Hesed: Mercy; the fourth Sefirah; corresponds to God's abundant blessings and Grace; the Divine name El (God); the Archangel Tzadkiel, and the angelic order of Hashmalim (speaking silences).

Hod: Splendor or submission; the eighth Sefirah; corresponds to God's glory within Creation; the Divine name Elohim Tzabaot (God of Hosts or God of Spirits); the Archangel Michael, and the angelic order of Beni Elohim (sons of God).

Hokmah: Wisdom; the second Sefirah; corresponds to God's principle of Life-force; the Holy Father (Abba); the Divine name Yah or Yahweh (Lord); the archangel Ratziel, and the angelic order of Ophanim (wheels).

Holy Spirit: Ruach Ha-Kodesh; a threefold Spirit; the Spirit of the prophets, Spirit of the initiates, and Spirit of the Messiah—three degrees of the enlightenment experience. It is the active power of the Divine presence, and at times is used to denote the serpent power in individuals; what in the Eastern schools is called Kundalini. The Holy Spirit and holy Shekinah in Gnostic Tradition bear much the same meaning as Shakti in Eastern Traditions. The Holy Spirit is the feminine power of the Divine.

Husks of Darkness: See Klippot.

Initiation: A ceremony (or other circumstances) through which an adept or master of the tradition is able to transmit something of his or her spiritual experience and power to others. An experience through which an aspirant is brought into a new level of consciousness and spiritual power or a new degree of enlightenment by an adept or master (incarnate or disincarnate), or directly by the Holy Spirit. A shared spiritual experience among initiates in which one or more is brought into a new level of awareness or a spiritual mystery is revealed. (There are many forms of initiation and initiation can transpire in many ways.)

Kabbalah: To receive; that which is received; the tradition; the mystical tradition of Judaism, which Sophian Gnosticism views as the heart of the teachings of Jesus.

Keter: Crown; the first Sefirah of the Tree of Life; corresponds to God's Will or desire; the Divine name Eheieh (I am or I shall be); the archangel Metatron, and the angelic order of Hayyot He-Kodesh (holy living creatures).

Klippah (singular): See Klippot.

Klippot (plural): Fragments of the vessels or structures left over from former cosmic cycles of creation in which sparks of the Divine Light are trapped; a Kabbalistic term indicating cosmic ignorance and cosmic forces of ignorance; also a term specifically referring to evil and unclean spirits or forces of evil.

Logos: The Word of God; the male aspect of the Christos; the generative or creative force of God; the aspect of the soul of the Messiah embodied in Lord Yeshua.

Ma'aseh Bereshit: Work of Creation; knowledge of the mysteries of Creation; the Divine powers of Creation and God the Creator. It also suggests the first part of spiritual practice, which is the generation of a vehicle for direct spiritual or mystical experience; the term "ma'aseh merkavah" denoting the experience itself. See ma'aseh merkavah in relationship to this term.

Ma'aseh Merkavah: Work of the Chariot; the actual spiritual or mystical experience of which the holy Kabbalah speaks; knowledge and experience of inner dimension of Creation, along with the realms and worlds of the inner dimensions and beings-forces that dwell in them, and may include visions of the Divine image; knowledge of how to generate prophetic states of consciousness.

Maggid (singular): This term typically means an archangel or an angel with whom an initiate experiences visitation(s). However, it may also be applied to a disincarnate adept or master with whom an initiate experiences visitation(s), or to a holy master of the tradition that has great power, or who is viewed as "otherworldly" in presence, perception, intelligence, or other qualities. Typically, when applied to an incarnate master it suggests that they are viewed as having a very high grade of attainment. It is not a term anyone would apply to him or herself, but rather is used by others to express their perception.

Maggidim (plural): This term typically means "archangels and angels," but it may also refer to masters of a supernal attainment, who "resemble holy angels."

Malkut: Kingdom; the tenth Sefirah; corresponds to God's principle of order in Creation; God's Divine presence in Creation, and the world when harmonious with the Divine order; the daughter (Nukva) or anointed bride (Kallah Messiah); the Divine name Adonai (Lord); the archangel Sandalphon, and the angelic order of Ashim (souls of fire).

Merkavah: Chariot; from the vision of Ezekiel; knowledge of how to form a vehicle for entrance into prophetic states of consciousness or metaphysical dimensions, or the term may refer to the vehicle itself. In Gnostic Christianity, the chariot is considered the Body of

Light, which initiates learn to generate and transform into various images or forms that correspond to different planes of existence or metaphysical dimensions of reality, such as the heavens, the world of Supernal Light, and so on. Creating the corresponding chariot or body to a metaphysical dimension of Creation, one is able to experience that dimension.

Messianic Consciousness: See Christ-consciousness.

Metaphysical: Beyond the physical or material reality; inner and subtle levels of reality.

Nefesh: Bestial or earthly soul; it is the personality and life-display, and the astral matrix within and behind it. There are two states of this part of the soul—Nefesh Behamit (the bestial or unregenerated state) and Nefesh Elokit (the godly or regenerated state); hence unenlightened or enlightened. The Nefesh does not survive death save through the supreme attainment, in which case the Nefesh embodying the Neshamah in full attains the eternal life of Neshamah.

Neshamah: Divine nature; also called the supernal soul, holy soul, and heavenly soul. It is the Divine image of Yechidah, and the presence and power of Yechidah. It is in the Neshamah that the Christ-self dwells, and for this reason it is called the Holy Abode.

Netzach: Victory or dominion; the seventh Sefirah; corresponds to Divine dominion of God within and beyond Creation; the Divine name Yahweh Tzabaot (Lord of Hosts or Lord of Spirits); the angelic order of the Elohim (creative powers).

Partzuf: Personification of the Divine; there are purely metaphysical partzufim (plural) related to the holy Sefirot, but partzufim include the person of Yeshua, Mother Mary, Mary Magdalene, John the Baptist, Lazarus, and other characters in the Gospel. The envisioned image of any prophet, saint, or angel may be a partzuf. A partzuf (a Divine persona or image) provides a vehicle that links an initiate to the Divine or through which an initiate may have something of a direct spiritual or mystical experience. The principle of the partzufim is far more complex and sublime than there is space to explain in a glossary.

Ransom: A specific Gnostic ceremony of initiation; an initiation into the magical arts of Christian Gnosticism; the practice of the magical arts of Christian Gnosticism that advance the process of self-realization in the Christos and serve to liberate visible and invisible spirits.

Root of Evil: Ignorance, specifically selfishness, greed, and hatred.

Ruach: Literally, "spirit"; the Divine or human intelligence that links the earthly and heavenly parts of the soul (Nefesh and Neshamah, respectively).

Sabbath: A day in which the initiate rests from mundane labors and seeks to commune in God's presence; a day of spiritual fellowship, prayer, meditation, ceremony, and spiritual worship, which is the cornerstone of spiritual practice and spiritual living in the Sophian Tradition. It is called the day of the Beloved and is associated with the Holy Mother and Bride.

Sacrifice: A way of drawing oneself near unto the Lord; drawing near.

Second Coming: The advent of supernal consciousness on earth; enlightenment in a larger collective of humanity. This is conceived by Gnostics as taking place through the incarnation of Christ the Sophia in a woman's form, specifically, via the soul of St. Mary Magdalene.

Second Death: The dispersal of the energy of unenlightened souls at the end of a cosmic cycle of manifestation.

Sefirah (singular): See Sefirot.

Sefirot: Holy vessels or emanations of God's presence and power; gradations of the Divine presence and power that link creature/ creation and God. They correspond to the Divine names of God or attributes of God and are ten in number. Knowledge of these holy Sefirot or Divine names enables the initiate to consciously bind his or her soul to God's presence and power, and likewise to bind the Divine presence and power to his or her soul. They are the vehicles through which God interacts with creature/ creation and through which a human being is able to consciously experience God's presence and unite him or herself with God. These relate to the image and likeness of God in which the human being is created.

Shekinah: The Divine presence and power, which is feminine.

Shema: A proclamation and invocation of Divine unity; "Shema Israel, Adonai Elohenu, Adonai Achad." Hear, O Israel, the Lord is your God, the Lord is One.

Sin: Missing the mark of Truth; anything that cuts oneself off from the Divine, or brings harm to oneself or others. Much that is sin for oneself is subjective—such as alcohol for the alcoholic. (Negativity in general; of what places one in a negative state).

Sophia: The Wisdom of God, both primordial or uncreated Wisdom and created Wisdom; the primordial ground or space of Creation; the matrix or womb of Creation; the formation power of God. primordial or uncreated Wisdom is represented by the person of the Holy Mother and created Wisdom is represented by the holy bride, St. Mary Magdalene. Sophia is the female aspect of the Christos; the aspect of the soul of the Messiah embodied in Lady Mary Magdalene.

Spiritual Sun: A Gnostic term for the Christos, Logos, and Sophia. It may also be used as a symbol of the indwelling Christ presence.

Talmud: A vast body of rabbinical commentary on the Torah and practices of Judaism.

Tau: A Gnostic elder or holy apostle; one who is a master of the tradition, or who embodies something of a higher consciousness. One who is an initiate of an advanced grade of initiation and is able to teach and initiate others.

Tiferet: Beauty; the sixth Sefirah; corresponds to the underlying unity of God in Creation; the Son (Eben) or Messiah (Anointed One); the Divine names Yahweh Eloah Ve-Da'at (Lord my God and knowledge) and Yeheshuah (Yahweh delivers); the archangel Raphael, and the angelic order of the Malachim (messengers).

Tikkune: The correction, repair, redemption, mending, or healing of the soul; the redemption, mending or healing of the world and

Creation; the fulfillment of the Divine plan in Creation; the completion of the creative process by way of conscious evolution.

Tree of Life: The underlying metaphysical structure of creatures and Creation.

Tree of Life Glyph: A diagram and set of correspondences used to teach the esoteric Wisdom of the holy Kabbalah.

True Gnosis: A state of enlightenment or self-realization; the three grades of Christ-consciousness, which are Gnosis of the indwelling Christ, Gnosis of the Cosmic Christ, and Gnosis of the primordial Christ (supernal being); higher Gnosis that comes into being through an experience of conscious unification with the Divine.

Tzaddik: An adept or master of the tradition; literally "righteous one"; a term often applied to an elder or tau of the Sophian Tradition or to an individual who embodies something of a higher consciousness. Such a person may be incarnate or disincarnate, and thus the term may be applied to "saints." In essence, it is a Hebrew term for a saint.

Tzaddikim: Plural form of tzaddik; see Tzaddik.

Unmaker: Gnostic term for the Demiurgos; a suggestion of the "second death." See Cosmic Ignorance and Second Death.

Vehayah: Literally, "And it shall come to pass." A word of power derived from the Tetragrammaton that affirms a prayer or invocation at its conclusion, or affirms the manifestation of what one has asked for or visualized by the power of faith in the one Life-power.

Wedding Feast: See Eucharist.

Wickedness: Denotes negative thoughts, feelings/emotions, or dark imaginings that are acted upon (a state of ignorance).

Yechidah: Holy or Divine spark; the essence or inmost part of the holy soul; the holy spark of the soul of the Messiah within the soul; the I am or Christ-self or Divine self. It is through Yechidah that the holy soul, God, and Godhead are united.

Yeheshuah: Joshua, Hebrew for Jesus; initiates of the Sophian Tradition use the Hebrew form of the blessed name to draw out the esoteric meaning of the name. It literally means "Yahweh delivers," and mystically holds the meaning "The truth will set you free" or "That which binds is that which liberates." It is the same as the word or name Yahweh, with the addition of one Hebrew letter (Shin).

Yeshua: Aramaic for Jesus; Jesus being the name of the Master in Greek. Initiates of the Sophian Tradition often use this form of the blessed name as it is more likely the pronunciation originally used. Likewise, it tends to indicate a view of Jesus different from that of typical orthodoxy. See Yeheshuah.

Yesod: Foundation; the ninth Sefirah; corresponds to God's connecting power between the material and spiritual worlds; the Divine name Shaddai (Almighty), El Shaddai (God Almighty), and Shaddai El Hai (Almighty Living God); the archangel Gabriel, and the order of the Kerubim (strong ones).

Yetzirah: Universe of formation; the third Kabbalistic universe following Beriyah; associated with the angelic hosts; often called the world of angels (and demons).

Zohar (Sepher Ha-Zohar): Book of Splendor; a source-work of Kabbalistic teachings composed of several volumes of mystical commentary on the Torah.

SUGGESTED READING
AND REFERENCES

Barnstone, Willis, general editor. *The Other Bible*. Harper & Row, New York, 1984.

Douglas-Klotz, Neil. *The Hidden Gospel*. Quest Books, Wheaton IL, 1999.

———. *Prayers of the Cosmos*. HarperCollins, New York, 1990.

Frankiel, Tamar. *Gift of the Kabbalah*. Jewish Lights, Woodstock VT, 2001.

Fox, Matthew. *Coming of the Cosmic Christ*. Harper & Row, New York, 1988.

Kaplan, Aryeh. *Meditation and the Bible*. Weiser, York Beach Maine, 1978.

Kushner, Lawrence. *The River of Light*. Jewish Lights, Woodstock VT, 1981.

Matt, Daniel C. *The Essential Kabbalah*. HarperCollins, New York, 1995.

———. *God & The Big Bang*. Jewish lights, Woodstock VT, 1996.

Pagels, Elaine. *The Gnostic Gospels*. Random House, New York, 1979.

Ravindra, Ravi. *The Yoga of the Christ*. Element Books, Great Britain, 1990.

Robinson, James M., general editor. *The Nag Hammadi Library*. HarperCollins, New York, 1978.

To Write to the Author

If you wish to contact the author or would like more information about this book, please write to the author in care of Llewellyn Worldwide and we will forward your request. Both the author and publisher appreciate hearing from you and learning of your enjoyment of this book and how it has helped you. Llewellyn Worldwide cannot guarantee that every letter written to the author can be answered, but all will be forwarded. Please write to:

Tau Malachi
C/o Llewellyn Worldwide
P.O. Box 64383, Dept. 0-7387-0499-7
St. Paul, MN 55164-0383, U.S.A.

Please enclose a self-addressed stamped envelope for reply,
or $1.00 to cover costs. If outside U.S.A., enclose
international postal reply coupon.

Many of Llewellyn's authors have websites with additional information and resources. For more information, please visit our website at http://www.llewellyn.com.